Twentieth-Century East Asia

Modern History in Comparative and Transnational Perspectives

Edited by Todd A. Henry
University of California, San Diego

SAN DIEGO

Bassim Hamadeh, CEO and Publisher
Seidy Cruz, Specialist Acquisitions Editor
Kaela Martin, Project Editor
Celeste Paed, Associate Production Editor
Jess Estrella, Senior Graphic Designer
Michael Skinner, Senior Licensing Specialist
Natalie Piccotti, Director of Marketing
Kassie Graves, Vice President of Editorial
Jamie Giganti, Director of Academic Publishing

Cover image source: https://commons.wikimedia.org/wiki/File%3AEngagement_first_sino-japanese_war_%28oil_painting%29.jpg

9781793518125

3970 Sorrento Valley Blvd., Ste. 500, San Diego, CA 92121

Contents

PART III
SHADOWS OF THE COLD WAR
(1945–1999)

PART I

EXPRESSIONS OF SELF-DETERMINATION

(1900 – 1931)

GOOD-BYE ASIA (DATSU-A), 1885

By Fukuzawa Yukichi
Edited by David J. Lu

*I*n the transmission of knowledge concerning the West, no one had a greater impact than Fukuzawa Yukichi (1834–1901). Born in a lower samurai family, Fukuzawa studied in Nagasaki and became a student of Dutch studies. In 1860 when the Tokugawa bakufu sent its first official mission to the United States, he was retained as a translator. In 1862 when a bakufu mission was sent to Europe, he was again asked to accompany it. In 1867, he again went to the United States to acquire new knowledge. After his return he established a private academy called Keiō Gijuku and engaged in teaching and writing to enlighten his fellow countrymen. In 1868 he moved the site of his school to Mita and concentrated on educational activities. He taught the dignity of the individual and attempted to inculcate in his students a spirit of independence. He spoke of pragmatic approaches to social issues and renounced old customs and practices. His stress on utilitarianism and political economy paved the way for Keiō graduates to advance in the business world. Fukuzawa shunned governmental service and was content with publishing his own newspaper, Jiji Shimpō (in 1882), as a means of persuading the public toward acceptance of his political philosophy of gradualism. He was a prolific writer with one hundred volumes to his credit. Among his major works were Conditions of the West (Seiyō Jijō, 1886) and An Outline of Civilization (Bummeiron no Gairyaku, 1875). Document 1 is taken from his Encouragement of Learning (Gakumon no Susume). Chapter 5, from which this selection is taken is less well known than the popular Chapter 1. In this chapter, he spoke of a spirit of independence that would insist on independence from governmental interference and on adherence to academic freedom. Broadly interpreted, it was also the spirit that could eventually make Japan equal to other civilized nations.

In 1885, which was the eighteenth year of Meiji and nine years before the coming of the Sino-Japanese war, Fukuzawa wrote an article "Datsu-a Ron" (On Saying Good-bye to Asia, Document 2) urging his fellow country-men to cast away the shackles of East Asian traditions. Around that time the notion of pan-Asianism became intellectually respectable, with pundits suggesting Japan assume the leadership role over other East Asian nations. It implied Japan retain much of the East Asian traditions and become aligned with China and Korea. In Fukuzawa's view, it would have presented another obstacle to the path to bummei kaika. He wanted a clean break from the past, accompanied by changes in attitudes and perspectives, so that Japan would truly become part of the civilized world of the West.

GOOD-BYE ASIA (DATSU-A), 1885[*]

Transportation has become so convenient these days that once the wind of Western civilization blows to the

_____

[*] Fukuzawa Yukichi, *"Datsu-a Ron"* (On Saying Good-bye to Asia), reprinted in Takeuchi Yoshimi, ed., *Azia Shugi (Asianism)*

East, every blade of grass and every tree in the East follow what the Western wind brings. Ancient Westerners and present-day Westerners are from the same stock and are not much different from one another. The ancient ones moved slowly, but their contemporary counterparts move vivaciously at a fast pace. This is possible because present-day Westerners take advantage of the means of transportation available to them. For those of us who live in the Orient, unless we want to prevent the coming of Western civilization with a firm resolve, it is best that we cast our lot with them. If one observes carefully what is going on in today's world, one knows the futility of trying to prevent the onslaught of Western civilization. Why not float with them in the same ocean of civilization, sail the same waves, and enjoy the fruits and endeavors of civilization?

The movement of a civilization is like the spread of measles. Measles in Tokyo start in Nagasaki and come eastward with the spring thaw. We may hate the spread of this communicable disease, but is there any effective way of preventing it? I can prove that it is not possible. In a communicable disease, people receive only damages. In a civilization, damages may accompany benefits, but benefits always far outweigh them, and their force cannot be stopped. This being the case, there is no point in trying to prevent their spread. A wise man encourages the spread and allows our people to get used to its ways.

The opening to the modern civilization of the West began in the reign of Kaei (1848–58). Our people began to discover its utility and gradually and yet actively moved toward its acceptance. However, there was an old-fashioned and bloated government that stood in the way of progress. It was a problem impossible to solve. If the government were allowed to continue, the new civilization could not enter. The modern civilization and Japan's old conventions were mutually exclusive. If we were to discard our old conventions, that government also had to be abolished. We could have prevented the entry of this civilization, but it would have meant loss of our national independence. The struggles taking place in the world civilization were such that they would not allow an Eastern island nation to slumber in isolation. At that point, dedicated men (*shijin*) recognized the principle of "the country is more important than the government," relied on the dignity of the Imperial Household and toppled the old government to establish a new one. With this, public and the private sectors alike, everyone in our country accepted the modern Western civilization. Not only were we able to cast aside Japan's old conventions, but we also succeeded in creating a new axle toward progress in Asia. Our basic assumptions could be summarized in two words: "Good-bye Asia *(Datsu-a)*."

Japan is located in the eastern extremities of Asia, but the spirit of her people have already moved away from the old conventions of Asia to the Western civilization. Unfortunately for Japan, there are two neighboring countries. One is called China and another Korea. These two peoples, like the Japanese people, have been nurtured by Asiatic political thoughts and mores. It may be that we are different races of people, or it may be due to the differences in our heredity or education; significant differences mark the three peoples. The Chinese and Koreans are more like each other and together they do not show as much similarity to the Japanese. These two peoples do not know how to progress either personally or as a nation. In this day and age with transportation becoming so convenient, they cannot be blind to the manifestations of Western civilization. But they say that what is seen or heard cannot influence the disposition of their minds. Their love affairs with ancient ways and old customs remain as strong as they were centuries ago. In this new and vibrant theater of civilization when we speak of education, they only refer back to Confucianism. As for school education, they can only cite [Mencius's] precepts of humanity, righteousness, decorum, and knowledge.[*] While professing their abhorrence to ostentation, in reality they show their ignorance of truth and principles. As for their morality, one only has to observe their unspeakable acts of cruelty and shamelessness. Yet they remain arrogant and show no sign of self-examination.

Gendai Nihon Shisō Taikei (Great Compilation of Modern Japanese Thought), vol. 8 (Tokyo: Chikuma Shobō, 1963), pp. 38–40.

[*] In Japanese, *jin, gi, rei, chi,* and in Chinese *jen, i, li, chih (ren, yi, li, zhi).*

In my view, these two countries cannot survive as independent nations with the onslaught of Western civilization to the East. Their concerned citizens might yet find a way to engage in a massive reform, on the scale of our Meiji Restoration, and they could change their governments and bring about a renewal of spirit among their peoples. If that could happen they would indeed be fortunate. However, it is more likely that would never happen, and within a few short years they will be wiped out from the world with their lands divided among the civilized nations. Why is this so? Simply at a time when the spread of civilization and enlightenment (*bummei kaika*) has a force akin to that of measles, China and Korea violate the natural law of its spread. They forcibly try to avoid it by shutting off air from their rooms. Without air, they suffocate to death. It is said that neighbors must extend helping hands to one another because their relations are inseparable. Today's China and Korea have not done a thing for Japan. From the perspectives of civilized Westerners, they may see what is happening in China and Korea and judge Japan accordingly, because of the three countries' geographical proximity. The governments of China and Korea still retain their autocratic manners and do not abide by the rule of law. Westerners may consider Japan likewise a lawless society. Natives of China and Korea are deep in their hocus pocus of nonscientific behavior. Western scholars may think that Japan still remains a country dedicated to the *yin* and *yang* and five elements, Chinese are mean-spirited and shameless, and the chivalry of the Japanese people is lost to the Westerners. Koreans punish their convicts in an atrocious manner, and that is imputed to the Japanese as heartless people. There are many more examples I can cite. It is not different from the case of a righteous man living in a neighborhood of a town known for foolishness, lawlessness, atrocity, and heartlessness. His action is so rare that it is always buried under the ugliness of his neighbors' activities. When these incidents are multiplied, that can affect our normal conduct of diplomatic affairs. How unfortunate it is for Japan.

What must we do today? We do not have time to wait for the enlightenment of our neighbors so that we can work together toward the development of Asia. It is better for us to leave the ranks of Asian nations and cast our lot with civilized nations of the West. As for the way of dealing with China and Korea, no special treatment is necessary just because they happen to be our neighbors. We simply follow the manner of the Westerners in knowing how to treat them. Any person who cherishes a bad friend cannot escape his bad notoriety. We simply erase from our minds our bad friends in Asia.

The "Fourteen Points" and the "Four Points"

By President Woodrow Wilson

The "Fourteen Points" and the "Four Points." President Wilson's Fourteen Points, from his address to the Joint Session of Congress, January 8, 1918. President Wilson's Four Points, from his address at Mount Vernon, July 4, 1918.

We entered this war because violations of right had occurred which touched us to the quick and made the life of our own people impossible unless they were corrected and the world secured once for all against their recurrence. What we demand in this war, therefore, is nothing peculiar to ourselves. It is that the world be made fit and safe to live in; and particularly that it be made safe for every peace-loving nation which, like our own, wishes to live its own life, determine its own institutions, be assured of justice and fair dealing by the other peoples of the world as against force and selfish aggression. All the peoples of the world are in effect partners in this interest, and for our own part we see very clearly that unless justice be done to others it will not be done to us. The programme of the world's peace, therefore, is our programme; and that programme, the only possible programme, as we see it, is this:

I. Open covenants of peace, openly arrived at, after which there shall be no private international understandings of any kind but diplomacy shall proceed always frankly and in the public view.

II. Absolute freedom of navigation upon the seas, outside territorial waters, alike in peace and in war, except as the seas may be closed in whole or in part by international action for the enforcement of international covenants.

III. The removal, so far as possible, of all economic barriers and the establishment of an equality of trade conditions among all the nations consenting to the peace and associating themselves for its maintenance.

IV. Adequate guarantees given and taken that national armaments will be reduced to the lowest point consistent with domestic safety.

V. A free, open-minded, and absolutely impartial adjustment of all colonial claims, based upon a strict observance of the principle that in determining all such questions of sovereignty the interests of the populations concerned must have equal weight with the equitable claims of the government whose title is to be determined.

VI. The evacuation of all Russian territory and such a settlement of all questions affecting Russia as will secure the best and freest cooperation of the other nations of the world in obtaining for her an unhampered and unembarrassed opportunity for the independent determination of her own political development and national policy and assure her of a sincere welcome into the society of free nations under institutions of her own choosing; and, more than a welcome, assistance also of every kind that she may need and may herself desire. The treatment accorded Russia by her sister nations in the months to come will be the acid test of their good will, of their comprehension of her needs as distinguished from their own interests, and of their intelligent and unselfish sympathy.

VII. Belgium, the whole world will agree, must be evacuated and restored, without any attempt to limit the sovereignty which she enjoys in common with all other free nations. No other single act will serve as this will serve to restore confidence among the nations in the laws which they have themselves set and determined for the government of their relations with one another. Without this healing act the whole structure and validity of international law is forever impaired.

VIII. All French territory should be freed and the invaded portions restored, and the wrong done to France by Prussia in 1871 in the matter of Alsace-Lorraine, which has unsettled the peace of the world for nearly fifty years, should be righted, in order that peace may once more be made secure in the interest of all.

IX. A readjustment of the frontiers of Italy should be effected along clearly recognizable lines of nationality.

X. The peoples of Austria-Hungary, whose place among the nations we wish to see safeguarded and assured, should be accorded the freest opportunity of autonomous development.

XI. Rumania, Serbia, and Montenegro should be evacuated; occupied territories restored; Serbia accorded free and secure access to the sea; and the relations of the several Balkan states to one another, determined by friendly counsel along historically established lines of allegiance and nationality; and international guarantees of the political and economic independence and territorial integrity of the several Balkan states should be entered into.

XII. The Turkish portions of the present Ottoman Empire should be assured a secure sovereignty, but the other nationalities which are now under Turkish rule should be assured an undoubted security of life and an absolutely unmolested opportunity of autonomous development, and the Dardanelles should be permanently opened as a free passage to the ships and commerce of all nations under international guarantees.

XIII. An independent Polish state should be erected which should include the territories inhabited by indisputably Polish populations, which should be assured a free and secure access to the sea, and whose political and economic independence and territorial integrity should be guaranteed by international covenant.

XIV. A general association of nations must be formed under specific covenants for the purpose of affording mutual guarantees of political independence and territorial integrity to great and small states alike.

In regard to these essential rectifications of wrong and assertions of right we feel ourselves to be intimate partners of all the governments and peoples associated together against the Imperialists. We cannot be separated in interest or divided in purpose. We stand together until the end.

We have spoken now, surely, in terms too concrete to admit of any further doubt or question. An evident principle runs through the whole programme I have outlined. It is the principle of justice to all peoples and nationalities, and their right to live on equal terms of liberty and safety with one another, whether they be strong or weak. Unless this principle be made its foundation no part of the structure of international justice can stand. The people of the United States could act upon no other principle; and to the vindication of this principle they are ready to devote their lives, their honor, and everything that they possess. The moral climax of this the culminating and final war for human liberty has come, and they are ready to put their own strength, their own highest purpose, their own integrity and devotion to the test.

PRESIDENT WILSON'S FOUR POINTS.

From His Address at Mount Vernon, July 4. 1918.

I. The destruction of every arbitrary power anywhere that can separately, secretly, and of its single choice disturb the peace of the world; or, if it cannot be presently destroyed, at the least its reduction to virtual impotence.

II. The settlement of every question, whether of territory, of sovereignty, of economic arrangement, or of political relationship upon the basis of the free acceptance of that settlement by the people immediately concerned, and not upon the basis of the material interest or advantage of any other nation or people which may desire a different settlement for the sake of its own exterior influence or mastery.

III. The consent of all nations to be governed in their conduct toward each other by the same principles of honor and of respect for the common law of civilized society that govern the individual citizens of all modern States in their relations with one another; to the end that all promises and covenants may be sacredly observed, no private plots or conspiracies hatched, no selfish injuries wrought with impunity, and a mutual trust established upon the handsome foundation of a mutual respect for right.

IV. The establishment of an organization of peace which shall make it certain that the combined power of free nations will check every invasion of right and serve to make peace and justice the more secure by affording a definite tribunal of opinion to which all must submit and by which every international readjustment that cannot be amicably agreed upon by the peoples directly concerned shall be sanctioned. These great objects can be put into a single sentence. What we seek is the reign of law, based upon the consent of the governed and sustained by the organized opinion of mankind.

Yoshino Sakuzō's Minpon Shugi

Edited by David J. Lu

In attempting to articulate the nature of democracy for Taishō Japan, Yoshino Sakuzō (1878–1933) had to face the problem of seemingly irreconcilable concepts of the sovereignty of the emperor, as enunciated in the Meiji constitution, and the sovereignty of the people. Yoshino resolved this problem by stating that democracy in the sense of sovereignty residing in the people (minshu shugi) could not apply to Japan. On the other hand, whether a country be a monarchy or a democracy, that country should have a government organized for the people, serving their welfare, and decisions reached by it should reflect the will of the people. This he called minpon shugi, which means an ideology having people as the base, or loosely translated, "democracy" in a more narrow and confined sense.

After his graduation from Tokyo University, Yoshino studied in England, Germany and the United States. Upon his return he became professor of political science at Tokyo University and began contributing to the Chūo Kōron, the prestigious journal of opinion. He organized Reimeikai, a study group, to promote the cause of democracy and later joined the Asahi newspapers. The following article first appeared in 1914, justifying antigovernment demonstrations and advocating openness in the conduct of government affairs. It signaled a fit beginning for Taishō democracy.

I
ON DEMONSTRATION, 1914[*]

Following a set pattern, there was a demonstration in Hibiya [a centrally located district of Tokyo facing the Imperial Palace] in February of this year. The demonstration was held against the Siemens affair in which high-ranking naval officers were alleged to have received bribes for warship construction. A subsidiary issue was the question of tax reduction. A similar demonstration took place during the month of February in 1913. It was a more militant one than this year's and resulted in the ouster of Prince Katsura from his premiership. … Both of these demonstrations shared one thing in common. They were staged for the purpose of effecting changes in our political system. …

It is a source of concern to us to see the masses assembling and creating disturbances. On the other hand, however, some people argue that demonstrations are beneficial to the development of constitutional rule in Japan. I, for one, welcome demonstrations if they can make the judgment of the people become the final arbitrator in interpreting political issues or in conferring or accepting political powers. If the will of the people

---

[*] Yoshino Sakuzō, "*Minshuteki Shijiundō o Ronzu* (On Democratic Demonstrations)," reprinted in *Chūo Kōron*, November 1965, pp, 366–75.

can become a preponderant influence in our politics, then demonstrations can be justified.

Of course, even in the past, the judgment of the people was not completely ignored in politics. In most instances, people could not participate in the process of making binding final decisions. ... Even after the promulgation of the constitution, changes in government were never conducted in full public view and in an aboveboard manner. For some time, it has been asserted that the Cabinet should be a transcendental one, existing above politics and above any shift in the balance of power within the Diet. ... Around the time the constitution was promulgated, changes in the Cabinet were effected in most instances by decisions made secretly by the clan oligarchs (*hanbatsu*). No one outside the oligarchs' circle could tell why the Kuroda Cabinet had to be replaced by the Itō Cabinet. In any event, the will of the people, or the power blocks in the Diet that represented the will of the people, had nothing to do with changes in government. ...

The development of political parties, especially the emergence of strong parties such as the Seiyūkai, was an occasion for hope that the government would have to recognize the power of the people and be influenced by it in determining changes in government. It was felt that the power of the political parties could not be ignored. Before long, however, party executives began entering into secret deals with the government and started conferring or accepting political power in a manner lacking fairness. ... This is not the way constitutional rule should develop or function. We must somehow destroy this political secrecy.

To destroy it, there is no other recourse but to rely on the power of the people. When there is a blatant abuse of power, and normal means cannot destroy it, one is forced to resort to demonstration. If demonstrations become more prevalent, they can revitalize the stale undercurrent in the political world and deepen the understanding of politics by the people. In this sense, demonstrations can contribute toward the development of a constitutional government. ...

There are many obstinate people in this world who look with disdain on acquisition of power by the people. They somehow deem the extension of power to the people as something akin to a socialistic or subversive thought, or at times associate it with the disturbances created by the mobs in the French Revolution. ... This type of mind set is prevalent among older people, and it is also ingrained in the so-called bureaucrats. However, when we observe the background of these people with obstinate ideas, it is not difficult to discover that they are usually fearful of losing their own power base when the power of the people is expanded. In order to maintain their present position they have to suppress the rise in people's power. ...

Unfortunately these people's thoughts are clouded by a one-sided view. Everything has its positive and negative aspects, and indeed democracy has certain shortcomings. If we are to speak of shortcomings, however, we must also recognize the existence of shortcomings in oligarchy. In fact, if the two are compared, oligarchy will be found to contain more shortcomings. Oligarchy by its nature stresses secrecy, and wrongdoings may not become readily apparent. In contrast, democracy is conducted in full public view, and any wrongdoing can immediately be called to the attention of the observers. Thus people tend to name the shortcomings of democracy and forget similar shortcomings existing in oligarchy. If one happens to be a member of the clan oligarchy, no matter how knowledgeable he may be, he is not likely to discover the ills of oligarchy.

Politics of a nation must first of all abide by the principles of justice, unencumbered by secrecy. ... However, if only a few professional politicians, whose power is not based on the support of the people, can make secret deals, there is bound to be some personal considerations. ... For example, when an officer purchases certain items, if the purchase is made in full public view, there can be no wrongdoing. However, once the purchase is made only from a certain special party, wrongdoing can occur. This was evident in the bribery case of the navy. Who would have doubted the loyalty and devotion of the officers of the imperial navy? Yet a very clear case of corruption existed because their procurement was done behind the dark screen of secrecy. If the navy could be made into a glass box open to inspection from every corner, then the corruption would not have taken place. There are many other similar instances. ...

If we subscribe to this view, then regardless of certain merits it possesses, oligarchy cannot compare favorably with democracy. Once a person gains political power, he wishes to monopolize it. ... To safeguard the purity of politics, we must insist on recognizing the power of the people. In this sense, I am pro-democracy, and I also applaud the recent demonstrations.

However, several rebuttals are put forward against this view. The first one states that the view just expressed is not consistent with the national polity of Japan and is contrary to the Japanese constitution. ... The national polity of Japan does not permit the will of the people to become the final arbitrator. However, we must consider this: When the Emperor exercises his power, he invariably consults someone. He does not exercise his power alone and has an option of consulting a small number of people or a large number of people. The fact that the Emperor consults the opinion of the people in exercising his power does not go counter to the national polity. If one maintains that democracy is contrary to the national polity, then oligarchy is also contrary to the national polity. As we have indicated, the difference lies merely in the number of people the Emperor consults. ... The Charter Oath of Emperor Meiji states that "a deliberative assembly shall be convoked on a broad basis, and all matters of state shall be decided by open discussion." If anyone denies that democracy is consistent with the national polity of Japan, it must be remembered that this thought comes from an archaic notion that the nobility must be placed between the Emperor and the people to defend the former from the latter. ...

The notion that democracy is contrary to the constitution stems from a confusion between legality and politics. ... The function of law is to show a certain direction, but in its application it must be entirely flexible. Thus within the framework of law, political precedents have their rightful place. For example, one of the constitutional principles states that the Emperor has the power to appoint or dismiss his ministers. However, within the framework of this principle, a precedent can be established that can permit formation of a party Cabinet. It is true that in the final analysis, the Emperor possesses the power to appoint his ministers. But in practice, the Emperor has never appointed his ministers by solely relying on his own judgment. The Emperor normally acts on the recommendations of several persons. If consultation is to be made with a certain group, then a precedent can also be established to make the political parties perform that function. ...

The second objection to democracy stems from a notion that participation in the political process by ignorant people is too dangerous a step to take. ... Some people maintain that participation in the political process requires understanding of the nature of that participation and adequate knowledge of politics. There is no doubt that democracy can grow only among the people who are sufficiently advanced. However democracy in the final analysis does not require advance in political knowledge as the necessary prerequisite. Politics is often incomprehensible not only to the common people but also to those who have received higher education. ... For example, lately we have been debating the desirability of abolishing the business tax, or the desirability of reducing the land tax. We must judge these issues from the perspectives of our overall national interest, but I wonder how many college students or even representatives will not be baffled by the complexity of these issues. If we insist on allowing participation in politics only to those people who can determine the pros and cons of these technical questions we have to subscribe to the idealism of Plato in which only philosophers can govern.

Under a democratic form of government, people select as their representatives those persons in whose qualifications they have confidence. The candidates for office state their views and appeal to the people for their support. ... It does not follow that people can always pass judgment on the views expressed by the candidates. ... The minimum requirement that democracy makes of the people is to pass judgment on the personality of the candidates, determining which one of the candidates is a better person, more dependable, or can be entrusted with the affairs of state. ... The ability to discern the personality of the candidates does not require special training in politics, law, or economics. I am sure this is not an excessive requirement.

... Often those people who are closer to certain basic issues are not necessarily the best judges of the problems involved. They may not be able to transcend immediate issues and render impartial judgment. Thus occasionally it may be better to have educated guesses of outsiders.

For example, many strategic decisions are made by staff officers far removed from the battle scene and not by those who are in actual command. The analogy permits us to stress from a different perspective the importance of having a representative government. ...

The third objection to the democratic form of government comes from those people who insist that democracy brings forth many incidences of corruption and other ills. What are they referring to? Lately in Japan, some people say that the United States is suffering from mob rule and presents a sorry example of the ills of democracy. This type of argument either stems from an emotional outburst against the United States because of her recent Japanese exclusion act or from a complete ignorance of the political development of the United States in recent years. It is true that the United States shows all the ills of democracy in their extremes. But on the other hand, she is also an outstanding showcase of democracy. Oftentimes, the good points are replaced by bad ones, and vice versa. But in general the ills are few and the country benefits from the advantages given by a democratic form of government. One can look at the condition of the federal government with envy. Not a single one of its Cabinet secretaries has been under suspicion of corruption.

In short, democracy is not something to be disdained, as some people fretfully insist, but it must be welcomed. Setting aside the question of advantages and disadvantages, we must not forget that democracy is one of the rising forces in the world today. Whatever constitutional lawyers or defenders of the clan oligarchy may say, the power of the people is on the rise day after day. There is nothing one can do except to help nurture it. Assuming that democracy is not desirable, still one cannot suppress it totally. We must recognize this fact in planning the future of our nation.

There are, however, some phenomena that give us great concern. Democratic movement is a great asset to politics when it is conducted spontaneously and positively. It is not desirable if the masses congregate and indulge in demonstrations without having any concrete proposals. The demonstration against the conclusion of the Treaty of Portsmouth in September 1905 cannot be considered fully spontaneous. However, there was a definite demand among the people. There were many

instances of deplorable violence, but they had certain meanings. However, most of the recent demonstrations cannot be considered positive or spontaneous. I suspect some men who witnessed the strength of the people who were united for a cause in 1905 are now organizing demonstrations to utilize that strength for other self-serving purposes. These recent demonstrations appear to have agitators behind them. ...

If we are committed to democracy as our ultimate goal [and eliminate causes for the recurrence of demonstrations], we must remove existing inequities and work toward betterment of our constitutional government. ...

Among the two major approaches, the first is to institute certain reforms in the implementation of our constitutional government. Disturbances occur when the constitutional government is not smoothly functioning. ... There are several ways in which we can bring about that smooth functioning of our government. The first is expansion of the right to vote to a larger segment of our population and equitable redistribution of electoral districts. ... The second is the establishment of party government ... which in turn may require rivalry by two major political parties. Only future events can determine if political parties can be organized into two groups. It cannot be legislated as in the case of suffrage. What we must do at the present time is to eliminate those existing conditions that are detrimental to the development of party government. ...

The second approach concerns the development of people themselves. This can again be divided into two main topics. The first is, of course, economic development. If life is difficult, people tend to give in to agitation and can be taken advantage of by demagogues. In the olden days we spoke of "those who have permanent treasure have steady hearts." To stabilize the strength of our people in a healthy manner, we must enact certain social legislations in order to secure livelihood for the lower class of people. ...

Another point we must consider is the nurturing of people's intellectual and spiritual development. The first thing that comes to mind is encouragement of political education which is not done at all today. In the Western world, political parties are organized in such a way that they must continuously appeal to the people for their support. They do not neglect to reach the people by all available means. They may not make political education one of their major goals, but they conduct speeches, publish newspapers, and issue tracts and pamphlets on current problems. How poorly our political parties compare with them.

Another aspect deals with moral education of the people. We must enlighten the people, make them understand the voice of justice, and make their minds receptive to justice. Without this, democracy may not be able to rise above the abyss of corruption. On this point I am most impressed with an example set by the United States. In New York, there is a political organization called Tammany Hall, making a mockery of the municipal government. Abuses were rampant, but when some reformers began decrying against such evils, people responded by showing their determination to eradicate once for all the atmosphere of corruption. Indeed, the voice of justice should find a harmonious chord in the moral fiber of the nation. A young man in his early thirties was elected mayor after he hoisted the banner of reform.* His reforms are unorthodox but heartwarming. When I hear that he is succeeding in eradicating many existing ills, my heart is filled with envy. We must guide our people to attain this level of understanding. True, this can influence politics only indirectly, but I think it is the most essential condition in the development of democracy. On this point, I beseech the help and collaboration of educators and religious leaders with great expectation.

---

* The thirty-four-year-old Fusion candidate, John Purroy Mitchell, was elected mayor of New York in November 1913.

National Culture During the Colonial Period

and

The Nationalist Movement

Edited by Yongho Ch'oe, Peter H. Lee, and William Theodore De Bary

THE STUDY OF THE KOREAN LANGUAGE AND *HANGŬL*

Shortly after the March First movement, the Society for Research in the Korean Language (Chosŏnŏ Yŏnguhoe) was formed by the disciples of Che Sigyŏng (1876–1914), the great pioneer in the study of the Korean language and *hangŭl*, the Korean alphabet. This was a close-knit and active group whose members considered it their patriotic duty to study their national language. They were also interested in promoting the study and use of the Korean language and *hangŭl*, and to that end in 1926 they designated the anniversary of the promulgation of *hangŭl* in 1446 as *Hangŭl* Day (now celebrated on 9 October), staging an elaborate, if private, celebration. In 1927 they began publication of the first scholarly journal on the Korean language, *Hangŭl*. The editorial in the journal's inaugural issue, an excerpt of which is presented here, called upon the people to treasure and develop their linguistic heritage.

By 1931 the group had adopted a new name, the Korean Language Society (Chosŏnŏ Hakhoe), and launched a series of ambitious projects. Foremost among them was a plan to publish a comprehensive dictionary of the Korean language. It was to be a monumental project requiring an enormous amount of painstaking work. With limited manpower and budget, the undertaking was time-consuming and difficult. Along the way, they passed a few significant milestones: the orthographic

rules for *hangŭl* spelling were adopted after three years of intense deliberations (1933); a dictionary of the standard vocabulary was published (1936); and the rules for transcribing foreign words were announced after nearly ten years of preparation (1940). Because of the accelerated pace of the "Japanizing" programs, the Korean dictionary project became a race against the clock, and printing proceeded in sections as soon as portions of the manuscript, prepared in two copies, were completed. But the Japanese authorities decided to strike before the dictionary project could be consummated. In 1942 they labeled the Korean Language Society a subversive group plotting Korea's independence and arrested twenty-one linguists including Yi Kŭngno (1893–1978), Ch'oe Hyŏnbae (1894–1970), and Yi Hŭisŭng (1896–1989). A dozen of them were eventually convicted and sentenced. Those who survived prison had to wait for the nation's liberation before they could resume their work.

YI YUNJAE: INAUGURAL EDITORIAL FOR *HANGŬL*

[From *Hangŭl* 1:3]

The journal *Hangŭl* suspended publication soon after its first issue in 1927 but was resurrected in 1932 and published the "inaugural" issue, dated 1 May 1932. Yi Yunjae (1888–1943), a linguist and the editor of the journal, was also known for his nationalistic convictions. In 1942 he was arrested for the second time by the Japanese for his role in the Korean Language Association; he died in prison the following year.

At present when all fields of science, scholarship, and culture of the society are progressing daily, everything depends on the spoken and written word. We need not belabor how important and precious speech and scripts are in our life and how indispensable they are every minute of the day. Every nation has its own speech and scripts, which its people love greatly.

We, the Koreans, have a fine speech and scripts. Our scripts, *hangŭl* in particular, are excellent; they have unchanging sounds, they look attractive, and they are easy to learn and use. Nevertheless, we have long despised and mistreated them. *Hangŭl* letters have thereby failed to develop into a superb writing system as they should have. Instead, they have become untidy and unsightly.

We are happy for the sake of the future of *hangŭl* that some forty years ago, Chu Sigyŏng, our great teacher, opened the right path, which not a few disciples chose to follow with the full intention of working diligently for the promotion of *hangŭl*.

The demand for better knowledge of our own script has lately become louder. We should lose no time in recovering our *hangŭl* from long neglect and restoring it to its original correct and unsullied form. To this end, some of us began the publication of the magazine *Hangŭl* four years ago, but we regretfully had to abandon the project until today because we lacked the wherewithal to continue, as is often the case with many things nowadays. We are now publishing this *Hangŭl* magazine in response to the demands of the times and also in pursuit of the mission of our association. We believe that a rearranged and unified system of *hangŭl* writing can now be perfected. We trust that everyone who speaks and writes in the Korean language will support the project. Let us be united in our determination and join our strength in making our speech and letters shine brighter. On this occasion of publishing *Hangŭl*, we make this statement of our intentions.

HKK

DEVELOPMENT OF NEW LITERATURE

In literature, Yi Kwangsu (b. 1892) helped introduce a new era by publishing a series of modern novels in the late 1910s and thereafter that combined nationalism and humanism in a new popular, if didactic, format and style. *Mujŏng* (The heartless, 1917) and *Hŭk* (The soil, 1932–1933) appeared relatively early in his literary career and are often characterized as "the literature of enlightenment" *(kyemong munhak)*. Yi was also a political activist during and after the March First movement, taking part in the activities of the Korean Provisional Government in Shanghai. Yi's literary fame also made him the prime target in the Japanese effort to pressure prominent Koreans into collaboration with their "Japanization" campaign.

Among Yi's contemporaries, two other names deserve mention here as literary trailblazers. Kim Tongin (1900–1951) helped publish the first writers' magazine, called *Ch'angjo* (Creation), and wrote short stories such as "Kamja" (Potato, 1925), which was acclaimed for its underlying theme of naturalism.* Yŏm Sangsŏp (1897–1963) was a writer in the tradition of literary realism; his novel *Samdae* (Three Generations, 1931) depicts in careful detail the sometimes sordid and disillusioning conditions of Korean society.

Romanticism and sentimentalism were also represented in the Korean literary scene at that time, as seen in the pages of the literary magazines *Ch'angjo, P'yehŏ* (Ruins), and *Paekcho* (White Tide). The long shadow of Chinese literary tradition and Confucian ethos had now been replaced by "Korean" literature written in the vernacular but influenced by the literary trends of the West as well as by Westernized Japan.

In the 1920s and subsequent decades still other themes became current in literary works. A sense of social awareness and national identity was dominant in the poems of Han Yongun (1879–1944), a nationalistic Buddhist and one of the thirty-three signers of the 1919 Declaration of independence. His poems in

---

* For a translation of "Potato" by Kim Tongin, see Peter H. Lee, ed., *Modern Korean Literature: An Anthology* (Honolulu: University of Hawaii Press, 1990), pp. 16–23. Hereafter cited as *MKL*.

Nim ŭi ch'immuk (The Silence of Love, 1926) expressed profound love for his nation.* In the magazine *Creation*, Kim Sowŏl (1903–1934) published lyric poems, such as "Chindallae kkot" (The Azalea, 1922), that expressed a sense of sorrow directly touching the heart of the subjugated people of Korea.† Yi Sanghwa (1901–1943), a nationalistic poet who died in self-imposed exile, writes here of his intense love for a land under alien occupation. A patriotic verse by Sim Hun (1901–1936), also represented here, wistfully anticipates the day of freedom and independence for his homeland.

Radical left-wing ideologies also found their echoes in literary works. Class conflict and protest against the existing socioeconomic order were the motivating forces for members of the Korean Artists Proletariat Federation (1925–1935), who considered art as a weapon for class revolution. Such overt politicization of literary activities invited critical reactions from those who advocated art for art's sake. The onset of World War II, however, engulfed Korea as part of the Japanese empire and effectively ended the development of modern literature as an expression of Korean, culture and art.

Yi Sanghwa:
"Does Spring Come To Stolen Fields?"

[From *Wŏnjŏn taegyo Yi Sanghwa chŏnjip*, pp. 16–17]

The earlier works of Yi Sanghwa (1901–1943), a founding member of the little magazine *Paekcho* (White Tide), tended to be "romantic," but beginning in 1924 he published poems of strongly nationalistic tenor, such as the one below, which appeared in the journal *Kaehyŏk* (Genesis) in June 1926.

The land is no longer our own.
Does spring come even to the stolen fields?

Along a paddy path like a part in the hair,
I walk, sun-drenched, as if in a dream,
Toward where blue sky and green fields meet

Sky and fields with closed lips!
I don't feel I came out on my own.
Have you enticed me or has someone else called?

Winds whisper,
Shaking my coat's hero to urge me forward.
A lark laughs in the clouds like a girl singing behind
   the hedge.

O bountifully ripening barley fields,
You washed your long thick hair in a fine rain
That fell past midnight—I too feel buoyant.

Alone I will walk
On the good ditch around the dry paddy,
My shoulders dancing, I sing a lullaby.

Butterflies and swallows, don't be boisterous
But greet cockscombs and wild hemp flowers,
I want to see the fields where girls with castor-oiled hair
   weeded.

I want a scythe in my hands.
I want to stamp on this soil, soft as a plump breast,
Until my ankle aches and I stream with sweat.

What are you looking for? My soul,
Endlessly darting like children at play by the river,
How amusing, answer me: Where are you going?

Filled with the color of grass, compounded
Of green laughter and green sorrow,
Limping along, I walk all day as if possessed by the
   spring devil:

But now these are stolen fields, and even our spring will
   be taken.

* See Peter H. Lee, ed., *The Silence of Love: Twentieth-Century Korean Poetry* (Honolulu: University Press of Hawaii, 1980).

† For a translation of "The Azalea" see *MKL*, p. 29.

PL

SIM HUN: "WHEN THAT DAY COMES"

[From *Sim Hun munhak chŏnjip* 1:53–54]

Sim Hun (1901–1936) studied in Hangchow, China, before working as a reporter for a Korean daily in Seoul. He was also active as a script writer, actor, and film director. In addition, he wrote fiction, such as the prize-winning novel on the rural enlightenment movement, *Sangnoksu* (The Evergreen, 1936). In 1932 a collection of his poems, entitled "When That Day Comes," was not published because of Japanese censorship. He died of typhoid on 16 September 1936.

When that day comes, when that day comes,
Mount Samgak will rise and dance,
the waters of Han will rise up.
If that day comes before I perish,
I will soar like a crow at night
and pound the Chongno bell with my head.
The bones of my skull
will scatter, but I shall die in joy without regret.
When that day has come at last, O that day,
I'll roll and leap and shout on the boulevard
and if joy still stifles within my breast
I'll take a knife
and skin my body and make
a large drum and march with it
in the vanguard. O procession!
Let me once hear that thundering shout,
Even if I fall headlong,
my eyes can close then.

PL

THE NATIONALIST MOVEMENT

For thirty-five years, from August 1910 until August 1945, Japan occupied Korea and imposed a harsh colonial rule that was supported by the presence of powerful army, gendarmerie, and police forces. At the apex of the colonial hierarchy was a governor-general who had a wide range of executive, legislative, and judicial powers and, until 1919, command authority over the military forces as well. Of the nine men who served as governor-general, one was a navy admiral, and all the others were army generals.

Five of them were appointed prime minister of Japan either before or after their Korean tour. They reported directly to the Japanese emperor through the prime minister, an arrangement that reflected their status in Korea as a virtual "king."

The colonial bureaucracy was a tightly knit hierarchy governed in part by certain laws of Japan but mostly by administrative ordinances issued by the governor-general. As Japanese officials filled an overwhelming majority of higher executive posts, there was only token participation of Korean bureaucrats. No elective assemblies were created during this colonial period, and Koreans had no opportunity to elect their representatives at any level of administration.

The ultimate purpose of the Japanese administration was twofold: to perpetuate Japanese rule and to develop Korea as a source of human and material resources for the expanding empire of Japan. Politics that purportedly sought these ends were, however, often contradictory. Officially the Japanese colonial regime called for a full amalgamation of the two peoples; but in fact it suppressed, exploited, and discriminated against the Korean people. Economically, Japanese capital, know-how, and managerial skills brought about modernization, with the development of heavy industries taking place primarily after the Manchurian incident of 1931. In the Japanese scheme, the Korean economy was to integrate with and complement Japan's economy. To say that the economic and social well-being of the Korean people per se was not Japan's ultimate objective would be an understatement. At the same time, it cannot be denied that Korea went through a modernizing metamorphosis.

It is customary to divide the colonial years into three periods: 1910–1919, 1920–1931, 1931–1945. During the first period, the primary objective of the colonial administration was to bring about the complete submission of Koreans to the new ruler. A harsh military rule based on brute force was the means to this end. The so-called Conspiracy Case of 1911 that sent one hundred and five Korean nationalists to torture and imprisonment on the false charge of plotting to assassinate the first Japanese governor-general was typical of the policy of intimidation and suppression. Freedom of the press, association, and assembly were severely curtailed. Most Korean newspapers were closed down, and all organizations that had been active in the patriotic enlightenment movement were disbanded. Public assemblies, including children's athletic events on primary school playgrounds, had to be approved in advance. Private schools were taken over and converted to public schools in order to turn out subjects loyal to the Japanese emperor. A 1911 rule on business incorporation encouraged Japanese entrepreneurs and discouraged Koreans from launching business careers. A land survey of 1910–1918 required formal registration of landownership or leases. When many Korean landowners and tenants failed to register due to fear or ignorance, they lost their long-standing rights to the land. This benefited newly arriving Japanese settlers and large-scale commercial farmers. The Japanese gendarmerie exercised civil police powers, thereby becoming the ubiquitous object of fear and hatred.

Koreans who were dispossessed or otherwise could not endure the colonial rule left Korea for China, particularly southeastern Manchuria, and the Russian Maritime Province. Along the northeastern border of Korea, a number of Korean armed groups were organized to continue the armed resistance against Japan. Within Korea armed struggle ceased rather quickly, but underground activities for the nation's independence continued.

THE MARCH FIRST MOVEMENT

The March First movement of 1919 would not have been possible had it not been for the widespread and intense antipathy against Japanese colonialism. It is true that President Woodrow Wilson's Fourteen Points declaration had raised Korean hopes for national self-determination. It is also true that ex-Emperor Kojong's death and impending funeral in early March 1919 helped mobilize the crowd. In the final analysis, however, the millions of Koreans who paraded through the streets all over Korea shouting *"manse"* (long live Korean independence) did so because of their wish to end the degrading and harsh alien rule. Without doubt, it was the most massive demonstration of nationalism in the modern history of Korea. But preparations for the demonstration involved only a handful of activists and a surprisingly short period of time. First there was

a meeting of Korean students in Tokyo on 8 February 1919 where a declaration of Korean independence was read aloud. An eloquent statement declaring Korea's independence to the world, the first selection in this chapter, was quickly drafted by Ch'oe Namsŏn, and thirty-three "representatives of the Korean people" (sixteen Christians, fifteen leaders of Ch'ŏndogyo, and two Buddhists) signed it.

At noon on 1 March the declaration was read at a large gathering of students in Seoul's Pagoda Park, signaling the beginning of nationwide demonstrations that mobilized men and women of all ages and social backgrounds. Taken by surprise, the Japanese police and troops reacted with fury. But despite a large number of casualties, the massive wave of demonstrations went on for months. Official Japanese figures listed over one million participants in 3,200 demonstrations, resulting in about 20,000 arrests.[*] Korean sources give much higher estimates: more than two million participants in the first three months alone, almost 47,000 arrests, 7,509 deaths, and 15,961 injured among the demonstrators.[†]

The impact of the March First movement was profound and long-lasting, although it failed to achieve its stated aim of Korean independence. It was a powerful, if costly, display of Korean nationalism that belied the Japanese profession of benevolence and goodwill toward the colonized people. Worldwide publicity and criticism of the colonial system in Korea led directly to certain measures of appeasement, the self-styled "Cultural Policy" from the newly appointed Japanese governor-general. One of the best known of these measures was the partial lifting of the ban against Korean language newspapers. The *Tonga ilbo* (East Asia Daily) and the *Chosŏn ilbo* (Korea Daily) began publication.

---

[*] An official report entitled "The Ideology and Movement of the Korean Disturbances (Chōsen sōjō jiken)" prepared by the Secretarial Office of the Governor-General appears in Japan Provost Marshal in Korea, ed., *Chosen sanichi dokuritsu sōjō jiken* (March 1st. independence disturbances in Korea), reprinted by Gannandō shoten (Tokyo, 1969), p. 438.

[†] *Munhwa sa*, pp. 284, 288; Pak Ŭsik, *Hanguk tongnip undong chi hyŏlsa* (Shanghai: Weihsinshe, 1920), 2:26–43.

The March First movement also spurred patriotic Koreans overseas to redouble their efforts. A Korean national congress was organized near Vladivostok on 17 March 1919 by the representatives of more than half a million Korean residents in Manchuria and Siberia, and it proceeded to name the leaders of a provisional government. Similar efforts toward creating a government council and adopting a constitution were made at a secret conference of provincial representatives meeting in Seoul in April 1919. Earlier in the same month, in the relative safety of the French concession area in Shanghai, dozens of Korean activists had gathered for a series of meetings that proclaimed the establishment of a provisional government of the "Korean Republic" (Taehan Minguk). The conferees—men of diverse social and ideological backgrounds—selected yet another slate of cabinet officials and proclaimed another constitution, the second selection presented in this chapter. The Shanghai organization proved to be more broadly based and durable than the others, and until 1945 it served as the rallying point for the Korean independence movement.

The provisional constitution adopted in Shanghai provided for a republican form of government consisting of a legislative council and an executive council, the former to be headed by Yi Tongnyŏng and the latter by Yi Sŭngman (Syngman Rhee). In order to maintain close contacts with nationalists in Korea, the provisional government established a clandestine communication network. Moreover, it sent emissaries to present the Korean case before various international gatherings, including the Versailles Peace Conference, and created a commission for Europe and America (Kumi wiwŏnhoe).* The provisional government also established military headquarters in southern Manchuria in preparation for armed conflict with Japan. In August

1919 it began publishing a paper, *Tongnip sinmum* (The Independence News).†

SON PYŎNGHŬI AND OTHERS: DECLARATION OF INDEPENDENCE

[From *Korean Studies* 13:1–4]

The Declaration of Independence, dated 1 March 1919, was drafted in a few days by a twenty-nine-year-old scholar-publisher, Ch'oe Namsŏn (1890–1957). Ch'oe himself did not sign the declaration, however, professing a disinclination to become openly involved in the national independence movement. All the same, he was imprisoned for nearly three years after the March First movement. He devoted most of his later years to writing Korean history, but his wartime collaboration with the Japanese tainted his image in Korean eyes. The declaration is written in a literary form that was modern by 1919 standards but relied heavily on the classical Chinese style of writing in which Ch'oe excelled. The list of signatories began with the name of Son Pyŏnghui, the Ch'ŏndogyo leader. The "pledges" were allegedly drafted and appended to the Declaration of Independence by Han Yongtin (1879–1944), a Buddhist leader and one of the thirty-three signers of the declaration.

We hereby declare that Korea is an independent state and that Koreans are a self-governing people. We proclaim it to the nations of the world in affirmation of the principle of the equality of all nations, and we proclaim it to our posterity, preserving in perpetuity the right of national survival. We make this declaration on the strength of five thousand years of history as an expression of the devotion and loyalty of twenty million people. We claim independence in the interest of the eternal and free development of our people and in accordance with the great movement for world reform based upon the awakening conscience of mankind. This is the clear command of heaven, the course of our times, and a legitimate manifestation of the right of all nations

---

* The text of "The Petition of the Korean People and Nation for Liberation from Japan and the Reconstitution of Korea as an Independent State" submitted to the Versailles Conference by Kiusic Kimm (Kim Kyusik) appears in Donald G. Tewksbury, comp., *Source Materials on Korean Politics and Ideologies* (New York: International Secretariat, Institute of Pacific Relations, 1950), pp. 56–63.

---

† *Munhwa sa*, pp. 290–291.

to coexist and live in harmony. Nothing in the world can suppress or block it.

For the first time in several thousand years, we have suffered the agony of alien suppression for a decade, becoming a victim of the policies of aggression and coercion, which are relics from a bygone era. How long have we been deprived of our right to exist? How long has our spiritual development been hampered? How long have the opportunities to contribute our creative vitality to the development of world culture been denied us?

Alas! In order to rectify past grievances, free ourselves from present hardships, eliminate future threats, stimulate and enhance the weakened conscience of our people, eradicate the shame that befell our nation, ensure proper development of human dignity, avoid leaving humiliating legacies to our children, and usher in lasting and complete happiness for our posterity, the most urgent task is to firmly establish national independence. Today when human nature and conscience are placing the forces of justice and humanity on our side, if every one of our twenty million people arms himself for battle, whom could we not defeat and what could we not accomplish?

We do not intend to accuse Japan of infidelity for its violation of various solemn treaty obligations since the Treaty of Amity of 1876. Japan's scholars and officials, indulging in a conqueror's exuberance, have denigrated the accomplishments of our ancestors and treated our civilized people like barbarians. Despite their disregard for the ancient origins of our society and the brilliant spirit of our people, we shall not blame Japan; we must first blame ourselves before finding fault with others. Because of the urgent need for remedies for the problems of today, we cannot afford the time for recriminations over past wrongs.

Our task today is to build up our own strength, not to destroy others. We must chart a new course for ourselves in accord with the solemn dictates of conscience, not malign and reject others for reasons of past enmity or momentary passions. In order to restore natural and just conditions, we must remedy the unnatural and unjust conditions brought about by the leaders of Japan, who are chained to old ideas and old forces and victimized by their obsession with glory.

From the outset the union of the two countries did not emanate from the wishes of the people, and its outcome has been oppressive coercion, discriminatory injustice, and fabrication of statistical data, thereby deepening the eternally irreconcilable chasm of ill will between the two nations. To correct past mistakes and open a new phase of friendship based upon genuine understanding and sympathy—is this not the easiest way to avoid disaster and invite blessing? The enslavement of twenty million resentful people by force does not contribute to lasting peace in the East. It deepens the fear and suspicion of Japan by the four hundred million Chinese who constitute the main axis for stability in the East, and it will lead to the tragic downfall of all nations in our region. Independence for Korea today shall not only enable Koreans to lead a normal, prosperous life, as is their due; it will also guide Japan to leave its evil path and perform its great task of supporting the cause of the East, liberating China from a gnawing uneasiness and fear and helping the cause of world peace and happiness for mankind, which depends greatly on peace in the East. How can this be considered a trivial issue of mere sentiment?

Behold! A new world is before our eyes. The days of force are gone, and the days of morality are here. The spirit of humanity, nurtured throughout the past century, has begun casting its rays of new civilization upon human history. A new spring has arrived prompting the myriad forms of life to come to life again. The past was a time of freezing ice and snow, stifling the breath of life; the present is a time of mild breezes and warm sunshine, reinvigorating the spirit. Facing the return of the universal cycle, we set forth on the changing tide of the world. Nothing can make us hesitate or fear.

We shall safeguard our inherent right to freedom and enjoy a life of prosperity; we shall also make use of our creativity, enabling our national essence to blossom in the vernal warmth. We have arisen now. Conscience is on our side, and truth guides our way. All of us, men and women, young and old, have firmly left behind the old nest of darkness and gloom and head for joyful resurrection together with the myriad living things. The spirits of thousands of generations of our ancestors protect us; the rising tide of world consciousness shall assist us. Once started, we shall surely succeed: With this hope we march forward.

Three Open Pledges

1. Our action today represents the demand of our people for justice, humanity, survival, and dignity. It manifests our spirit of freedom and should not engender antiforeign feelings.
2. To the last one of us and to the last moment possible, we shall unhesitatingly publicize the views of our people, as is our right.
3. All our actions should scrupulously uphold public order, and our demands and our attitudes must be honorable and upright.

HKK

PROVISIONAL CONSTITUTION OF THE KOREAN GOVERNMENT IN EXILE

[From *Hanguk tonghip undong sa* 3:326]

By the will of God, the people of Korea, both from Seoul and the provinces, have united in a peaceful declaration of their independence in the Korean capital, and for over a month have carried on their demonstrations in over three hundred districts. A provisional government, organized in complete accord with popular faith, proclaims a provisional constitution that the provisional council of state has adopted in order to pass on to our posterity the blessings of sovereign independence.

*Provisional Constitution of The Korean Republic** *

1. The Korean Republic shall be a democratic republic.
2. A provisional government shall govern the Korean Republic in accordance, with the decision of a provisional legislative council (Imsi Ŭijŏngwŏn).

3. There shall be no class distinctions among the citizens of the Korean Republic, and men and women, noble and common, rich and poor, shall have complete equality.
4. The citizens of the Korean Republic shall have personal and property rights including the freedoms of faith, speech, writing, publishing, association, assembly, and dwelling.
5. A citizen of the Korean Republic, unless disfranchised, shall have the right to vote or to be elected.
6. The citizens of the Korean Republic shall be subject to compulsory education, taxation, and military conscription.
7. The Korean Republic shall join the League of Nations in order to demonstrate to the world that its creation has been in accord with the will of God and also to make a contribution to world civilization and peace.
8. The Korean Republic shall extend favorable treatment to the former imperial family.
9. The death penalty, corporal punishment, and open prostitution shall be abolished.
10. Within one year following the recovery of the national land, the provisional government shall convene a national assembly.

President, Provisional Legislative Council:
   Yi Tongnyŏng
Prime Minister, Provisional Government:
   Syngman Rhee†
Minister of Home Affairs: An Ch'angho
Minister of Foreign Affairs: Kim Kyusik
Minister of Judicial Affairs: Yi Siyŏng
Minister of Financial Affairs: Ch'oe Chaehyŏng
Minister of Military Affairs: Yi Tonghwi
Minister of Transportation: Mun Ch'angbŏm

HKK

---

* The South Korean state is today called "Taehan Minguk" or the Republic of Korea. In order to avoid confusion, the name "Taehan Minguk" that appears here is translated as "the Korean Republic."

† Syngman Rhee and his cabinet colleagues named here, with only one exception, were not present in Shanghai at that time. Their election is explained as an attempt "to select the most renowned figures among Koreans abroad and thus endow the organization with legitimacy"; see Chong-sik Lee, *The Politics of Korean Nationalism,* p. 131.

STRATEGIES FOR REGAINING NATIONAL INDEPENDENCE

The strategy for regaining Korea's independence was an issue of crucial importance. It was also a divisive issue that fractionalized the independence movement. Basically three alternatives were discussed: diplomacy, armed struggle, and self-strengthening. Diplomacy was to solicit foreign powers' support for Korea through lobbying, propaganda, and diplomatic representation at international conferences. Syngman Rhee (1875–1965), the first "provisional president" of the exile government and later the head of its Commission for Europe and America, was among those who advocated diplomacy. The third selection in this chapter, an appeal to America adopted by members of the First Korean Congress assembled in Philadelphia in April 1919, is an example of these diplomatic efforts.

An Ch'angho (1878–1938), a widely respected nationalist leader, conceded that armed struggle was necessary. But as a prerequisite to such direct action, An cautioned, Koreans must first build up their own strength through education and mutual cooperation. Sin Ch'aeho (1880–1936), whose fervent nationalism was reflected in his writings on Korean history as discussed in an earlier chapter, was critical of both the "diplomacy" and the "preparation first" strategies. His "Declaration of Korean Revolution," a manifesto of the Righteous Patriots Corps (Ŭiyŏltan),* was a strident call for violent struggle against Japan.

Organized anti-Japanese military campaigns were centered in the Kando (Chien-tao) region just across the northeastern border of Korea, but there were similar campaigns in other parts of Manchuria and in the Russian Maritime Province. A score of military groups were active at one time or another. General Hong Pŏmelo (1868–1943) led a "Korean Independence Army" (Taehan Tongnip Kun) to victory in the battle at Pongodong in 1920. Later in the same year, General Hong and General Kim Chwajin (1889–1930) led their units in a battle at Ch'ŏngsanni that dealt a humiliating defeat to a large Japanese force.[†]

In China, Korean efforts to create an anti-Japanese army began to bear fruit only after the outbreak of the Sino–Japanese War in 1937. The Provisional Government of the Korean Republic, now headed by Kim Ku (1876–1949), created a military commission in 1937 and, with active support from the Nationalist government of China, created the Korean Restoration Army (Hanguk Kwangbok Kun) in 1940.

The Korean Congress in the U.S.: An Appeal To America

[From *First Korean Congress* (Philadelphia 1919), pp. 29–30]

Upon hearing the news of the March First movement, Sŏ Chaep'il convened and chaired a three-day meeting in Philadelphia that was attended by about seventy Koreans residing in the United States, Hawaii, and Mexico. Syngman Rhee was an active participant in this conference, the avowed purpose of which was to publicize the Korean cause and solicit American sympathy.

We, the Koreans in Congress assembled in Philadelphia on 14–16 April 1919, representing eighteen million people of our race who are now suffering untold miseries and barbarous treatment by the Japanese military authorities in Korea, hereby appeal to the great and generous American people.

For four thousand years our country enjoyed absolute autonomy. We have our own history, our own language, our own literature, and our own civilization. We have made treaties with the leading nations of the world; all of them recognized our independence, including Japan.

In 1904, at the beginning of the Russo–Japanese War, Japan made a treaty of alliance with Korea, guaranteeing

---

*   The Righteous Patriots Corps was an anti-Japanese terrorist organization that was organized after the March First movement by Kim Wŏnbong (b. 1898), a left-leaning Korean revolutionary. The corps' members were implicated in several bombing attacks on the colonial government offices. On Kim, see Robert A. Scalapino and Chong-sik Lee, *Communism in Korea* (Berkeley: University of California Press, 1972), 1:173–178 et passim.

†   *Munhwa sa*, pp. 296–297.

the territorial integrity and political independence of Korea, to cooperate in the war against Russia. Korea was opened to Japan for military purposes and Korea assisted Japan in many ways. After the war was over, Japan discarded the treaty of alliance as a "scrap of paper" and annexed Korea as a conquered territory. Ever since, she has been ruling Korea with that autocratic militarism whose prototype has been well illustrated by Germany in Belgium and northern France.

The Korean people patiently suffered under the iron heel of Japan for the last decade or more, but now they have reached the point where they are no longer able to endure it. On 1 March of this year some three million men, mostly of the educated class and composed of Christians, Heaven Worshipers,* Confucians, Buddhists, students of mission schools, under the leadership of the pastors of the native Christian churches, declared their independence from Japan and formed a provisional government on the border of Manchuria. Through the news dispatches and through private telegrams we are informed that so far thirty-two thousand Korean revolutionists have been thrown into dungeons by the Japanese, and over one hundred thousand men, women, and children have been killed or wounded. The Koreans have no weapons with which to fight, as the Japanese had taken everything away from them since the annexation, even pistols and fowling pieces. What resistance they are offering now against the Japanese soldiers and gendarmerie is math pitchforks and sickles. In spite of this disadvantage and the horrible casualties among the Koreans, these people are keeping up their resistance, and this demonstration is now nationwide, including nearly all provinces. Japan has declared martial law in Korea and is butchering these unfortunate but patriotic people by the thousands every day.

The Koreans in the United States and Hawaii have sent their representatives to Philadelphia, the Cradle of Liberty, to formulate a concerted plan with a view to stop this inhuman treatment of their brethren by the "Asiatic Kaiser," and to devise ways and means to help along the great cause of freedom and justice for our native land.

---

* Refers to the Ch'ŏndogyo believers.

We appeal to you for support and sympathy because we know you love justice; you also fought for liberty and democracy, and you stand for Christianity and humanity. Our cause is a just one before the laws of God and man. Our aim is freedom from militaristic autocracy; our object is democracy for Asia; our hope is universal Christianity. Therefore we feel that our appeal merits your consideration.

You have already championed the cause of the oppressed and held out your helping hand to the weak of the earth's races. Your nation is the Hope of Mankind; therefore we come to you.

Besides this, we also feel that we have the right to ask your help for the reason that the treaty between the United States and Korea [signed in 1882] contains a stipulation in article 1, paragraph 2, which reads as follows:

"If other powers deal unjustly or oppressively with either government, the other will exert their good offices, on being informed of the case, to bring about an amicable arrangement, thus showing their friendly feelings."

Does not this agreement make it incumbent upon America to intercede now in Korea's behalf?

There are many other good and sufficient reasons for America to exert her good offices to bring about an amicable arrangement, but we mention only one more, which is a new principle recently formulated at the peace conference in Paris. We cannot do better than to quote President Wilson's words, who is one of the founders of this new international obligation.

"The principle of the League of Nations is that it is the friendly right of every nation [that is] a member of the League to call attention to any thing that she thinks will disturb the peace of the world, no matter where that thing is occurring. There is no subject that touches the peace of the world that is exempt from inquiry or discussion."

We, therefore, in the name of humanity, liberty, and democracy, in the name of the American–Korean treaty, and in the name of the peace of the world, ask the government of the United States to exert its good offices to save the lives of our freedom-loving brethren in Korea and to protect the American missionaries and their families who are in danger of losing their lives and property on account of their love for our people and their faith in Christ.

We further ask you, the great American public, to give us your moral and material help so that our brethren in Korea will know that your sympathy is with them and that you are truly the champions of liberty and international justice.

AN CH'ANGHO: GRAND STRATEGY FOR INDEPENDENCE

[From *Hanguk tongnip undong sa* 3:372–388]

This statement was printed in the 8 January 1920 edition of *Tongnip sinmum* (The Independence), an organ of the Korean Provisional Government (Taehan Minguk Imsi Chŏngbu) in Shanghai that had begun publication in August 1919. This paper should not be confused with the paper of the same name published by the Independence Club between 1896 and 1899.

Because of illness I find it difficult to speak to you. There are six major issues on which our people must act resolutely today: military affairs, diplomacy, education, judicial affairs, finance, and unity. Before I get to the main topic, there are a few other things I must mention first.

The Relationship Between Government and People

Isn't there an emperor in our country today? The answer is yes. In the past there was only one emperor in our country, but now every one of the twenty million Koreans is an emperor. Where you are sitting at this moment is the royal throne, and what you are wearing on your head is the royal crown. What is an emperor? He is the one who holds the sovereign power. In the past one person held the sovereign power; now all of you have that power. In the past when one person held the sovereign power, the rise and fall of the nation depended on that person; today, they depend on the entire people. Government officials are servants; hence, the president and the prime minister are all your servants. The sovereign people most learn how to guide their servants, and the government officials must learn how to serve the sovereign people. …

Military Affairs

Let me now discuss the main subject. These six major issues are most crucial. In order to carry out our work, there must first be rational study; this alone produces a clear-cut decision. Our job is to destroy a ferocious Japan and regain our nation. Ours is a huge task, and naturally it needs careful study. Let me ask you, how many times a day do you think about our country? Every day, every hour, we must think and study. …

The big problem we face right now is whether we should conduct our independence campaign in a peaceful way or through war. The advocates of peaceful means as well as those of war are all sincere in their patriotic devotion.

The peace advocates argue that we can only express our thoughts and that war is as useless, when one compares our strength with theirs, as hitting a stone with an egg. It is best, they say, to appeal to world opinion.

The war advocates argue that Koreans will not be accused of being extremists even if they should declare war. Others have fought for their independence; isn't it natural that we should fight for ours? Comparing our strength with theirs is folly. We are not to calculate the chances for victory or defeat. It is natural to risk our own death as we watch our fellow countrymen being killed, maimed, or dishonored, it is natural to risk one's own death. Moral duty and human feeling compel us to fight. Moreover, Japan today is faced with an unprecedented crisis due to serious foreign complications and internal schism. We therefore can win according to these war advocates.

Considering the circumstances of our time and our moral obligations we have no other option but to fight. But should we go to battle now or after completing our preparations? Some say that we cannot wait for preparations because a revolution is not like a business venture. Nevertheless, preparations are necessary.

When I say preparations, I do not mean bringing our strength up to the level of the enemy's. But some preparations there must be. Even in a private gang fight, each side prepares its battle plans. To march to battle without preparations is to disparage the significance of the revolutionary war. Allowing, twenty *chŏn** to feed a

_____

* One-hundredth of a *wŏn*.

soldier a day, sixty thousand *wŏn* would be needed to feed ten thousand men for a month. If we go to war without preparations, we may starve to death before the enemy can kill us.

Therefore, if you should be in favor of war, you must understand that preparations are absolutely necessary. Some say, "Don't talk about preparations. For the last ten years we haven't been able to do anything because we have been preparing." But the truth is that we could not march to war due to lack of preparations caused by incessant talk about marching, not because we were busy with preparations. Had we talked less about marching and more about preparing, we might have marched forth already. ...

If one fully realizes the shame of enslavement, however, even death may not appear too dreadful Let us not be too anxious to survive long enough to see the day of independence; rather, let our death build the foundation for national independence. Let us not join the independence army merely by our words but by our deeds. We must vow to wage the war of independence successfully by all means at our command.

For the purpose of bringing about a fighting war, we have to continue waging a peaceful war. What is a peaceful war? The *manse* demonstrations would be an example.

Needless to say, *manse* alone will not bring about independence. Yet the power of *manse* has been enormous: it affected the entire population at home and the entire world abroad. In the past, the people of the United States prodded their government and Congress on our behalf; now the government and Congress must prod the people. I have seen a pamphlet being circulated in the Senate on our behalf. Is this not a result of the peaceful war? To induce our fellow countrymen who became public officials under enemy rule to leave their positions would be an example of the peaceful war. If the general public should refuse to pay tax to the enemy and pay to the government of the Korean Republic instead, if they should hoist the flag of the Korean Republic instead of the Japanese flag, if they should boycott the Japanese currency, if they should stop dealing with Japanese government agencies for adjudication or other settlements—all these would be examples of the peaceful war. Are these not cases of vigorous warfare?

Even if only a part of our population, not to mention all of the people, should behave in this manner, how effective they would be! Some argue that this would not be enough. Nevertheless we must continue on this course until the outbreak of a major war. The peaceful war may cost hundreds of thousands of lives. It too is a war of independence.

HKK

SIN CH'AEHO: DECLARATION OF KOREAN REVOLUTION

[From *Tanjae Sin Ch'aeho chŏnjip* 2:35–46]

Sin Ch'aeho, also known for his historical writings, which show intense nationalism, wrote this statement at the request of a Korean direct action group, the Righteous Patriots Corps (Ŭiyŏltan), headed by Kim Wŏnbong. This is an excerpt from the lengthy mission statement of this organization, which was responsible, among others, for a bombing assault on the head office of the Oriental Development Company (Tongch'ŏk) by Na Sŏkchu (1892–1926).

The Japanese burglars wiped out the name of our nation, seized the powers of our government, and deprived us of all necessary sustenance for survival. They took away the lifelines of our economy, ranging from forests, rivers, railroads, mines, and fishing grounds to the raw materials for petty handicraft industries, thereby smashing our production capacity to pieces. They levied a land tax, house tax, poll tax, cattle tax, surtax, local tax, liquor and tobacco taxes, fertilizer fax, seed tax, business tax, sanitation tax, income tax, and others that were raised frequently and relentlessly, sucking away the last drop of our blood. Korean businessmen became mere intermediaries to sell Japanese products to Koreans but face eventual demise due to concentration of capital The majority of our people—the peasants—work day and night only to see the fruits of their labor going to the Japanese burglars rather than to feed their wives and children. They became like draft animals condemned to work for eternity to enrich the Japanese. Even the life of draft animals has become impossible, and as a growing number of Japanese settlers quickly poured into Korea, our people lost the land to live on and had to migrate over land and water to western Kando, northern Kando,* or Siberia. Starving souls have thus become roving souls without a home.

Our children must attend schools—that is, training centers for slaves—where Japanese is called the national language and Japanese script is referred to as the national script. A Korean wanting to read Korean history will end up reading what the Japanese have fabricated—such as the assertion that the Tangun was a brother of Susanoo† or that the territories south of the Han River belonged to Japan during the Three Kingdoms period. Newspapers and magazines carry only semi-Japanized slavelike writings that praise the oppressive rule. A child born with intellectual endowment faces two choices: either the pressure of circumstances reduces him to pessimism and despair, resulting in total ruination, or he is incarcerated on a trumped-up charge of conspiracy and subjected to all manner of barbaric tortures that kill or maim him for the rest of his life.

On the basis of these facts, we declare that the oppressive Japanese rule, rule by an alien race, is the enemy that jeopardizes Korea's national survival. We further proclaim that we are entitled to employ revolutionary means to exterminate the Japanese enemy who threatens our survival. ...

At present, because of the Japanese political and economic oppression, the economy experiences growing difficulties, all the production facilities have been taken away, and the means to feed and clothe the people have been exhausted. How, then, can industries be developed? With what resources? How can education be expanded? Where and how many soldiers can we train? Even if such training should be possible, is it possible to train as many as one-hundredth of the Japanese armed forces? This argument is indeed illusory.

For these reasons, we discard the illusions of "diplomacy" and preparations." We proclaim that we shall carry out a people's direct revolution.

In order for the Korean people to survive, they must expel Japan; to expel Japan, only revolutionary means will succeed. There is no other way.

How should we go about carrying out a revolution? In the past, the people were the servants of the state under the control of the ruling lord—the privileged group. A revolution was merely a change of the name of the privileged group. ... Today's revolution is carried out by the people for their own benefit. We therefore call it "a people's revolution" or "a direct revolution." Due to the direct participation of the people, the intensity and magnitude of such a revolution can exceed the usual bounds, and its outcome can go beyond the normal expectations in warfare: the people without funds or arms can bring down a monarch who commands a million troops and immense wealth, or they may expel foreign invaders. The first step for our revolution is, therefore, to arouse the people. How then can the people be aroused? ...

Those who awoke first must serve as the revolutionary pioneers for the benefit of the entire people. If the people who suffer from hunger, cold, deprivation, pain, taxes, debt, restrictions on their freedom of movement, and so on, to the point of absolute despair should see the destruction of the perpetrator of such an oppressive rule or demolition of the oppressors' installations, and if the welcome news should spread and strike a sympathetic chord among the general public, then the people would realize that, instead of starving to death, they have another option—namely, revolution. ... In order to awaken our people, to smash this oppressive colonial rule, and to give a new life to our people, one exploding bomb would be more effective than training a hundred thousand soldiers, and one uprising would be more eloquent than millions of pages written in newspapers and magazines. ...

The targets of violence—assassination, destruction, uprising—include:

1. The governor-general of Korea and various officials in the colonial government
2. The emperor and government officials of Japan

---

* The Chien-tao region in southeast Manchuria, bordering Korea.

† The younger brother of the Sun Goddess in Japanese mythology.

3. Spies and traitors
4. All physical installations of the enemy

In addition, any leading citizens and wealthy persons in various communities who, by words or deeds, attempt to moderate or slander our activities, not to mention actively impede our revolutionary work, will meet with our violence, Japanese immigrants in Korea who have become tools for the oppressive colonial rule, thereby threatening the survival of the Korean people, will be forcibly expelled.

The road to revolution starts with destruction. But destruction is not for destruction's sake; rather, it is for the sake of construction. … The Korean people and the Japanese burglars are locked in a conflict in which one or the other will perish. Since we know this, we, the twenty million people, must be united in marching forward on the road of violence and destruction.

The people are the main force of the revolution. Violence is the only weapon of our revolution.

HKK

Kim Ku: Declaration of the Korean Restoration Army

[From *Tongnip undong sa* 6:177–178]

After the outbreak of the full-scale Sino–Japanese War and as Japanese forces were moving deeper into China, the Korean Provisional Government in Shanghai had to follow the retreating Chinese government to Chungking. Kim Ku, president of the Korean Republic, had long been anxious to create a Korean army to fight the Japanese. On 15 September 1940 he issued this declaration announcing the first step toward that goal. Under the overall command of General Yi Ch'ŏngch'ŏn, some Korean units were later engaged in combat, albeit on a limited scale.

The Provisional Government of the Korean Republic hereby proclaims the creation of the Restoration Army (Kwangbokkun) of Korea and the establishment of the General Headquarters of the Restoration Army of Korea on 17 September 1940 pursuant to the Law on Military Organization promulgated by the government in 1919 and with special approval of Generalissimo Chiang Kai-shek, president of the Republic of China. The Restoration Army of Korea shall continue the war of resistance in cooperation with the people of the Republic of China and as part of the Allied Forces in order to defeat the Japanese imperialists, the common enemy, for the purpose of restoring the independence of our two nations.

For the past thirty years, when Japan ruled Korea, with a resolute spirit of independence our people have staged a heroic struggle against the brutal oppressors to secure a release from a shameful life of enslavement.

As the glorious campaign of resistance by the Chinese people reaches its fourth year, we have great hopes and firmly believe that the time has come to enhance our fighting capabilities for the independence of our fatherland.

We are pleased that Generalissimo Chiang Kai-shek, the supreme leader of the Republic of China, has adopted a far-sighted policy regarding the Korean people. We extend to him thankful praise. His moral support greatly encourages the movement for liberation of our nation and especially the preparations for armed resistance against the oppressive Japanese enemy.

We pledge that we shall continue our own ceaseless struggle in a united Korean–Chinese front to win freedom and equality for the peoples of the Far East and Asia.

HKK

THE NEW CULTURE MOVEMENT

Edited by William Theodore De Bary and Richard John Lufrano

s its name implies, the New Culture Movement was an attempt to destroy what remained of traditional Confucian culture in the republican era and to replace it with something new. The collapse of the old dynastic system in 1911 and the failure of Yuan Shikai's Confucian-garbed monarchical restoration in 1916 meant that, politically, Confucianism was almost dead. It had, however, been much more than a political philosophy. It had been a complete way of life, which nationalism and republicanism supplanted only in part. There were some even among republicans who felt that certain aspects of the old culture, Confucian ethics especially, should be preserved and strengthened, lest the whole fabric of Chinese life come apart and the new regime itself be seriously weakened. Others, with far more influence on the younger generation, drew precisely the opposite conclusion. For them, nothing in Confucianism was worth salvaging from the debris of the Manchu dynasty. In fact, whatever vestiges of the past remained in the daily life and thinking of the people should be rooted out; otherwise the young republic would rest on shaky foundations, and its progress would be retarded by a backward citizenry. The new order required a whole new culture. The political revolution of 1911 had to be followed by a cultural revolution. In this conflict of views many issues surfaced that reappeared in the 1980s and 1990s between those who advocated a return to

Confucianism and those who saw "modernization" as requiring liberation from the past.

During and just after World War I the intellectual spearhead of this cultural evolution went on the offensive, launching a movement that reached out in many directions and touched many aspects of Chinese society. Roughly, it may be divided into six major phases, presented below in more or less chronological order. They are (1) the attack on Confucianism, (2) the Literary Revolution, (3) the proclaiming of a new philosophy of life, (4) the debate on science and the philosophy of life, (5) the "doubting of antiquity" movement, and (6) the debate on Chinese and Western cultural values. Needless to say, these phases overlapped considerably, and certain leading writers figured prominently in more than one phase of the movement.

From the movement's anti-traditionalist character one may infer that its leaders looked very much to the West. Positivism was their great inspiration, science and materialism were their great slogans, and—in the early years especially—John Dewey and Bertrand Russell were their great idols. The leaders themselves were in many cases Western-educated, though not necessarily schooled in the West, since Western-style education was by now established in the East, in Japan, and in the new national and missionary colleges of China. Often college professors themselves, the leaders now had access to the lecture platform, as well as to the new organs of the public journalism and the intellectual and literary reviews that were a novel feature of the modern age. Above all, they had a new audience—young, intense, frustrated by China's failures in the past, and full of eager hopes for the future.

THE ATTACK ON CONFUCIANISM

The open assault on Confucianism, which began in 1916, was led by Chen Duxiu (1879–1942), editor of a magazine titled *The New Youth*. Earlier reformers had attacked certain of the concepts of Confucianism, often in the name of a purified and revitalized Confucian belief or, with less obvious partisanship, combining criticism of certain aspects with praise of others. Chen, by contrast, challenged Confucianism from beginning to end, realizing as he did so that he struck at the very heart of the traditional culture. For him, a partisan of "science" and "democracy," Confucianism stood simply for reaction and obscurantism. He identified it with the old regime, with Yuan Shikai's attempt to restore the monarchy, with everything from the past that, to his mind, had smothered progress and creativity.

Such an uncompromising attack was bound to shock many—those who had taken Confucianism as much for granted as the good earth of China or those who still held to it consciously, and with some pride, as an expression of cultural nationalism. But there were others upon whom Chen's bold denunciations had an electrifying effect—those, particularly young teachers and students, for whom Confucianism had come to hold little positive meaning as their own education became more Westernized; those for whom, in fact, it was now more likely to be felt in their own lives simply as a form of unwanted parental or societal constraint. Young people of this group, with Beijing as their center, *The New Youth* as their mouthpiece, and Chen as their literary champion, were glad to throw themselves into a crusade against this bugbear from the past and to proclaim their own coming of age in the modern world by shouting, "Destroy the old curiosity shop of Confucius!"

CHEN DUXIU: "THE WAY OF CONFUCIUS AND MODERN LIFE"

Through articles such as this, which appeared in December 1916, Chen Duxiu established himself as perhaps the most influential writer of his time. His popular review, *Xin qingnian* (*The New Youth*), had for its Western title *La Jeunesse nouvelle*, reflecting the avant-garde character of its editor, who had obtained his higher education first in a Japanese normal college and later in France. Here the Westernized and "liberated" Chen directs his fire at social customs and abuses that seemed to have Confucian sanction but have no place in the modern age. Here the man who was to found the Chinese Communist Party five years later speaks as an individualist, who attributes the lack of individualism in China to the traditional view of property as family-owned and -controlled rather than belonging to an individual

The pulse of modern life is economic, and the fundamental principle of economic production is individual independence. Its effect has penetrated ethics. Consequently, the independence of the individual in the ethical field and the independence of property in the economic field bear witness to each other, thus reaffirming the theory [of such interaction]. Because of this [interaction], social mores and material culture have taken a great step forward.

In China, the Confucians have based their teachings on their ethical norms. Sons and wives possess neither personal individuality nor personal property. Fathers and elder brothers bring up their sons and younger brothers and are in turn supported by them. It is said in chapter 30 of the *Record of Rites*: "While parents are living, the son dares not regard his person or property as his own" [27:14]. This is absolutely not the way to personal independence. ...

In all modern constitutional states, whether monarchies or republics, there are political parties. Those who engage in party activities all express their spirit of independent conviction. They go their own way and need not agree with their fathers or husbands. When people are bound by the Confucian teachings of filial piety and obedience to the point of the son not deviating from the father's way even three years after his death* and the woman not only obeying her father and husband but also her son,† how can they form their own political party and make their own choice? The movement of women's participation in politics is also an aspect of women's life in modern civilization. When they are bound by the Confucian teaching that "To be a woman means to submit,"‡ that "The wife's words should not travel beyond her own apartment," and that "A woman does not discuss affairs outside the home,"§ would it not be unusual if they participated in politics?

In the West some widows choose to remain single because they are strongly attached to their late husbands and sometimes because they prefer a single life; they have nothing to do with what is called the chastity of widowhood. Widows who remarry are not despised by society at all. On the other hand, in the Chinese teaching of decorum, there is the doctrine of "no remarriage after the husband's death."¶ It is considered to be extremely shameful and unchaste for a woman to serve two husbands or a man to serve two rulers. The *Record of Rites* also prohibits widows from wailing at night [27:21] and people from being friends with sons of widows. For the sake of their family reputation, people have forced their daughters-in-law to remain widows. These women have had no freedom and have endured a most miserable life. Year after year these many promising young women have lived a physically and spiritually abnormal life. All this is the result of Confucian teachings of ritual decorum.

In today's civilized society, social intercourse between men and women is a common practice. Some even say that because women have a tender nature and can temper the crudeness of man, they are necessary in public or private gatherings. It is not considered improper even

for strangers to sit or dance together once they have been introduced by the host. In the way of Confucian teaching, however, "Men and women do not sit on the same mat," "Brothers- and sisters-in-law do not exchange inquiries about each other," "Married sisters do not sit on the same mat with brothers or eat from the same dish," "Men and women do not know each other's name except through a matchmaker and should have no social relations or show affection until after marriage presents have been exchanged,"** "Women must cover their faces when they go out,"†† "Boys and girls seven years or older do not sit or eat together," "Men and women have no social relations except through a matchmaker and do not meet until after marriage presents have been exchanged,"‡‡ and "Except in religious sacrifices, men and women do not exchange wine cups."§§ Such rules of decorum are not only inconsistent with the mode of life in Western society; they cannot even be observed in today's China.

Western women make their own living in various professions such as that of lawyer, physician, and store employee. But in the Confucian Way, "In giving or receiving anything, a man or woman should not touch the other's hand,"¶¶ "A man does not talk about affairs inside [the household] and a woman does not talk about affairs outside [the household]," and "They do not exchange cups except in sacrificial rites and funerals."*** "A married woman is to obey" and the husband is the mainstay of the wife.††† Thus the wife is naturally supported by the husband and needs no independent livelihood.

---

* Referring to *Analects* 1:11.

† *Record of Rites* 9:24.
‡ Ibid.

§ Ibid. 1:24.

¶ Ibid. 9:24.

** Ibid. 1:24.

†† Ibid. 10:12.
‡‡ Ibid. 10:51.

§§ Ibid. 27:17.
¶¶ Ibid. 27:20.

*** Ibid. 10:12.

††† Ibid. 9:24.

A married woman is at first a stranger to her parents-in-law. She has only affection but no obligation toward them. In the West, parents and children usually do not live together, and daughters-in-law, particularly, have no obligation to serve parents-in-law. But in the way of Confucius, a woman is to "revere and respect them and never to disobey day or night,"* "A woman obeys, that is, obeys her parents-in-law,"† "A woman serves her parents-in-law as she serves her own parents,"‡ she "never should disobey or be lazy in carrying out the orders of parents and parents-in-law." "If a man is very fond of his wife, but his parents do not like her, she should be divorced."§ (In ancient times there were many such cases, like that of Lu Yu [1125–1210].) "Unless told to retire to her own apartment, a woman does not do so, and if she has an errand to do, she must get permission from her parents-in-law."¶ This is the reason why cruelty to daughters-in-law has never ceased in Chinese society.

According to Western customs, fathers do not discipline grown-up sons but leave them to the law of the country and the control of society. But in the Way of Confucius, "When one's parents are angry and not pleased and beat him until he bleeds, he does not complain but instead arouses in himself the feelings of reverence and filial piety."** This is the reason why in China there is the saying, "One has to die if his father wants him to, and the minister has to perish if his ruler wants him to."…

Confucius lived in a feudal age. The ethics he promoted is the ethics of the feudal age. The social mores he taught and even his own mode of living were teachings and modes of a feudal age. The objectives, ethics, social norms, mode of living, and political institutions did not go beyond the privilege and prestige of a few rulers and aristocrats and had nothing to do with the happiness of the great masses. How can this be shown? In the teachings of Confucius, the most important elements in social ethics and social life are the rules of decorum, and the most serious thing in government is punishment. In chapter 1 of the *Record of Rites*, it is said, "The rules of decorum do not go down to the common people and the penal statutes do not go up to great officers" [1:35]. Is this not solid proof of the [true] spirit of the Way of Confucius and the spirit of the feudal age?

[From Chen, "Kongzi zhi dao yu xiandai shenghuo," pp. 3–5—WTC]

THE LITERARY REVOLUTION

Paralleling the attack on Confucianism was the attack on the classical literary language—the language of Confucian tradition and of the old-style scholar-official. With the abandonment of the "eight-legged essay" examinations for the civil service in 1905, the discarding also of the official language, so far removed from ordinary speech, might have seemed inevitable. This was a time of rising nationalism, which in the West had been linked to the rise of vernacular literatures; an era of expanding education, which would be greatly facilitated by a written language simpler and easier to learn; a period of strong Westernization in thought and scholarship, which would require a more flexible instrument for the expression of new concepts. No doubt each of these factors contributed to the rapid spread of the literary revolution after its launching by Hu Shi, with the support of Chen Duxiu in 1917. And yet it is a sign of the strong hold that the classical language had on educated men, and of its great prestige as a mark of learning, that until Hu appeared on the scene with his novel ideas, even the manifestos of reformers and revolutionaries had kept to the classical style of writing as if there could be no other.

Hu Shi (1891–1962) had studied agriculture at Cornell on a Boxer Indemnity grant and philosophy at Columbia under John Dewey, of whom he became the leading Chinese disciple. Even before his return home he had begun advocating a new written language for China, along with a complete reexamination and

---

* *I-li*, ch. 2; Steele, 1:39.

† *Record of Rites* 41:6.

‡ Ibid. 10:3.

§ Ibid. 10:12.

¶ Ibid. 10:13.

** Ibid. 10:12.

reevaluation of the classical tradition in thought and literature. Chen Duxiu's position as head of the department of literature at Beijing National University, and his new political organ, *The New Youth*, represented strong backing for Hu's revolutionary program—a program all the more commanding of attention because its aim was not merely destructive of traditional usage but, ambitiously enough, directed to the stimulation of a new literature and new ideas. Instead of dwelling solely upon the deficiencies of the past, Hu's writings were full of concrete and constructive suggestions for the future. There was hope here, as well as indignation.

Hu's program thus looked beyond the immediate literary revolution, stressing the vernacular as a means of communication, to what came to be known as the literary renaissance. There can be no doubt that this movement stimulated literary activity along new lines, especially in the adoption of forms and genres then popular in the West. Yet there is real doubt whether this new literary output was able to fulfill all of Hu's expectations, given the political constraints to which it was later subjected. It excelled in social criticism and so contributed further to the processes of social and political disintegration. Also—and this is particularly true of Hu's own work—it rendered great service in the rehabilitation of popular literature from earlier centuries, above all, the great Chinese novels. But whether it produced in its own right a contemporary literature of great distinction and creative imagination is a question that must be left to historians and critics of the future with a better perspective on these troubled times.

Hu Shi:
"A Preliminary Discussion of Literary Reform"

Many people have been discussing literary reform. Who am I, unlearned and unlettered, to offer an opinion? Nevertheless, for some years I have studied the matter and thought it over many times, helped by my deliberations with friends; and the conclusions I have come to are perhaps not unworthy of discussion. Therefore I shall summarize my views under eight points and elaborate on them separately to invite the study and comments of those interested in literary reform.

I believe that literary reform at the present time must begin with these eight items: (1) Write with substance. (2) Do not imitate the ancients. (3) Emphasize grammar. (4) Reject melancholy. (5) Eliminate old clichés. (6) Do not use allusions. (7) Do not use couplets and parallelisms. And (8) Do not avoid popular expressions or popular forms of characters.

1. *Write with substance.* By *substance* I mean: (a) Feeling. … Feeling is the soul of literature. Literature without feeling is like a man without a soul. … (b) Thought. By *thought* I mean insight, knowledge, and ideals. Thought does not necessarily depend on literature for transmission, but literature becomes more valuable if it contains thought, and thought is more valuable if it possesses literary value. This is the reason why the essays of Zhuangzi, the poems of Tao Qian [365–427], Li Bo [689–762], and Du Fu [717–770], the *ci* of Xin Jiaxuan [1140–1207], and the novel of Shi Naian [that is, the *Shuihu zhuan* or *Water Margin*] are matchless for all times. … In recent years literary men have satisfied themselves with tones, rhythm, words, and phrases and have had neither lofty thoughts nor genuine feeling. This is the chief cause of the deterioration of literature. This is the bad effect of superficiality over substantiality, that is to say, writing without substance. To remedy this bad situation, we must resort to substance. And what is substance? Nothing but feeling and thought.

2. *Do not imitate the ancients.* Literature changes with time. Each period from Zhou and Qin to Song, Yuan, and Ming has its own literature. This is not my private opinion but the universal law of the advancement of civilization. Take prose, for example. There is the prose of the *Classic of History*, the prose of the ancient philosophers, the prose of [the historians] Sima Qian and Ban Gu, the prose of the [Tang and Song masters] Han Yu, Liu Zongyuan, Ouyang Xiu, and Su Xun, the prose of the *Recorded Conversations* of the Neo-Confucians, and the prose of Shi Naian and Cao Xueqin [d. ca. 1765, author *of The Dream of Red Mansions*]. This is the development of prose.

… Each period has changed in accordance with its situation and circumstance, each with its own characteristic merits. From the point of view of historical evolution, we cannot say that the writings of the ancients are all superior to those of modern writers. The prose of Zuo Qiuming [sixth century B.C., author of the *Zuozhuan*] and Sima Qian is wonderful, but compared to the *Zuozhuan* and *Records of the Historian*, wherein is Shi Naian's *Water Margin* (*Shuihu zhuan*) inferior? …

I have always held that colloquial stories alone in modern Chinese literature can proudly be compared with the first-class literature of the world. Because they do not imitate the past but only describe the society of the day, they have become genuine literature. …

3. *Emphasize grammar.* Many writers of prose and poetry today neglect grammatical construction. Examples are too numerous to mention, especially in parallel prose and the four-line and eight-line verses.

4. *Reject melancholy.* This is not an easy task. Nowadays young writers often show passion. They choose such names as "Cold Ash," "No Birth," and "Dead Ash" as pen names, and in their prose and poetry they think of declining years when they face the setting sun, and of destitution when they meet the autumn wind. … I am not unaware of the fact that our country is facing many troubles. But can salvation be achieved through tears? I hope all writers become Fichtes and Mazzinis and not like Jia Yi [201–169 B.C.], Wang Can [177–217], Qu Yuan[343–277 B.C.], Xie Gaoyu [1249–1295], and so on [who moaned and com-plained]. …

5. *Eliminate old clichés.* By this I merely mean that writers should describe in their own words what they personally experience. So long as they achieve the goal of describing things and expressing the mood without sacrificing realism, that is literary achievement. Those who employ old clichés are lazy people who refuse to coin their own terms of description.

6. *Do not use allusions.* I do not mean *allusion* in the broad sense. These are of five kinds: (a) analogies employed by ancient writers, which have a universal meaning … ; (b) idioms; (c) references to historical events … ; (d)quoting from or referring to people in the past for comparison … ; and (e) quotations. … Allusions such as these may or may not be used.

But I do not approve of the use of allusions in the narrow sense. By *using allusions* I mean that writers are incapable of creating their own expressions to portray the scene before them or the concepts in their minds, and instead muddle along by borrowing old stories or expressions that are partly or wholly inapplicable. …

7. *Do not use couplets and parallelisms.* Parallelism is a special characteristic of human language. This is why in ancient writings such as those of Laozi and Confucius, there are occasionally couplets. The first chapter of the *Daodejing* consists of three couplets. *Analects* 1:14, 1:15, and 3:17 are all couplets. But these are fairly natural expressions and have no indication of being forced or artificial, especially because there is no rigid requirement about the number of words, tones, or parts of speech. Writers in the age of literary decadence, however, who had nothing to say, emphasized superficiality, the extreme of which led to the development of the parallel prose, regulated *ci*, and the long regulated verse. It is not that there are no good products in these forms, but they are, in the final analysis, few. Why? Is it not because they restrict to the highest degree the free expression of man? (Not a single good piece can be mentioned among the long regulated verse.) To talk about literary reform today, we must "first establish the fundamental"* and not waste our useful energy in the nonessentials of subtlety and delicacy. This

---

* *Mencius* 6A:15.

is why I advocate giving up couplets and rhymes. Even if they cannot be abolished, they should be regarded as merely literary stunts and nothing to be pursued seriously.

There are still people today who deprecate colloquial novels as trifling literature, without realizing that Shi Naian, Cao Xueqin, and Wu Jianren [1867–1910]* all represent the main line of literature while parallel and regulated verse are really trifling matters. I know some will keep clear of me when they hear this.

8. *Do not avoid popular expressions or popular forms of characters.* When Buddhist scriptures were introduced into China, because classical expressions could not express their meanings, translators used clear and simple expressions. Their style already approached the colloquial. Later, many Buddhist lectures and dialogues were in the colloquial style, thus giving rise to the "conversation" style. When the Neo-Confucians of the Song dynasty used the colloquial in their *Recorded Conversations*, this style became the orthodox style of scholarly discussion. (This was followed by scholars of the Ming.) By that time, colloquial expressions had already penetrated rhymed prose, as can be seen in the colloquial poems of Tang and Song poets. From the third century to the end of the Yuan, North China had been under foreign races and popular literature developed. In prose there were such novels as *Water Margin* (*Shuihu zhuan*) and *Journey to the West* (*Xiyou ji*). In drama the products were innumerable. From the modern point of view, the Yuan period should be considered as a high point of literary development; unquestionably it produced the greatest number of immortal works. At that time writing and colloquial speech were the closest to each other, and the latter almost became the language of literature. Had the tendency not been checked, living literature would have emerged in China, and the great

---

* Author of *Ershi nian mu du zhi guai xianzhuang* (*Strange Phenomena Seen in Two Decades*).

work of Dante and Luther [who inaugurated the substitution of a living language for dead Latin] would have taken place in China. Unfortunately, the tendency was checked in the Ming when the government selected officials on the basis of the rigid "eight-legged" prose style and at the same time literary men like the "seven scholars" including Li [Mengyang, 1472–1529] considered "returning to the past" as highbrow. Thus the once-in-a-millennium chance of uniting writing and speech was killed prematurely, midway in the process. But from the modern viewpoint of historical evolution, we can definitely say that the colloquial literature is the main line of Chinese literature and that it should be the medium employed in the literature of the future. (This is my own opinion; not many will agree with me today.) For this reason, I hold that we should use popular expressions and words in prose and poetry. Rather than using dead expressions of three thousand years ago, it is better to employ living expressions of the twentieth century, and rather than using the language of the Qin, Han, and the Six Dynasties, which cannot reach many people and cannot be universally understood, it is better to use the language of the *Water Margin* (*Shuihu zhuan*) and *Journey to the West* (*Xiyou ji*), which is understood in every household.

[Hu, "Wenxue gailiang chuyi," in *Hu Shi wencun*, collection 1, ch. 1, pp. 5–16; original version in *Xin qingnian* 2, no. 5 (January 1917): 1–11—WTC]

CHEN DUXIU: "ON LITERARY REVOLUTION"

The movement of literary revolution has been in the making for some time. My friend Hu Shi is the one who started the revolution of which he is the vanguard. I do not mind being an enemy of all old-fashioned scholars in the country and raising to great heights the banner of "the Army of Literary Revolution" to support my friend. On this banner shall be written these three fundamental principles of our revolutionary army: (1) Destroy the aristocratic literature, which is nothing but literary chiseling and flattery, and construct a simple, expressive literature of the people. (2) Destroy the outmoded, showy, classical literature and construct a fresh and sincere literature of realism. (3) Destroy the obscure and abstruse "forest" literature* and construct a clear and popular literature of society. …

At this time of literary reform, aristocratic literature, classical literature, and forest literature should all be rejected. What are the reasons for attacking these three kinds of literature? The answer is that aristocratic literature employs embellishments and depends on previous writers and therefore has lost the qualities of independence and self-respect, that classical literature exaggerates and piles word after word and has lost the fundamental objective of expressing emotions and realistic descriptions; and that "forest" literature is difficult and obscure and is claimed to be lofty writing but is actually of no benefit to the masses. The form of such literatures is continuous repetition of previous models. It has flesh but no bones, body but no spirit. It is an ornament and is of no actual use. With respect to their contents, their horizon does not go beyond kings and aristocrats, spiritual beings and ghosts and personal fortunes and misfortunes. The universe, life, and society are all beyond their conception. These defects are common to all three forms of literature. These types of literature are both causes and effects of our national character of flattery, boasting, insincerity, and flagrant disregard of truth and facts. Now that we want political reform, we must regenerate the literature of those who are entrenched in political life. If we do not open our eyes and see the literary tendencies of the world society and the spirit of the time but instead bury our heads in old books day and night and confine our attention to kings and aristocrats, spiritual beings and ghosts and immortals, and personal fortunes and misfortunes, and in so doing hope to reform literature and politics, it is like binding our four limbs to fight Meng Ben [an ancient strong man].

[Chen, "Wenxue geminglun," pp. 1–4—WTC]

---

* An expression of Chen's for esoteric literature.

HU SHI: "CONSTRUCTIVE LITERARY REVOLUTION— A LITERATURE OF NATIONAL SPEECH"

A National Speech of Literary Quality

Since I returned to China last year, in my speeches on literary revolution in various places, I have changed my "eight points" [in the previous selection] into something positive and shall summarize them under four items:

1. Speak only when you have something to say. (A different version of the first of the eight points.)
2. Speak what you want to say and say it in the way you want to say it. (Different version of points 2–6.)
3. Speak what is your own and not that of someone else. (Different version of point 7.)
4. Speak in the language of the time in which you live. (Different version of point 8.)

The literary revolution we are promoting aims merely at the creation of a Chinese literature of national speech. Only when there is such a literature can there be a national speech of literary quality. And only when there is a national speech of literary quality can our national speech be considered a real national speech. A national speech without literary quality will be devoid of life and value and can be neither established nor developed. This is the main point of this essay. …

Why is it that a dead language cannot produce a living literature? It is because of the nature of literature. The function of language and literature lies in expressing ideas and showing feelings. When these are well done, we have literature. Those who use a dead classical style will translate their own ideas into allusions of several thousand years ago and convert their own feelings into literary expressions of centuries past. … If China wants to have a living literature, we must use the plain speech that is the natural speech, and we must devote ourselves to a literature of national speech. …

Someone says, "If we want to use the national speech in literature, we must first have a national speech. At present we do not have a standard national speech. How can we have a literature of national speech?" I will say, this sounds plausible but is really not true. A national language is not to be created by a few linguistic experts or a few texts and dictionaries of national speech. ... The truly effective and powerful text of national speech is the literature of national speech—novels, prose, poems, and plays written in the national speech. The time when these works prevail is the day when the Chinese national speech will have been established. Let us ask why we are now able simply to pick up the brush and write essays in the plain-speech style and use several hundred colloquial terms. Did we learn this from some textbook of plain speech? Was it not that we learned from such novels as the *Water Margin* (*Shuihu zhuan*), *Journey to the West* (*Xiyou ji*), *Dream of Red Mansions* (*Hongloumeng*) and *Unofficial History of the Scholars* (*Rulin waishi*)? This type of plain-speech literature is several hundred times as powerful as textbooks and dictionaries. ... If we want to establish anew a standard national speech, we must first of all produce numerous works like these novels in the national speech style. ...

A literature of national speech and a national speech of literary quality are our basic programs. Let us now discuss what should be done to carry them out.

I believe that the procedure in creating a new literature consists of three steps: (1) acquiring tools, (2) developing methods, and (3) creating. The first two are preparatory. The third is the real step to create a new literature.

1. *The tools.* Our tool is plain speech. Those of us who wish to create a literature of national speech should prepare this indispensable tool right away. There are two ways to do so:

    (a) Read extensively literary works written in the plain speech that can serve as models, such as the works mentioned above, the *Recorded Conversations* of Song Neo-Confucians and their letters written in the plain speech, the plays of the Yuan period, and the stories and monologues of the Ming and Qing times. Tang and Song poems and *ci* written in the plain speech should also be selected to read.

    (b) In all forms of literature, write in the plain-speech style. ...

2. *Methods.* I believe that the greatest defect of the literary men who have recently emerged in our country is the lack of a good literary method. ...

    Generally speaking, literary methods are of three kinds:

    (a) The method of collecting material. ... I believe that for future literary men the method of collecting material should be about as follows: (i) Enlarge the area from which material is to be collected. The three sources of material, namely, officialdom, houses of prostitution, and dirty society [from which present novelists draw their material], are definitely not enough. At present, the poor man's society, male and female factory workers, rickshaw pullers, farmers in the interior districts, small shop owners and peddlers everywhere, and all conditions of suffering have no place in literature [as they should]. Moreover, now that new and old civilizations have come into contact, problems like family catastrophes, tragedies in marriage, the position of women, the unfitness of present education, and so on, can all supply literature with material. (ii) Stress actual observation and personal experience. ... (iii) Use broad and keen imagination to supplement observation and experience.

    (b) The method of construction. ... This may be separated into two steps, namely, tailoring and laying the plot. ... While tailoring is to determine what to do, laying the plot is to determine how to do it. ...

    (c) The method of description. ...

3. *Creation.* The two items, tools and methods, discussed above are only preparations for the creation of a new literature. ... As to what constitutes the creation of a new literature, I had better not say a word. In my opinion we in China today have not reached the point where we can take concrete steps to create a new literature, and there is no need of talking theoretically about the techniques of creation. Let us first devote our efforts to the first two steps of preparatory work.

[Hu, "Jianshe di wenxue geminglun,"
Xin qingnian 4, no. 4 (April 1918): 290–306;
Hu Shi wencun, collection 1, pp. 56–73—WTC]

WHO IS AFRAID OF THE CHINESE MODERN GIRL?

By Madeleine Y. Dong

Edited by Alys Eve Weinbaum, Modern Girl Around the World Research Group

In Zhang Henshui's novel *Shanghai Express* (1935), the young protagonist Xuchun, on board the Beijing–Shanghai express, at first appears to be an ideal modern woman. Her tasteful dress, charming smile, graceful gestures, skillful handling of complicated situations, her eloquence, her independence, and her ability to read English, quickly catch the attention of Mr. Hu, an older, married businessman. Although Hu is attracted to Xuchun's modern appearance, it is her willingness to become a concubinelike secret lover and submit her life to his control that convinces him to enter a relationship with her. As the train dashes toward Shanghai, Hu falls asleep fantasizing that Xuchun will belong to him, but he wakes up only to find that she has disappeared with all his money and stocks. Now penniless in the big city Shanghai, Hu sees Xuchun in every modern-looking woman on the station platform and cries out warnings to all men.[1]

Zhang's story is a quintessential cautionary tale of the modern told through the figure of the Modern Girl. Its crux, the anxiety caused by a combination of attraction to and fear of the unknowable Modern Girl, was shared widely by her representations in news reports, literature, and visual culture.[2] While the Modern Girl was represented in advertisements as a beguiling icon of the glamour of modern life and happiness ostensibly achievable through consumption of industrial commodities, she also often appeared as a mystery and was seen as a threatening figure.[3] Modern Girl Xuchun, for

example, is nothing but artifice or performance. By the end of the novel, the reader learns nothing about this woman except her modern appearance. Her name is false, and all her history is bogus. She is the perfect con artist whose true identity is impossible to know, a woman as baffling as the modern city Shanghai itself. In addition, guarding against this Modern Girl also means fighting against one's own desires. Hu's warning about the Modern Girl, therefore, is also one against men's own fantasies toward the modern. In this sense, her attractiveness and men's inability to resist it conceal the real threat of the Modern Girl.

The prevalence of themes and plots such as those in *Shanghai Express* indicated the angst and titillation among the elite caused by the Modern Girl. In the first two sections of this chapter, I examine how the "Modern Girl look" facilitated the crossing of class boundaries and how the elite tried to salvage this look to defend its privilege to be modern. In a third section I discuss how the Modern Girl upset social conventions in her relations with her male counterpart, the modern man. Historically, the "superficiality" of the Modern Girl has been the focus of her criticisms from all sides. The last section of the chapter considers the historical and historiographical effects of such a focus.

In order to understand the Modern Girl figure, it is necessary to confront the issue of the dominance of male perspectives in her representations. Major changes in Republican-era Chinese social practices—such as the establishment of the nuclear family as the norm; young men and women receiving education or joining in the work force in integrated public spaces away from their parents' homes; and the emergence of an urban culture targeting the young—opened up potential spaces for single young women to play new roles in society. These public roles for women involved unprecedented visibility and shifts in representation, including Modern Girl fashions, attitudes, and images. The forms and meanings of these representations gave rise to a host of disputes, anxieties, and marketing schemes. The representations of the Modern Girl in stories, cartoons, and pictures were a major staging ground shaping these images and people's actions in relation to them. Though women were key actors in the social changes, this world of image production and interpretation was controlled and shaped mainly by men and capitalist forces. Hence, the main focus became the male issues of desire and fear and an all-or-nothing vision of the Modern Girl as emasculating or confirming modern masculinity. This chapter treats the bias in such male perspectives as an entry point to unravel how, through the figure of the Modern Girl, the desires, fantasies, and disillusionments of young women and men of the post-May Fourth period were not separated, but deeply entangled.

WHO WERE THESE MODERN-LOOKING WOMEN?

The Modern Girl look, with its painted face, bobbed or permed hair, fashionable *qipao*, and high-heel shoes, was so widely adopted by women of diverse social groups, including high school and college students, professionals, young wives of the upper and middle classes, and prostitutes, that by the 1930s it had become a passport to opportunity and a dress code of necessity for young female city dwellers. In an article written in 1933, Yunshang argued that the Modern Girl phenomenon had spread from the "leisure class" to the "middle class" and then led to the emergence of dance girls, masseuses, waitresses, saleswomen, all of whom were seen as prostitutes in disguise.[4] If a woman's appearance is often the first quality used to identify her in the modern city, the Modern Girl look was nonetheless often considered as veiling more than it revealed. While they reflected the

new urban anonymity, representations of the Modern Girl as a mysterious figure also indicated anxiety over her blurring of class and status lines.

The magazine *Young Companion (Liang Yu)* stood out in featuring images of modern-looking women. Established in 1926, this popular pictorial was set apart from contemporary magazines through high-quality printing and avoidance of tabloid-style content. Reports on international news and eminent figures on the national stage, fiction, advertisements for cosmetics, cigarettes, fabrics, and other "modern" commodities filled its pages. The magazine juxtaposed photos of real women with advertising images and fashion sketches and created a space for imagining the modern by blending reality, desire, and fantasy.

After featuring female movie stars and two young female students on the covers of its first few issues, the magazine received the following response from a reader, which it published in its eleventh issue: "The magazine focuses on women visually and uses them as ornaments, but the texts treat them as subjects for jokes. Does this elevate women's status, or does it treat them as playthings?" The editors defended the magazine by arguing that it was the deteriorating social conditions that distorted the meaning of women's physical beauty. But the editors admitted that they once offended a high school student by publishing her picture without her consent. The editors observed, "Her attitude is typical of the mentality of the majority of people who consider all females whose pictures appear in magazines, except old ladies with white hair and wrinkled skin, cheap women of low moral quality."[5]

This mentality changed by the end of 1927 when a Chinese "high society" took form following the reunification of China and the establishment of the Nationalist government in Nanjing. The magazine developed its high-class reputation, and it became acceptable, even honorable, for young women to have their pictures published in *Young Companion*. A column named "Women's Page" *(Funü zhi ye)* featured images of modern Chinese women around the world. Appearing in hairstyles, fashions, and makeup identical to those of Modern Girls in ads, the women in *Young Companion* were graduates of elite high schools, college students from around the country, daughters of eminent families in China and overseas Chinese communities, or young wives of famous men. The word "debutante" often accompanied the photos. In some cases, the young women in the pictures were attached to well-known families, but most of the time they were identified only by their own names. In other words, they were not defined in relationship to patrilineal families but as free and available young women in a public space. The only guarantee that they were "respectable," "good," and "high-class" was the highbrow medium in which their pictures were displayed. In contrast, newspapers and magazines published during the same period targeting a relatively lower-class audience, such as *Shanghai huabao* (*Shanghai Pictorial*, published in 1925), *Fu'ermosi* (*Sherlock Holmes*, published in 1926), and *Jingbao* (*Crysta*, published in 1929) displayed no such photos of young women.

While the magazine apparently intended its covers and the Women's Page to showcase debutantes and high-class women, those whose images were chosen sometimes turned out to possess surprising qualities or even scandalous associations. The cover of *Young Companion's* issue no. 130, published in July 1937, the month when Japan officially began its invasion of China, featured a charming and confident young woman. The magazine identified her as Ms. Zheng.[6] Zheng appeared in the perfect Modern Girl look: permed hair, careful makeup, bright smile, and form-fitting floral qipao. She could have been just another debutante, except that three years later, instead of marrying an eminent man, she was executed by Chinese collaborators with the Japanese occupation army for being a spy for the nationalists. Zheng's Modern Girl appearance played a major role in her disarming of Ding Mocun, who headed the intelligence agency of the collaboration force and was a target of assassination by the nationalists, but that appearance belied a political commitment for which she was ready to sacrifice her life. Contemporary reports, expectedly, stressed her love affair with Ding, and it was widely rumored that she was executed at the urging of officials' wives who considered her and women like her a major threat to their families.[7]

9.1 Zheng Pingru on the cover of *Young Companion: no. 130, 1937.*

If the Modern Girl on the cover of *Young Companion* could be a national hero but also a "threat to families," Ms. Peiying, whose photos appeared in the magazine's Women's Page in 1929, became an example of all that had gone wrong with "women's liberation movement." In this case, under the Modern Girl look was a college student who descended into a cabaret dancer and was "forced by a dance partner to drink poison." An editorial in the same issue commented: "There is no longer any doubt that we have to break the old moral codes; but what is the solution for women after their liberation? Some have indeed achieved happiness through liberation, but opposite cases are abundant … For example, one woman eloped with a janitor; some left school and became prostitutes. They would claim that they had done it out of love and were breaking vulgar social codes."[8] The lesson the magazine's readers were expected to draw from the story was that the wrong kind of "liberation" could be dangerous. The editor clearly made a connection between "women's liberation" and achieving a higher class status; careless Modern Girls could easily slip down the social ladder, and "they will become excuses for the conservatives and turn into barriers to women's liberation." [9]

9.2 "Sir … I am here to interview for the position for a woman clerk," by Lu Shaofei.
Shidai Manhua, **1934.**

For women who worked in government institutions, schools, companies, and stores as teachers, clerks, secretaries, saleswomen and typists, the Modern Girl look was a necessity. Yang Gonghuai noted the difficulty for women to find jobs and explained that their employment often resulted from an employer's desire to use the women to "improve the atmosphere of the office." When interviewing female applicants, employers paid much less attention to their knowledge and abilities than to their "look" (*maixiang,* literally "selling appearance"), as shown in a cartoon printed in 1931 (see

figure 9.2). Consequently, working women uniformly wore penned hair, fashionable clothes, high heels, as well as powder, rouge, and lipstick. Yang is critical of these women and of the social environment. He recognizes that the women had to endure harassments from both their bosses and the customers. On the other hand, he criticized the women for preferring to spend their leisure time shopping, in movie theaters, or dining in restaurants but not doing housework or studying, which he considered an indication of their flawed moral character.[10]

The Modern Girl look also reached women workers living along the heavily polluted Suzhou Creek, an area of shacks housing the city's poorest labor forces. While, spending little on food, these workers invested their money in dressing up. In the mid-1930s, it became popular in schools to elect "queens" and "school flowers." Following this example, factory workers elected as factory flowers women who displayed three attributes: pretty faces, good relationships with co-workers, and talent in singing, dancing, and the art of conversation. As a folk song puts it, "Her fragrance wafts three miles, and so white is her face powder." When participating in social events, factory flowers dressed up in a "modern" (*modeng*) style, donning qipao or Western suits and leather shoes and wearing permed hair. They looked like high-class "young ladies *[xiaojie]* at aristocratic schools" and "people could not tell that they came from factory worker backgrounds at all." "Factory workers" then were transformed into "modern metropolitan girls" *[dushi modeng nülang).* In one case, a teacher allegedly fell in love with a factory flower, but she dumped him and became a dance hall girl and "made very good money."[11]

Stories about rural women's transformations into urban Modern Girls also frequently appeared in major Chinese-language newspapers such as *Shenbao.* One article described a married woman from Suzhou who worked as a maid in Shanghai. She spent all her income on clothes and jewelry until she "did not look like a country woman at all." She attracted a man working at the customs and moved in with him, bluntly telling her husband, who came to Shanghai to look for her, that she no longer loved him.[12] Another report, titled "Country Girl Suddenly Became Fashionable," told the story of a nineteen-year-old country girl who went to work in a

Shanghai silk textile factory and became an outstanding worker. Having been promoted and making a decent income, she began dating a young man in her neighborhood and spending all her wages on clothing. One day, she bought a pink qipao and Western-style shoes and had a perm at a hair studio in the concessions. About her new look her aunt commented, "A country girl should not dress like this." Enraged, she left the house she shared with her uncle and aunt.[13]

9.3 "When penned hair became popular," by Zhang Guangyu. *Manhua daguan, 1931. The women's clothes indicate that they are of the lower class.*

What made these cases scandalous and newsworthy was that these women were using the Modern Girl look to enter the society to which they did not belong, disturbing the social order. There was no sure way to tell the class of a young woman sporting the Modern Girl look, nor was there any guarantee of her high moral standing. Even *Young Companion*, among the most elitist magazines at the time, juxtaposed pictures of famous wives and debutantes with those of movie stars and Peiying, the college student who deteriorated into a dance hall girl. Young unmarried women within the elite class were disturbing marriages as they enjoyed their "provisional space." "Low-class" women workers and rural migrant women dressed up as Modern Girls to "seduce" respectable young men of higher class.

While "bad women" of lower classes were sneaking into the elite marriage market, good women could fall out of it because the Modern Girl look led them down a path toward disreputable actions or dangers. Both were class slippages based on the inability of women and men to see beyond the artifice of the Modern Girl look to the reality of a woman's character. The Modern Girl look, then, blurred class and status lines and threatened the purity of the elite marriage market. The life path prescribed for young women in *Young Companion* aimed at securing the patrilineal family within the status quo: attending school, coming out as a debutante, marrying a successful man, and enjoying children as a young mother. But in reality, this ideal was hard to maintain and social boundaries were difficult to police.

MOLDING THE IDEAL MODERN WOMAN

The role the Modern Girl look played in blurring class boundaries and its serving as a means for female upward social mobility made it an object of scrutiny by the social and cultural elites, who considered it their privilege and duty to define the meaning of being modern. Their efforts at crafting a more skilled reading of appearances to distinguish "true" from "false" modern involved two not necessarily harmonious, and at times even conflicting, goals. Fighting to maintain their privilege to be the "truly" modern, "cosmopolitan elites" took it upon themselves to separate "high-class" modern women from the rest. The scrutiny applied to the Modern Girl, in this sense, indicated a struggle between the attempt to cross the class boundaries and the need to establish and maintain them. Meanwhile, through commercial publications, the social and cultural elites were also molding the "modern women" according to their own aesthetic and moral criteria.

Furen huabao (Women's Pictorial), published from 1933 to 1935, offered a complete manual on how to be a "real" modern woman. Guo Jianying served as the chief editor. Interested in Japanese modernist literature, and a close friend of the New Perceptionist writer Liu Naou, Guo published a fair number of translations as well as his own writings in the literature journal *Xin wenyi (New Literature,* 1929). His drawings of modern urban life began to appear in Shanghai's newspapers and magazines in 1931 and were published as a collection in 1934. Shunning the politicized terms for women at the time, *funü* or *nüxing*, Guo chose the more neutral *furen* for the title of his magazine. At the peak of its publication, in contrast to most contemporary popular magazines, which used photographs of Chinese beauties on their covers, *Furen huabao* featured line drawings to achieve a more cosmopolitan look (see figure 9.4). Complaining about the rarity of "ideal modern women" in Shanghai, Guo designed the magazine to teach Chinese women to distinguish "high-class" *(gaoguide)* from "native and vulgar" *(xiangtuqide)* modernity. The magazine presented a plethora of information on fashion, makeup, fragrance, foreign and Chinese movie stars, fiction, poetry, essays, and cartoons by the most eminent modernist artists. As a finishing school on paper, it provided the knowledge for the "truly modern woman."[14]

The magazine paid close attention to details of women's appearance and behavior. Many articles and images instructed the readers how to care for their facial skin, eyebrows, hair and hands, and how to apply cosmetics. A large portion of the magazine was devoted to pointing out fashion mistakes made by the Chinese Modern Girl and how to correct those following Western role models. Readers were encouraged to pay attention to European and American fashion magazines such as *Vogue*, for inspiration on what kinds of dress and shoes to wear for different occasions. Every issue of the magazine featured articles and images informing readers of the latest fashion trends in Europe and the United States, especially Paris, so that they would not be confused by any "low-class taste."[15] Guo's special column, "Modeng shenghuo xue jiangzuo" (Forum on modern life), took references from *Vanity Fair, College Humor*, and Japanese women's magazines to teach the proper etiquette in various social situations such as dating, dancing, dining, walking in the street, or riding the bus.[16] The "ideal modern woman" was one "without any trace of modern," a standard hard to meet by just any woman who, often out of necessity, wore a qipao, a pair of high heels, and lipstick.[17]

9.4 Guo Jianying's line drawing for the cover of *Furen huabao*, no. 22, 1934.

The colonial worship of things foreign (including foreign women) had a strong impact on the modernity of the Chinese Modern Girl. *Furen huabao* clearly defined the ideal modern Chinese woman as authentically or properly Westernized in her appearance, behavior, education, and mentality. Using her Western counterparts as role models, the Chinese Modern Girl was expected to be beautiful, healthy, energetic, cheerful, and lively. A number of articles in the magazine concurred that traditional Chinese standard of beauty—oval face, willow leaf eyebrows, long thin eyes, small cherry-like mouth, and slim fragile-looking body—had been replaced by one featuring big eyes, long thin eyebrows, broad mouth with fine white teeth, and an agile, energetic body.[18] Ten contemporary Hollywood actresses were presented as examples of ideal feminine beauty.[19]

The modernist writer Ouwai Ou scrutinized the faces and bodies of Chinese women in great detail. Their faces, in contrast to those of Caucasian women, lacked shadow due to the flatness of their noses and eye sockets. The only way for them to compensate for this flaw was to learn from Western movie actresses how to make their faces more expressive. The author noted approvingly that Chinese women had in fact gleaned from movie close-ups how to improve their expressions by presenting a "Hollywood screen face." "Urban women's faces are no longer authentically Chinese," he wrote. "It is not an exaggeration to say that they now reflect international beauty beyond national boundaries."[20] Ouwai also suggested that all Chinese women needed the help of surgical measures to reshape their eyebrows and make them similar to those of Caucasian women. On the other hand, he praised straight black hair and "yellow" skin color as the special advantages of East Asian and Chinese women. Ouwai's comments exemplify the numerous contemporary critiques of the appearance of the Chinese Modern Girl and of Chinese women in general. Although not always espousing conventional Western racial schemes, these critiques are nonetheless racial. The creation of the ideal "look" for the Chinese Modern Girl thus involved both class and racial discourses—being high-class meant being properly Westernized, socially and physically.

In addition to the correct "modern look," the magazine also inculcated its readers with the idea that a truly modern woman was expected to develop her "internal qualities by attaining a certain level of taste for modern life." Specifically, she needed to have sufficient knowledge in film, sports, readings (weighted equally among modern literature, classical literature, self-development, the domestic arts, and contemporary magazines), social dancing (but not at dance halls that hired commercial dancing girls), music (the ability to play an instrument, and an album collection made up of 40 percent jazz and 60 percent classical), and handicrafts (such as knitting).[21]

The new meaning of "morality," apparently, settled heavily on domesticity. Women readers were admonished not to forget the ultimate purpose of all this self-polishing—to attract men and to become their worthy companions.[22] The magazine warned that indulgence in youthful fun might divert attention from marriage until it was too late. Letters from "old maidens" regretting their missed opportunities in marriage were published

as warning lessons for young women.[23] An article written in 1934 by Xu Xinqin in *Shidai manhua* (Times Cartoon), a popular Shanghai magazine, confirmed that marriage was considered the proper destiny for the Modern Girl. Xu observed, "The first concern on people's minds for the future of a *shidai xiaojie* [modern young lady/Modern Girl] is her marriage ... In the way this world is still organized, a woman always belongs to a family ... Society considers being a wife the proper destiny for a *xiaojie* ... It is commonly recognized that it is difficult for a *xiaojie* to avoid becoming a *taitai* [wife]." The author admitted that there were young women who did not want to become "slaves of the family" but pointed out that it was extremely difficult for them to make a living on their own.[24]

One purpose of creating the "real modern woman," then, was to prepare her for marrying the modern man. The ubiquitous appearance of young, unmarried women in the city was preceded and accompanied by the urban influx of young men for education and work, away from their extended families. As Susan Glosser argues, in spite of the radicalism of the May Fourth moment, young, educated urban men still defined themselves through marriage and family. Glosser points out that socioeconomic issues, rather than nationalism or individualism, drove the young urban man to challenge traditional family structure and authority and to be "passionately involved in redefining himself as a member of an industrializing economy and a modernizing state."[25]

> Because it was so important to a man's identity as a modern, enlightened individual to make a freely chosen love-marriage, the quality of his marriage and his wife became absolutely essential to his self-image. Consequently, despite the rhetoric about women's rights to independence and full personhood, these men were most interested in creating women who met male demands for educated, enlightened companionship. And men complained bitterly when women failed to meet their husbands' expectations.[26]

Thus, the primary motivation of marrying a "modern woman" was to achieve and maintain social status. It was not new to preserve the status quo through marriage. As Susan Mann points out in her study of texts and practices on marriage in eighteenth-century China, discourses on preparing young women for marriage were often "metonymic comment on larger social issues of mobility and class."[27] Mann argues that through protecting the purity of the marriage market, elites "sought to fix the fluidity of social change that threatened to erode the boundaries defining their own respectability."[28] Since wives and daughters carried forward the status of elite families and the honor of their class, the elites were always "discovering ways to valorize the states of brides and wives in their class and to emphasize the differences that separated marriageable women from concubine and women of lower rank."[29]

Like their eighteenth-century counterparts, the twentieth-century elites also attempted to control the marriage market; the difference lay in the new tensions and means in defining class boundaries. One quality *Furen huahao* considered important for modern Chinese women to develop was openness in their interaction with men. American college students—healthy, energetic, lively, and sexy—were presented as their role models.[30] Modern women should not be constrained by traditional cultural codes. But this was considered a privilege reserved for elite women. Xu Xinqin distinguished between "modern young ladies" *(modeng xiaojie)* and "old style young ladies" *(jiushi xiaojie)*. Modern young ladies determined their own marriage; parents and family could only play the role of consultants. "Girls of modest and working class families" had adopted some ideas from the *"modeng xiaojie"* and "put on some love tragedies." But they never ended up well: eventually, they were either taken home by their parents to be disciplined or sold to brothels in far-away cities.[31] While elite women should be "modern" and practice free love, women of lower classes needed to adhere to more traditional standards with trenchant (and dull) fervor. Again, as with the Modern Girl look, the correct practice of love also had to be class specific. In the Republican period, free love was a luxury to be enjoyed only by the elites. Without the scrutiny by the extended family and arranged marriage as the first line

of defense, and as elite men were beginning to make their own choices and decisions in marriage, the pool of candidates for "free love" must be kept pure. Elites such as the editors of *Furen huahao* were fighting to take control of the double-edged sword of the Modern Girl look that served as the new status marker in the city but could also slash open class lines.

THE MODERN GIRL AND THE MODERN MAN

Although the Modern Girl phenomenon touched upon a wide social milieu, it involved most directly urban upper-class and middle-class women and men. The modern urban men expressed paradoxical feelings toward the Modern Girl: both longing and fear. Such an attitude was most clearly expressed in their anxieties over the Modern Girl as lover and wife. In this section, I discuss the representation of the Modern Girl in love and marriage in social cartoons by a group of modernist artists.[32]

Manhua (satirical image, caricature, and cartoon) emerged in China at the end of the nineteenth century, following the development of lithograph printing, newspapers, and pictorials. An emergent and ever-growing middle class provided a willing market for stereotypical images in which it recognized itself. By the 1920s and 1930s, caricature had become a staple item in almost all newspapers and magazines across China. From 1934 to 1937, the number of cartoon magazines increased dramatically—Shanghai alone had nineteen.[33] Representative of this trend was *Shanghai manhua (Shanghai Sketch)*, a large-size color lithographic cartoon magazine founded and financed by Shao Xunmei, the modernist poet and quintessential modern boy who earned himself the name "Shanghai dandy."[34] It was first published from 1928 to 1930, during which time each of its more than one hundred issues sold about 3,000 copies. It was then folded into *Shidai manhua* and continued to be published for three more years in the early 1930s.[35]

Unlike earlier cartoons that focused on national politics, a large number of social caricatures appeared in these magazines through which the artists hoped to observe and express "the richness of Shanghai life."[36] Relationships between the sexes constituted a major theme for these social cartoons on urban life; in particular, the artists focused on the Modern Girl and her relationship with the modern man in both the public and private realms of city life. These caricatures, as interpretations of gender relations with an attitude, provide unique lenses for examining the role of the Modern Girl in creating new gender relations.

Most of the pieces in the magazines were by young male cartoonists who also worked for advertising agencies. Ding Song was employed by the advertising department of the British American Tobacco Company (BAT) in Shanghai, whose calendar posters featuring the Modern Girl created a new genre of commercial art in China.[37] Dan Duyu painted the Modern Girl in his advertisements and calendar posters, as did Lu Shaofei.[38] Ye Qianyu contributed his fashion drawings to *Young Companion*, while Guo Jianying's appeared in *Furen huabao*. These artists simultaneously created an idealized image of the Modern Girl in their advertisements, fashion drawings, and film while at the same time they critiqued her in their cartoons. From their constant shifting of position emerged a complex image of the Modern Girl, to her male counterpart, as a source of both fantasy and fear. The caricatures reflected ambivalence between desire for and resistance to the Modern Girl and incited self-recognition in their satirical depictions of flawed fellow beings. In so doing, the caricatures provoked humorous laughter that reflected a new kind of male identity created through the Modern Girl. As Ainslie McLees points out, "Social caricature is thematically affiliated with genre painting, which by definition portrays types rather than individuals, and modest, often domestic, situations rather than the exalted personages of history painting."[39] The caricatures thus created stereotypical images of modern urban women and communicated the artists' attitude toward them through the Modern Girl, an attitude that they believed would echo the sentiments of their audience.

The Modern Girl was seen as part of the scenery of the modern city. Guo Jianying claimed: "The youth of Shanghai women is endowed with energy and creativity. How boring and bleak Shanghai streets would be without the youthfulness of the women."[40] Much of Guo's work depicted the Modern Girl as spectacle. His artistic style reflects the influence of Aubrey Beardsley, who was

himself impacted by Japanese erotic prints and in turn inspired Chinese artists with his black and white pen and ink drawings. His illustrations for *Salome*, which was translated and staged by the Southern Society together with *Pan Jinlian* and *A Doll's House* in 1926, became familiar to Chinese intellectuals. Beardsley's depictions of women are often grotesque; his influence on Chinese artists, however led to the creation of a very soft genre, *shuqing hua* (lyrical drawings), of which Guo was a practitioner. In figure 9.5, a cartoon of a scene on a bus, although the Modern Girls are making the man nervous, they are depicted in a way that is decorative, feminine, and not austere. Guo apparently intended to depict women and modern urban life as "lively, vigorous, and refreshing."[41]

In these male depictions of the Modern Girl, the man's desire for her is apparent, but so is hers for him. Many of the caricatures show the male gaze at her. In public and private spaces—at work, in the streets, on balconies, on the bus, in the classroom, in front of the camera, and in men's fantasies—the Modern Girl is always being looked at. While she is represented as an object of desire, fetishism, and voyeurism, she often does not appear to be passive but a desiring subject instead. She rarely shuns such gazes but instead blatantly ignores them, enjoys them, gazes back, or even purposely provokes and attracts them. She also gazes at herself: she is narcissistic and consciously makes herself sexually attractive. She is aware of the value of her charm and uses it in her relationship with men. What these caricatures say, essentially, is that the Modern Girl solicits male attention. In the male's projection of his desire through the Modern Girl, the young woman becomes a powerful figure because she, while an object of the gaze, also possesses the gaze and thus is capable of objectifying those who would objectify her.

When the Modern Girl is depicted as interacting closely with men instead of as a distant spectacle, the caricatures reveal a critical attitude in general: she appears to be calculating, flirtatious, venal, and greedy. She is a gold digger; the first thing she looks for in a relationship is the man's money.[42] She is a consumer who uses her checkbook compulsively.[43] Her conspicuous consumption of commodities, including cosmetics, leads to spousal tensions. The crisis caused by

9.5 "Brutal torture … A shy young man stepped on the trolley bus," by Guo Jianying. *Jianying manhua ji,* **1934.**

9.6 "The photographer thinks that these are his best lenses," by Lu Shaofei. *Manhua daguan,* **1931.**

9.7 "A new teacher has come to the school," by Wang Zhenhui. *Manhua daguan, 1931.*

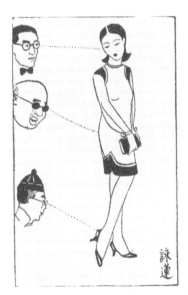

9.8 "Three stages of the gaze," by Yonglian. *Manhua daguan, 1931.*

transformation of the Chinese family from principally a unit of production to one of consumption is narrated through the spending habits of the Modern Girl. She does not know how to do housework or take care of a baby.[44] She is treacherous, entertaining her husband's friends when he is on a trip.[45] She is unchaste; premarital

9.9 "Memos of love," by Guo Jianying. *Manhua daguan, 1931.*

sex and simultaneous relationships with multiple men are normal for her. In Guo Jianying's "Memos of Love," a Modern Girl keeps information about men—names, ages, looks, physiques, wealth—and assigns a grade to each item under each name. When she wants a man who knows how to have fun, she calls Wang and extracts "unlimited pleasure from this handsome young man." When she needs money, she writes Shen because "this old man's wallet is always full." When she wants to take a walk, she calls Lin; and if she needs someone with strength, she turns to Chen.[46]

In these cartoons, men's experience with urban life appears to be totally different from the Modern Girl's. The cartoon images of the Modern Girl are highly dramatic and dramatized—these young women are always in public or places of entertainment: coffee shops, shoe stores, university campuses, dance halls, parks, beaches, and city streets. In contrast, quotidian and mundane themes are reserved for the male figures, who are often depicted as trapped in domestic, private spaces. The men are the ones who have to worry about the responsibilities of family and domestic life: mending socks, taking care of babies, bringing home the bread, and, as shown in figure 9.11, paying for the wife's expenditures to keep up her "modern" look.

The Modern Girl's aura of romance provokes male longing, but also fears. Just like Mr. Hu in *Shanghai Express*, the male figures in the caricatures appear to be trapped between their desire for the charming femininity of the Modern Girl and the danger of that charm. They are often overwhelmed by fears: of contracting sexually transmitted diseases; of competing with other men for women's attention; of dysfunctional relationships; and of rejection, emotional pain and loneliness. For men, urban life means both anxiety resulting from their own desires and fears caused by the constant presence of temptation. Men appear in these cartoons to be the victims in this new gender relation. In contrast to the confident Modern Girl who is totally at ease with and in command of modern urban life, her male counterpart seems to have difficulty living up to her challenge.

A reversal of power relations between the sexes and the contrast between powerful women and powerless men are clearly evident in these cartoons. The men do not assume the usual postures that signal power; for example, they do not stand in the conventional male stance, with legs apart and feet parallel. When their arms are outstretched from their bodies, their gesture does not signal power and authority but petty mean-ness or surprise. The body language of the women also reflects a break with traditional roles. They occupy no less, and very often even more, space than men, and their stance is neither modest nor less affected than that of men. Women are rarely shown with feet together or arms held close to their torsos—except where the artists depict ideal types. Female gestures are not responsive; instead, women often initiate actions and interactions with men. Their facial expressions are more individual-ized and articulated than those of men. The Modern Girl does not keep to herself. She gazes directly and smiles flirtatiously. With her slender waist, polished nails, painted red lips, plucked eyebrows, careful makeup, fashionable attire, and delicate high heels, the Modern Girl is a perfect image of seductive aggressiveness. She is always romantically involved with men but turns a deaf ear to male professions of love and is a threat to the patrilineal household—she does not cook, clean, sew, or have babies. In these cartoons, women conquer men; women, no male playthings, treat men as their playthings; husbands take on what should have been wives' work; men follow women; and women's images loom larger than men's. If the young, educated urban men sought their version of ideal marriage in modern

9.10 "Mama is not home," by Zhang Guangyu. *Manhua daguan, 1931.*

9.11 "Clothing, food, and housing," by Zhang Guangyu. *Manhua daguan, 1931. Inside the house, a woman with the Modern Girl look is gazing at herself in a mirror.*

9.12 "Playthings of different times," by Shen Baohui. *Manhua daguan, 1931.*

women, then the Modern Girl figure was used to stand in for these women who, in reality, often turned out to be "imperfect" companions in the eyes of their male counterparts.

In these cartoons, the social imbalances with which the hapless men have to cope make them, instead of the women, objects of laughter. Caricatures speak in coded language whose deciphering releases recognition and understanding in the audience. The resulting laughter reveals that the observer recognizes in the image before him his own imperfection and despairs over it while triumphing over it aesthetically.[47] The cartoonists apparently believed that their audience would understand and identify with the images and captions. The expected, knowing chuckles of the male readers thus indicate a common understanding of male identity that would not have existed without the image of the Modern Girl. She might have been comfortingly fictional but she played a central role in defining modern masculinity.

THE "SUPERFICIALITY" OF THE MODERN GIRL

The Chinese Modern Girl was criticized fiercely by many of her contemporaries, including the leftists, nationalists, and different strands of feminists. All the criticisms of her, however, share a common vocabulary, focusing on her "superficiality." She was "degenerated" *(duoluo),* "indulgent" *(xiangle),* "comfort-seeking" *(anyi),* "parasitic" *(jisheng),* "decadent" *(tuifei),* "vain" *(xurong),*

"extravagant" *(shechi),* "impetuous" *(ganqingyongshi),* and "slavish to foreign (products)." Her sexuality was commodified *(xing shangpin hua),* which made her a prostitute in disguise *(changji bianxing).* Four aspects of the Modern Girl, in particular, were singled out by her critics. First of all, her appearance solicits male attention. She wears qipao, high heel shoes, and permed hair. She applies face powder, rouge, and lipstick. She chases after new fashions. Her behavior was also scrutinized. She dances, frequents cinemas, enters men's rooms, and makes appearances in public gatherings. Her marriage, love, and sexuality received condemnation. She prefers to stay single, feels negative about family life, and refuses to have children. Or, otherwise, she is flirtatious, cohabits with men without getting married, and becomes pregnant out of wedlock. Sometimes the Modern Girl even practices homosexuality. She openly seeks sexual pleasure, plays emotional games with men, and pays too much attention to their appearance. She was also denounced for her consuming imported clothes and cosmetics and Indulging in good food and wine.[48]

To the leftists, the Modern Girl and her male counterparts such as Shao Xunmei were products of colonial culture. As Louise Edwards argues, the Modern Girl was a site where leftist intellectuals attempted to define women's modernity by rescuing the New Woman from her shallow counterpart. The Modern Girl, to them, usurped personal style as a political tool and depoliticized it. Challenging conventional dress codes had been a radical act for youth of the May Fourth period;

choosing to have natural feet and bobbed hair and wearing the short skirt adopted by students could make a young woman a social outcast or even cost her life. Edwards argues that the May Fourth modern woman was conceived as "politically aware, patriotic, independent, and educated." In contrast,

> By the late 1920s and early 1930s, big Shanghai companies used the modern woman as an enticement to purchase and consume "modern" goods and services. In this commercial framework, the modern woman was glamorous, fashionable, desirable, and available. Thus, two decades after their first appearance in 1918, the modern woman became a symbol of a national modernity that was commercially rather than politically centered. Commercial power usurped the reformist intellectual's guardianship of the modern woman.[49]

In distinguishing a real from a pseudomodern woman, intellectuals in the post-May Fourth era dismissed external manifestations of modernity such as clothing, hairstyles, and shoe styles as superficial trappings. A truly modern woman, they argued, had inner qualities centering on an abiding concern for China's national welfare. This preoccupation with the moral attributes of the modern woman, Edwards argues, was an attempt by some reformist intellectuals to reclaim their role as enlightened moral guardians and therefore leading advisers for the nation.[50] Sarah Stevens also points out that women's bodies were used to enact the struggle between conflicting aspects of modernity. The Modern Girl and the New Woman serve different functions in literary texts. The New Woman is always linked to the positive aspects of modernity. She symbolizes the vision of a future strong nation and her character highlights the revolutionary qualities of the modern women *(nüxing)*. As Stevens puts it, "The contrasts between the figures of the New Woman and the Modern Girl illustrate the tensions inherent within the very construction of modernity itself."[51]

The Nationalists and leftists, although political rivals, shared commonalities in their criticisms of the Modern Girl. The heyday of the Chinese Modern Girl roughly overlapped with the "Nanjing Decade" from the Nationalist government's reunification of China in 1927 to the Japanese invasion in 1937. In addition to purging radical intellectuals and silencing the left, the new nationalist government began to regulate daily life as soon as it took control of the cities. "Cloth demons"—women in "Westernized" fashions—were to be banned from public spaces.[52] Many cities, including Beijing, Shanghai, Nanjing, Tianjin, and Hankou, organized "Brigades of Destroyers of the Modern" *(Modeng pohui tuan)*, whose members patrolled the streets and cut women's clothes if they appeared too "modern" and "strange."[53] The government also enforced the regulation by policing public spaces and arresting women in "strange clothes."[54]

The policing of women's fashion reached a peak during the New Life Movement in 1934. Inspired by German and Italian Fascism, this was an attempt to mobilize the masses during a time of national crisis by fostering in them qualities such as frugality, self-discipline, and a spirit of self-sacrifice. During the New Life Movement, the Modern Girl look was considered un-Chinese, and her consumerism once again became an object of criticism and reform.[55] Song Meiling, wife of Nationalist leader Chiang Kai-shek, claimed that Chinese women should not wear permed hair, which was banned, together with nail polish, especially among professional women.[56] Women were required to abide by dress codes that limited the length of dress, jacket, and skirt, and to abandon "modern" *(modeng)* fashions.[57] These bans and codes, however, were not very effective and rarely followed. Public morality and national mobilization were excuses for these restrictions, and the national economy was another. The Modern Girl's consumption of imported luxury goods allegedly hurt China's economy. Men and women were told to wear plain clothes made of China's own fabric.[58] The year 1935 was designated "Year of National Products for Women" and the Modern Girl image, including photos of movie stars like Hu Die (Butterfly Wu), was widely mobilized to promote Chinese products. Here, the Nationalist government apparently attempted to recruit the Modern Girl as citizen, albeit still through consumption.

Unlike what had been historically considered models for women's liberation—the good wife and wise mother of the late Qing, the radical Nora, the professional women, and the working-class women—the Modern Girl was seen by most feminists as pulling the movement a step back. The May Fourth and New Culture Movement encouraged young women to venture into the public realm, to pursue modern education, to break away from the patriarchal family, and to struggle for free love and marriage. The Modern Girl appeared to be fulfilling most of these conditions. But what the Chinese Nora left was her father's house, and from there she was expected to walk into the "small family" of her husband. The Chinese Modern Girl did not revolutionize or abolish marriage but rather sought to negotiate "a better marriage," which was the main trend during this time. To Lu Xun's answer to his own question, "What happens after Nora leaves home?"—that she would either return, or become a prostitute—the Chinese Modern Girl provided an alternative. She undermined the patrilineal household from inside and brought changes to gender relations in everyday interactions with men and through new expectations for marital relations. In this way, the romance she offered posed a major threat to the patrilineal family. As Sally Mitchell points out, "Girl's culture suggested new ways of being, new modes of behavior, and new attitudes that were not yet acceptable for adult women. It authorized a change in outlook and supported inner transformations that had promise for transmuting women's 'nature.'"[59]

The Modern Girl and the modern man, the next generation of the May Fourth youth, together created new gender relations and entangled interests, as well as hopes and disillusionment for the urban nuclear family. The Modern Girl's aura of romance, together with the modern man's attraction to it, destabilized the patrilineal family. Beneath her consumerist façade, the ebullient, uncontainable Modern Girl challenged, historically and historiographically, male-centered conceptions of "youth" and commandeered societal expectations of the "girl-wife-mother" life cycle. The Modern Girl herself rarely voiced protest against criticism, but her having fun in the modern city with a smile on her face definitively caused plenty of fear.

NOTES

I am indebted to Susan Fernsebner, Joshua Goldstein, and the Modern Girl Around the World Research Group at the University of Washington for their comments and suggestions.

1. Zhang, *Shanghai Express.*
2. Shih, *The Lure of the Modern.*
3. Laing, *Selling Happiness.*
4. Yunshang, "Lun Modeng nülang zhi suo you chansheng" in *Funü gongming*, June 1933, 2–6.
5. *Young Companion*, no. 11, 1.
6. Ma, *Liangyou yi jiu*, 236–37.
7. Lo, "Historical Narrative and Literary Representation," 47–98.
8. Liang Desuo, "Bianhou yu" in *Young Companion*, no. 50, 2.
9. Ibid.
10. Yang Gonghuai, "Shanghai zhiyejie de nüzhiyuan," *Shanghai shenghuo*, no. 4 (1939): 20–21. Goodman, "The Vocational Woman and the Elusiveness of 'Personhood' in Early Republican China," 265–86.
11. Xu Xing, "Shanghai de nügong," *Shanghai shenghuo*, no. 4 (1939): 24–25.
12. *Shenbao*, 23 January 1930, 15.
13. *Shenbao*, 13 January 1930, 15.
14. "Opening remarks" in *Furen huabao* 1, no. 1.
15. Zhang Lilan, "Liuxing jie de bei xi ju," *Furen huabao* 25 (1935): 9–10.
16. Jianying, "Modeng shenghuo xue jiangzuo," *Furen huabao* 1, no. 1 (1933): 16.
17. Ms. Zhao Lianlian, "Ruguo wo shi ge nanzi," *Furen huabao* 16 (1934): 17.
18. Hu Kao, "Zhongguo nüxing de zhizhuo mei" and Moran, "Waken muzhong zhi Zhongguo nüxing mei" in *Furen huabao* 1, no. 4 (1933), special issue on beauty of Chinese women, 10–1 2.
19. "Biaozhun meiren," *Furen huabao* 1, no. 1 (1933): 18.
20. Ouwai Ou, "Zhonghua ernü mei zhi gebie shenpan," *Furen huabao* 1, no. 4 (1933), special issue on beauty of Chinese women, 12–16.
21. Zhang Lilan, "Nide xiandai shenghuo quwei yingyou zenyang de chengdu ne?" *Furen huabao*, 25 (1935): 13.

22. Ma Guoliang, "Shidai nüxing shenghuo zhi jiepou," *Furen huabao* 15 (1934): 9–11.

23. Huang Jiade, "Lao chunü de houhui," *Furen huabao* 27 (1935): 6–7.

24. Xu Xinqin, "Shidai xiaojie de jiangiai," *Shidai manhua* 1, inaugural issue (1934).

25. Glosser, "The Truth I Have Learned," 121.

26. Ibid., 139.

27. Mann, "Grooming a Daughter for Marriage," 94.

28. Ibid.

29. Ibid., 101.

30. Huang Jiade, "1934 nian de Meiguo nu daxue sheng," *Furen huabao* 14, special issue for the New Year (1934), 25–26.

31. Xu Xinqin, "Shidai xiaojie de jiangiai," 6.

32. The discussion in this section is based mostly on cartoons collected in Ye Qianyu, ed., *Manhua daguan*, published in Shanghai in 1931, unless otherwise referenced.

33. Bi and Huang, *Zhongguo manhua shi*, 93.

34. Hutt, "La Maison D'or," 111–42.

35. Bi and Huang, *Zhongguo manhua shi*, 86.

36. Ibid.

37. Ibid., 43.

38. Ibid., 56–57, 116. .

39. McLees, *Baudelaire's "Argot flastique"* 15.

40. Guo, *Modeng Shanghai*, 16.

41. Chen Zishan, "Modeng Shanghai de xiantiao ban: Guo Jianying qiren qihuaj" in Guo, *Modeng Shanghai* (no page).

42. Lu Zhixiang, "Her Hope," in Ye, *Manhua daguan*, 64.

43. Lu Shaofei, "Woman's Checkbook: To Save or Not to Save?" in Ye, *Manhua daguan*, insert, 4.

44. Guo, "No Need to Worry," in Guo, *Modeng Shanghai*, 20.

45. Lu Shaofei, "Jihui," in Ye, *Manhua daguan*, 75.

46. Guo, "Ai de beiwang lu," in Ye, *Manhua daguan*, 71.

47. McLees, *Baudelaire's "Argot flastique"* 33–40.

48. Yunshang, "Lun Modeng nulang zhi suo you chansheng," 2–6. Also see Sachiko Egami, "Xiandai Zhongguo de 'xin funü' huayu yu zuowei 'modeng nülang' daiyanren de Ding Ling," *Zhongguo xiandai ivenxue yanjiu congkan*, no. 2 (2006): 66–88.

49. Edwards, "Policing the Modern Woman in Republican China," 116.

50. Ibid., 115.

51. Stevens, "Figuring Modernity," 86.

52. Beiping Municipal Government, *Jingshi jingcha gongbao*, 25 June 1927 (no page number).

53. Beiping Municipal Government, *Shizheng pinglun*, 1 June 1934, 58–59.

54. *Jingsbi jingcha gongbao,* 16 July 19.27.

55. Gao Long, "Tantan funü biaozhun fuzhuang," *Funü yuebao* 1, no. 5 (June 1936): 9–10.

56. "Shi Jiaoju jinzhi nü jiaoyuan tangfa tuzhi," *Funü yuebao* 2, no. 8 (September 1936): 20.

57. "Bang Xinyunhui qedli funü qizhuang yifu," *Funü yuebao* 1, no. 3 (April 1935): 53–54; and "Guangzhou qiangzhi zhixing qudi qizhuang yifu," *Funü yuebao* 1, no. 9 (October 1935): 31–33.

58. "Shi Shanghui chengqing qudi qizhung yifu," *Funü yuebao* 1, no. 7 (August 1935): 35.

59. Mitchell, *The New Girl*, 3.

PART II

The Fifteen Year War in Asia-Pacific

(1931 – 1945)

EMPIRE AND WAR

Edited by William Theodore De Bary, Carol Gluck, and Donald Keene

The occupation of Manchuria, planned by Kwantung Army officers in 1931/1932, set in motion nearly a decade and a half of Japanese territorial expansion and military aggression on the Asian mainland and in the western Pacific. To be sure, Japan had already become an imperialist power in the late Meiji period. After winning wars with China in 1894/1895 and with Russia in 1904/1905, its colonial possessions stretched from Taiwan in the south through Korea to southern Sakhalin in the north, and under the provisions of the "unequal treaty" system Japan enjoyed the same rights and privileges in China as did the other imperialist countries. None of the Western powers, except perhaps for Russia, had contested these acquisitions, nor did they try to check Japan's expansion. On the contrary, with varying degrees of enthusiasm, they welcomed Japanese power as a "civilizing force" in East Asia.

By the early 1930s, the world had changed. The rise of anticolonial and anti-imperialist movements in European colonial territories like India and French Indochina had found sympathetic support in the newly established Soviet Union, whose leaders proclaimed their own anti-imperialist ideology. The world revolution, declared the Soviet leader Lenin, would begin not in the capitalist home countries but in the colonies or semicolonial areas where their power was weakest. This idea also appealed to Chinese nationalist intellectuals and activists, who embraced a radical anti-imperialist nationalism as they struggled to reunite and strengthen their country after the republican revolution of 1911/1912. In 1924 Soviet advisers helped the Guomindang, the leading nationalist organization, to reorganize, and members of the fledgling Chinese Communist Party joined it in a "united front" against the forces of imperialism and reaction in China.

Imperialism, colonialism, and territorial expansion were no longer unquestioned or unchallenged by Western leaders, either. A critical turning point in Western attitudes came with the peace settlement at the end of World War I. President Woodrow Wilson, who had declared the conflict a "war to end all wars," insisted that the victorious powers respect the right of all nationalities to "national self-determination" and proposed a new system of collective security based on the League of Nations. His idealistic vision was attractive to many Japanese political leaders, who welcomed a respite from the international competition that had driven the country for nearly two generations. During the 1920s, civilian-dominated political party cabinets cooperated with the American and British governments in constructing a diplomatic framework to reduce international tensions in East Asia and to phase out imperialist rights and privileges in China.

Other Japanese leaders, however, found the Wilsonian vision hypocritical and self-serving. Despite its call for "national self-determination," it was clear that Western colonial powers were willing neither to abandon their own colonies nor to include a "racial equality" clause in the League of Nations charter. And when the United States Congress passed legislation in 1924 restricting immigration from both Japan and the rest of Asia, an incensed Japanese press called it a "day of national humiliation." Many politicians called for a "positive" foreign policy more assertive of Japan's strategic interests and more independent of the Anglo-American powers. As Guomindang military forces moved northward in the mid-1920s in an effort to reunite China and unilaterally put an end to imperialist privilege, the Japanese public had become deeply divided over foreign policy issues. It was in this context that the Kwantung Army seized the initiative in Manchuria.

Japan's rapid and successful occupation of Manchuria enjoyed enormous political support and popular enthusiasm at home. But as the country embarked on its new imperialist expansion in the 1930s, Japanese political leaders, intellectuals, and journalists had to explain their policies to themselves, to the Japanese domestic public, and to the world in terms that suited the anti-imperialist temper of the times. Since the late Meiji period, advocates of expansion had been drawn to a Pan-Asian vision of an East Asia united under the Japanese leadership to counter the political, economic, and cultural intrusions of the Western countries, which some Japanese journalists sarcastically referred to as "the white peril." The ideology of Japanese imperialism in the 1930s and 1940s drew heavily on a similar rhetoric, stressing bonds of culture, language, values, and interests linking Japan to the countries it dominated. But imperialistic rhetoric increasingly insisted that Japan's mission was not simply to resist Western incursions but to liberate colonial and semicolonial regions of Asia from their Western oppressors.

The collapse of the world economy in the late 1920s and early 1930s provided another kind of rhetoric to justify Japan's expansion. The advance into Manchuria, for example, was touted as the opening of a new economic "frontier" or "lifeline" for a Japan struggling to overcome the impact of the world depression. During the 1930s, when Western countries adopted protectionist policies in their domestic and colonial markets to shore up their ailing economies, many Japanese political and intellectual leaders were convinced that the world would soon be dominated by a number of large regional economic and political blocs and that to survive in such a world, Japan would have to build a bloc of its own. The more optimistic saw building such a bloc as a major turning point in human history, with a triumphant Asia under Japanese leadership rising as the morally corrupt and economically defunct West went into decline. Indeed, many intellectuals spoke of the "world historical significance" of Japan's expansion in Asia, and political leaders quickly turned the phrase to their own uses.

In contrast to the late Meiji period, when the Western powers regarded Japanese imperialism with admiration tempered by apprehension, Japanese expansion in the 1930s turned the country into a diplomatic pariah. When the League of Nations issued a report in 1933 censuring Japan for its seizure of Manchuria, the Japanese government responded by withdrawing from the organization. Instead, it forged cordial relations with Nazi Germany and Fascist Italy, which were engaged in their own campaigns of territorial expansion in Europe and the Mediterranean region. Japan signed an anti-Communist pact with both countries in 1936 and then established a more formal diplomatic alliance in 1940. These actions put it on a collision course with Great Britain, France, and, ultimately, the United States.

After an undeclared war between China and Japan broke out in 1937, the government began to gear up the country for a long-term mobilization. Unlike Japan's earlier imperialistic wars, which were fought quickly and decisively, the war in China became a dreary and brutal war of attrition. To organize the population economically and politically, the cabinet of Konoe Fumimaro forced a national mobilization law through the Diet in 1938 and began a "spiritual mobilization" campaign to rally popular morale. When Konoe returned to power again in 1940, he proclaimed the need for a "new political order" to unite the country behind the emperor, and the political parties in the Diet dissolved themselves. While Japan never became a one-party totalitarian state like its allies, Germany and Italy, the country was transformed into a garrison state mobilized for "total war."

When the Japanese leadership decided to move into French Indochina in the fall of 1940 to end the military stalemate in China, Japan found itself face-to-face with the United States. After a series of unsuccessful negotiations intended to deflect American hostility, Japanese naval forces attacked the American naval base at Pearl Harbor, Hawaii, on December 7, 1941, and then launched a series of strikes that put Japan in control of much of Southeast Asia and the western Pacific. Significantly, the government designated the hostilities as the "Greater East Asia War," indicating that the deepest meaning of the war was the struggle to create an "Asia for Asians" by liberating the region from the thrall of "white imperialism" or "Anglo-American imperialism." In 1943 leaders from Japan together with those from Manchukuo (Manchuria) and several other territories under Japanese occupation issued a "Greater East Asia Declaration" outlining the goals of the war. Almost Wilsonian in tone, it committed the nations of the Greater East Asia Co-Prosperity Sphere to such principles as "coexistence and co-prosperity," "mutual respect for sovereign independence," "mutual cooperation and assistance," and the "elimination of racial prejudice."

THE IMPACT OF WORLD WAR I: A CONFLICT BETWEEN DEFENDERS AND OPPONENTS OF THE STATUS QUO

KONOE FUMIMARO

Konoe Fumimaro (1891–1945), the scion of an aristocratic family that traced its ancestry to the Heian period, served as prime minister during the outbreak of war with China in 1937 and later during the negotiations with the United States in 1941. He inherited a seat in the House of Peers from his father, Konoe Atsumaro, an ardent nationalist who argued for a strong stance toward Russia on the eve of the Russo-Japanese War. In 1918 Konoe, by then a protégé of Saionji Kinmochi, was appointed as a member of the Japanese delegation to the Paris Peace Conference. The following essay, written in November 1918, on the eve of his departure, summarizes a view of the world shared by many Japanese political and military leaders of his generation, who had grown up in a Japan that had emerged as a major world power but whose people still faced racial discrimination abroad.

"AGAINST A PACIFISM CENTERED ON ENGLAND AND AMERICA" (EI-BEI HON'I NO HEIWASHUGI O HAISU)

In my view, the European war has been a conflict between established powers and powers not yet established, a conflict between countries that found upholding the status quo convenient and countries that found overthrowing the status quo convenient. The countries that found upholding the status quo convenient clamored for peace, while the countries that found overthrowing the status quo convenient cried out for war. Pacifism does not always serve justice and humanism, and militarism does not always violate justice and humanism. All depends on the nature of the status quo. If the prewar status quo was the best possible and was consonant with justice and humanism, he who would destroy it is the enemy of justice and humanism; but if the status quo did not meet the criteria of justice and humanism, its destroyer is not necessarily the enemy of justice and humanism. By the same token, the pacifist countries that would uphold this status quo are not necessarily qualified to pride themselves on being the champions of justice and humanity.

Although England and America may have regarded Europe's prewar status as ideal, an impartial third party cannot acknowledge it to have been ideal in terms of justice and humanism. As the colonial history of England and France attests, they long ago occupied the less civilized regions of the world, made them into colonies, and had no scruples about monopolizing them for their own profit. Therefore not only Germany but all late-developing countries were in the position of having no land to seize and being unable to find any room for expansion. This state of affairs contravenes the principle of equal opportunity for all humanity, jeopardizes all nations' equal right to survival, and is a gross violation of justice and humanity. Germany's wish to overthrow this order was quite justified; the means it chose, however, were unfair and immoderate, and because they were based on militarism, with its emphasis on armed might, Germany received the world's opprobrium. Nevertheless, as a Japanese, I cannot help feeling deep sympathy for what Germany has to do.

The Need to Repudiate Economic Imperialism

At the coming peace conference, in joining the League of Nations Japan must insist at the very least, that repudiation of economic imperialism and nondiscriminatory treatment of Orientals and Caucasians be agreed upon from the start. Militarism is not the only thing injurious to justice and humanism. Although the world has been saved from the smoke of gunpowder and the hail of bullets by Germany's defeat, military might is not all that threatens nations' equal right to survival. We must realize that there is invasion through money, conquest through wealth. Just as we repudiate military imperialism, so in the same spirit we should naturally repudiate economic imperialism, which seeks to profit by monopolizing enormous capital and abundant natural resources and suppressing other nations' free growth without recourse to arms. I cannot avoid grave misgivings as to how far economic imperialism can be repudiated at the coming peace conference, led as it is by England and America, which I fear will unsheathe the sword of their economic imperialism after the war.

If we cannot subdue this rampant economic imperialism at the peace conference, England and America, which have profited most from the war, will promptly unify the world under their economic dominance and will rule the world, using the League of Nations and arms limitations to fix the status quo that serves their purpose. How will other countries endure this? Deprived of arms to express their revulsion and indignation, they will have no choice but to follow England and America, bleating in their wake like a flock of meek sheep. England has lost no time in trumpeting a policy of self-sufficiency, and many are advocating that other countries be denied access to its colonies. Such are the contradictions between what England and America say and what they do. This, indeed, is why I am wary of those who glorify England and America. If such a policy is carried out, needless to say it would be a great economic blow to Japan. Japan is limited in territory, [is] poor in natural resources, and has a small population and thus a meager market for manufactured products. If England closed off its colonies, how would we be able to assure the nation's secure survival? In such a case, the need to ensure its survival would compel Japan to attempt to overthrow the status quo as Germany did before the war.

If this is the fate awaiting all late-developing countries with little territory and no colonies, not only for the sake of Japan but for the sake of establishing the equal right to life of all nations of the world on the basis of justice and humanism, we must do away with economic imperialism and see that countries do not monopolize their colonies but accord other countries equal use of them both as markets for manufactured products and as suppliers of natural resources.

The next thing that the Japanese, especially, should insist upon is the elimination of discrimination between Caucasians and Orientals. There is no need to dwell on the fact that the United States, along with the English colonies of Australia and Canada, opens its doors to Caucasians but looks down on the Japanese and on Orientals in general and rejects them. This is something at which the Japanese have long chafed. Not only are Orientals barred from employment and forbidden to lease houses and farmland, but still worse, it is reported that in some places an Oriental wishing to spend the night at a hotel is required to have a Caucasian guarantor. This is a grave humanitarian problem that no defender of justice, Oriental or otherwise, should overlook.

At the coming peace conference, we must see that the English and Americans show deep remorse for their past sins and change their arrogant and insulting attitude, and we must insist, from the standpoint of justice and humanism, that they revise all laws that call for discriminatory treatment of Orientals, including of course rescinding immigration restrictions against Orientals. I believe that the coming peace conference will be the great test of whether the human race can bring itself to reconstruct a world based on justice and humanism. If Japan does not rashly endorse a pacifism centered on England and America but steadfastly asserts its position from the standpoint of justice and humanism in the true sense, it will long be celebrated in history as the champion of justice.

[Konoe, "Against a Pacifism," pp. 12–14; "Ei-Bei hon'i no heiwashugi o haisu." pp. 23–26]

A PLAN TO OCCUPY MANCHURIA

ISHIHARA KANJI

In 1931 Ishihara Kanji (1886–1949), a staff officer of the Kwantung Army, the Japanese garrison force stationed in southern Manchuria, plotted with fellow officers to seize control of the three northeastern provinces of China (commonly known as Manchuria) by military force. Research into military history had convinced Ishihara that the world faced an apocalyptic "final war" between a West unified by the United States and an Asia under the leadership of Japan. As a first step in preparation for this conflict, Ishihara wished to consolidate Japan's position on the Asian continent. The following position paper, written in May 1931, on the eve of the takeover of Manchuria, outlines his fundamental views on continental policy.

PERSONAL OPINION ON THE MANCHURIA–MONGOLIA PROBLEM (MANMŌ MONDAI SHIKEN)

The Value of Manchuria and Mongolia

A world dominated by the five superpowers that emerged from the Great War in Europe will eventually be united into one system. A struggle for supremacy between the United States, as the representative of the West, and Japan, as the champion of the East, will decide who will control it.

The basic principle of our national policy must be to acquire rapidly what we need to qualify as the champion of the East.

To overcome the current economic depression and to secure what we need to become the champion of the East requires rapidly expanding the borders necessary to maintain our sphere of influence. Although the Manchuria–Mongolia region is not suited to the solution of our population problem or endowed with sufficient natural resources for Greater Japan, at the present moment the solution of the so-called Manchuria–Mongolia problem should be our first priority, for the following reasons.

POLITICAL VALUE

1. For a nation-state to play an active role in the world, its most essential requirement is a favorable national defense position. The reason why Germany's defensive position is so unstable today is that the British hegemons established an advantageous defensive position in the nineteenth century. As the American navy grows, the British Empire in turn will find its defensive position seriously threatened; and as American economic power advances, the United States will become the champion of the Western peoples.

Our country must resist the encroachments of Russia to the north as it simultaneously confronts British and American naval power to the south. The Hulunbeier region in the Greater Xiangan Range [in northern Manchuria] is of especially important strategic value to Japan. If our country brings northern Manchuria under its influence, Russia will find it extremely difficult to advance to the east. It will not be difficult to [block Russia] simply by building up our strength in Manchuria and Mongolia. If our country is relieved of its burden to the north, depending on the dictates of national policy, it can then make bold plans for development toward China proper or toward the South Sea region.

The Manchuria–Mongolia region is of enormous strategic importance with respect to the destiny and development of our country.

If the Manchuria–Mongolia region is brought under our influence, then our control over Korea will be stabilized.

If our country shows firm determination by resolving the Manchuria–Mongolia problem through force, it can assume a position of leadership toward China; it can promote China's unity and stability; and it can guarantee peace in the East.

ECONOMIC VALUE

Agriculture in the Manchuria–Mongolia region is sufficient to solve the problem of food supplies for our people.

Iron from Anshan, coal from Fushun, and other resources [in Manchuria] are sufficient to build up our present heavy-industrial base.

Various business enterprises in the Manchuria–Mongolia region will enable us to break out of economic depression by helping those currently unemployed in our country. Even though the natural resources of the Manchuria–Mongolia region will not be enough to make us the champion of the East, they are sufficient to relieve our present plight and to build a foundation for a great leap forward.

The Solution of the Manchuria–Mongolia Problem

It is clear from the history of the past twenty-five years that it will be difficult to expect even limited development under the aegis of today's crafty Chinese politicos. To stabilize our national defenses as the guardian of the East against Russia, we must be aware that there is no solution to the Manchuria–Mongolia problem but to make the region our own territory.

The solution to the Manchuria–Mongolia problem rests on two assumptions: first, that making Manchuria–Mongolia into our territory is a just action; and, second, that our country has the power to carry this policy out resolutely.

Of course, we should heed those who argue that since Chinese society is finally making advances toward becoming a capitalist economy, our country should withdraw its political and military facilities from the Manchuria–Mongolia region and pursue our economic development in harmony with the revolution of the Han people. But on the basis of direct observation, I think that it is extremely doubtful that the Chinese will be able to build a modern nation-state by themselves. On the contrary, I firmly believe that if our country establishes peace and order, it will contribute to the natural development and well-being of the Han people [in Manchuria].

The mission of our Japan is to overthrow the warlords and bureaucrats who are the common enemy of the 30 million people living in Manchuria. Our country's control over the Manchuria–Mongolia region, moreover, will bring about the unification of China proper. This is also the best thing that could happen for the development of Western economic interests in China. But the Westerners, who are deeply envious of us, will almost certainly respond in a hostile manner. We must

anticipate military opposition from the United States and, depending on the circumstances, from Russia and Britain as well. The China and the Manchuria–Mongolia problems are not problems in our relations with China but in our relations with the United States. Unless we are determined to destroy this enemy, we will no more be able to solve this problem than we will be able to catch fish in a tree.

At first glance such a war may seem quite difficult for our country, but we must take into consideration geomilitary relations in East Asia. It will be extremely difficult for Russia to launch a powerful attack on us once it has withdrawn from northern Manchuria and we have occupied the same region. And it will be extraordinarily difficult for anyone to overcome our country by means of naval power.

Some [people] may be pessimistic about war from an economic point of view, but the costs will be slight. Since war expenses can be recovered in the war zone, we have little to fear financially, and if need be, we will resolutely establish a planned economy embracing both the homeland and the occupied territory. Naturally we may not be able to avoid a temporary major turmoil in the economic world, but eventually we will be able to overcome the economic crisis and progress to the same level as the advanced industrial countries.

It will be to our advantage to carry out this war by 1936 at the very latest, before Russia has recovered economically and before the United States has built up its naval power. This war will be a long one, however, so it is extremely important that the state devise war plans before it begins.

The Timing of the Solution

The present situation in our country raises concerns about how easy it will be to achieve national unity in the event of war. For that reason, at first it might seem logical to give priority to the domestic reconstruction of the country. But we fear that it will be difficult to achieve a so-called internal reconstruction and national unity and that it will take much time to achieve political stability. And even if political stability is achieved, it is clear from the experience of the Russian Revolution that since we do not yet have detailed and appropriate plans for reforming the economic structure, we must expect a temporary downturn in our country's economy.

If we can first draw up war plans and convince our capitalists that victory is possible, it will not be at all impossible to move the present political regime toward a positive foreign policy. History has shown that military success, especially at the early stage of a war, arouses and unites popular sentiment.

War will inevitably bring economic good times. If we encounter economic difficulties as the war goes on for an extended period, we will carry out various reforms under martial law. ... If we were confident that we could achieve political stability and establish concrete reform plans by 1936, then giving priority to internal reforms would not necessarily be a bad idea. But given current social and political conditions in our country, it is more appropriate to spur on the nation, charge on toward external development, and then, depending on the circumstances, firmly carry out domestic reforms at the same time.

[*Ishihara Kanji shiryō*, vol. 2, *Kokubō ronsaku*, in *Meiji Hyakunenshi shiryō*, vol. 18, pp. 76–79; PD]

AUTUMN NOTE

By Chu Tien Jen (1903–1947)
Translated by James C. T. Shu
Edited by Joseph S. M. Lau

CHU TIEN JEN (1903–1947)

Compared with Wu Cho-liu, Chu Tien-jen (pen name of Chu Shih-t'ou) lived a rather short and uneventful life. Not much is known about him. Following the example of Lai Ho, he chose to write in Chinese, which is only natural in view of the sentiments expressed in the story selected here. Though sharply different in educational background, the scholar in "Autumn Note" is a spiritual kin to the illiterate old woman in the previous selection, "The Doctor's Mother," in that they both cling to the memory of the old country as an assertion of their pride and their Chinese identity. To be sure, as a symbol of patriotic nobility the old scholar is overshadowed by the street hawker in "The Steelyard," who resorts to violence as a means of defiance. But as the editors of Taiwan Literature under the Japanese Occupation (Kuang-fu-ch'ien T'aiwan wen-hsüeh ch'uan-chi) *rightly observe: "At a time when the Japanese were in firm control of the island, the fact that Chu Tien-jen dared to subject his overlords to such relentless mockery and ridicule bespeaks uncommon courage. His fiction has therefore become a part of our valuable cultural heritage" (vol. 4, p. 33). His works are gathered in the afore-cited anthologies.*

AUTUMN NOTE

Master[1] Ton-wen concentrated his thought, held his breath, and practiced calligraphy by copying Wen T'ien'hsiang's "The Song of Righteousness."[2] The tip of his pen danced blithely on the paper, balancing the firm strokes with soft strokes. Every time his imitation approximated the calligraphy in the stone rubbings, he would put down the pen and spend some time comparing his work with the rubbings.

A while later, he moved on to reading. He read aloud "Peach Blossom Spring"[3] in a sing-song chant. Although he was over sixty years of age, his voice did not show the wear and tear of years: the clear, resounding recitation lingered and vibrated in the quiet of the morning.

This was Master Tou-wen's daily work, and it had gone uninterrupted for the past decades. As soon as he finished his work, he made his way across the yard where the unhulled rice was sunned. With a bamboo pipe in his mouth, he carried in his hand the *National News Weekly*, mailed to him from Shanghai by his grandson. He read as he walked.

It was just getting light in the east. The morning sun had yet to reveal itself; for the time being, it only sent a diffusion of pink hue across the sky above the hilltop in front of him.

A flock of ducks huddled beside the fence. As soon as they noticed some human movement, they stood up and quacked. A red-faced duck walked on its clumsy feet, its tail waggling, its neck stretching back and forth, until it came near his feet. It pecked aimlessly.

"Little beasts! Want to go out?" He opened the gate; the ducks started quacking again, and jostled their way out. He too went out through the open gate and sat under an old ch'ieh-tung tree[4] near the gate, smoking.

The sky over the eastern hill changed from pink to bright red. The fog that had been shrouding the earth was thinning out and, without his noticing it, finally vanished. The rice stalks, their clusters of grains having just been picked, were already half dried up and yellowed. The dew on the grass by the fields glittered like silver beads.

He smoked leisurely. The wisps of smoke coming out of his mouth fitted past the back of his head. He closed his left eye and looked at the chimney smoke rising from inside the hedge of bamboos ahead.

From the hedge of bamboos three people appeared, each carrying a small bundle. As they skirted a field and got to another hedge of bamboos closer by, another three people happened to emerge from it. Both parties paused, exchanged a few words, and then, making a turn together, walked along the edge of fields toward him.

"Aren't you Hsiu-ts'ai[5] Ch'en?" the leader asked. "Out early for some good air, eh?"

Since they were still some distance away, Master Tou-wen could not make out who they were. When he heard the greeting, he recognized it was from Wu Hsiang of the bamboo hedge farther back.

"You were up early, too!" By the time he made his answer, they were already close by. As he noticed that they were dressed in their New Year's best, he had the feeling that they were on a trip. "Hey, Hsiang. You're going to Taipei, aren't you?"

"Right. To see the Exhibit. Hsiu-ts'ai Ch'en, you should go, too. Come with us!"

"I don't want to go."

"It's really a shame not to go. I don't know about other villages, but in our village every family has someone going to see it. I heard that there are many tourist groups today. Maybe the train is going to be all jammed again. Hsiu-ts'ai Ch'en, life is short, and you're quite old. If you don't see it now, when are you going to

see it? Come on, let's go. Isn't it nice to see something different?"

"I don't want to go."

"You don't? Then, wait until we're back to tell you what it's like. Wow! It's late! We've got to hurry to get on the train."

Before the exhibit opened, the government[6] had done its best to propagandize for it. The press on the island also followed suit to give it good publicity. Railroad officials were even sent to the rural areas to promote it. And thus a very ordinary exhibit was transformed, through the magic of advertisement, into a raging sensation.

"Let's go! Go see the Exhibit in Metropolitan Taipei!" Everyone living outside Taipei had the idea that to go see it was a must in one's life, and a real pleasure at that.

"Grandpa! A policeman's coming!"

It was in an evening of early autumn, and Master Tou-wen was reading newspapers in his study when he heard his third grandson report, who rushed in all excited.

"Why didn't you tell him I've no time for visitors?"

"I did, but he wouldn't listen. He said something like he had to see you on business. Grandpa, what is 'on business'?"

"Very nice of him! Bothering you all the time! What damn business for today?"

Master Tou-wen came out, upset. He saw the old Japanese policeman Sasaki sitting in the living room, all smiles.

"You again."

"Hsiu-ts'ai Ch'en! Sorry, I know you're a busy man. Please sit down. I've something to tell you."

He had been working as a policeman for many years, a real old hand, and as he spoke, his Taiwanese was almost indistinguishable from that of a native of Taiwan.

"If you've something to tell me please hurry up."

"I'm taking the census today, and I'm just doing something extra on the side."

"Yes?"

"When will your grandson studying abroad in China be back?"

"No such thing! What's he coming back for?"

"Taiwan is having an exhibit. How can he not come back to take a look?"

"That's something I don't know."

"Well, so you don't know?" Sasaki paused at this point and changed his topic: "The Promotion Committee of the exhibit is recruiting members. A regular member is supposed to pay … five dollars. …"

"Wait a minute. I've nothing to do with the Promotion Committee. What are you coming to talk to me for?"

"Ha—ha, Hsiu-ts'ai Ch'en! You don't pay for any-thing. If you're a member, the committee will give you a membership card and a memorial badge. During the entire period of the exhibit you can drop in any time you want, and you can count on being entertained. …"

"So you want me to join?"

"You got it. Come on, join in. Come along and take a look at Taipei. How about taking a look at Japanese culture and your—no, Ch'ing dynasty culture.

"Ch'ing dynasty!" Upon hearing the two words "Ch'ing dynasty," Master Tou-wen felt as if his body had been hit with a jolt of electricity. Shivering all over, he stared blankly at the sky light, lost.

The exhibit had been open more than a dozen days now. The plowshare-wielding country people, who would consider such trivial things as two hens fighting each other a fit topic for conversation, were as jubilant about their visit to the island's capital and the exhibit as they would be about a visit to the moon. After their return, they lavished praise on it, making themselves the envy of those who could not go. Even though Master Tou-wen was not impressed, he would listen intently every time they praised. But what was surprising and disap-pointing was that most Taipei streets, as they mouthed them, were no longer under their old names.

"That's strange. Can Taipei change so fast?" Sometimes he would wonder, and felt the urge to go to Taipei. But Taipei was no longer the same city that used to fascinate him! So, he dropped the idea every time he thought of going. Then, more recently, he unexpectedly received a letter from a classmate of his grandson. It read as follows:

October 25

Dear Master Tou-wen:

As the summer was gone, I returned to this southern country with the autumn. My reasons for returning were first, to see my family and second, to see the Exhibit. Your grandson was so preoccupied with his study he didn't want to come, but he asked me to insist that you go to Taipei to take a look at the Exhibit.

Respectfully yours,
Wang Pei-fang

The few words helped Master Tou-wen make up his mind to go north. But he made no fuss over it; he did not even tell his family. Because he did not want to meet any of his acquaintances, he quietly took an unusual route to get on the 9 A.M. train from Station A.

It happened to be Sunday, and the train had long been packed with mixed crowds. As Master Tou-wen stepped into the car, somehow all the eyes were sponta-neously trained on him. Into the atmosphere of modern dress in the car—kimonos, Taiwanese tunics, Western clothes—Master Tou-wen's old-fashioned dress made its surprise inroad. He wore a black bowl-shaped cap, a black gown, and black cloth shoes—this, together with the bamboo pipe in his mouth and the pigtail that hung from the back of his head, made him look like a stork joining a flock of chickens.

He took the people's stares as an affront. For a short while he felt very upset. But pretty soon he got over it, and defiantly, he gave the people a going-over. He then sat down with composure.

Time for departure. As the station master began to blow his whistle, Master Tou-wen hurried to cover both his ears to shut out the noise of the siren of the train. This caused an uproar of laughter in the car.

The train began to move slowly. The village, where Master Tou-wen felt at home, began to recede. Instantly he felt empty. Out of boredom he opened the pages of *The Records of the Ten Continents of the World*,[7] which he had brought with him, and mechanically set the book on his knees. Even though his eyes fell on the book, he failed to catch the words; the conversations in the car very naturally entered his ears. Slowly, he looked up. The train was going at full speed alongside sugarcane fields.

"Liu, where are you going?"

"Taipei."

"Hey! What made a thrifty fellow like you want to go to Taipei!"

"Well, partly because I can't help it."

"You yourself wanted to go. What do you mean by 'I can't help it'?"

"The police in our village forced me to go."

"Well, is that right? Anyway, Liu, don't feel put out. They say the exhibit is the greatest fun there ever was in Taiwan; see it once and you can afford to depart from this world in peace!"

"See it once and you can afford to depart from this world in peace!" Master Tou-wen repeated after him like a parrot. His trip north would be worthwhile if Taipei was the Taipei that people looked forward to, he thought. He seemed to have forgotten all the changes in Taipei. Fu-Front Street,[8] Fu-Center Street, Fu-Back Street—former city streets appeared one after another in his mind. The faster the train went, the deeper he indulged in the fantasy.

"Mang-ka![9] Mang-ka!"

Upon hearing the cry, he came back to himself from the reverie.

"Ah, Mang-ka! The Mang-ka of 'First, Fu; second, Lu; third, Mang-ka'!"[10] His heart beat fast, as if he had met a long-separated old friend.

The train went past the Wan-hua station. After it went past two intersections, its windows reflected the imposing Sugar Industry Building, Exhibit Hall No. 1. As the exhibit hall was announced, the passengers in the car all scrambled to the windows to take a look. Master Tou-wen also stood on his toes to look. Ah! Right on the former site of the city walls of Taipei was the Exhibit Hall. His heart was pounding like a jackhammer as he fell weakly into his seat.

The train arrived at the Taipei station at three o'clock. The passengers, exhausted from the long hours of sitting in the train, fought their way to get off, pushing and jostling one another. Master Tou-wen followed the human wave through the exit gate. In the confusion of the milling crowd, as he hobbled along, his toes could not help touching other people's heels at each step. Finally he found himself pushed by the human wave into a corner on the left side. He looked up at the streets.

Lots of cars were weaving their way in the streets. At an intersection towered an arch, on which he caught the words: "In Celebration of the Fortieth Anniversary of New Government." Instantly he recovered from his trepidation. The imposing structure towering before him seemed to grin at him maliciously. He shook his head, recalling the lines, "Recently erected are the mansions of the new nobility; changed in style is the court dress from that of the *ancien régime*."[11] He was filled with a sense of nostalgia and loss.

Master Tou-wen was a smart student in his younger days. He became a hsiu-ts'ai at the age of nineteen. He then worked for the provincial administration of Taiwan under the Ch'ing dynasty.[12] At age twenty-seven, when he was about to take the provincial-level examination, Taiwan was ceded to Japan.[13] Consequently, his journey to success was cut short. He gave up the hope of bureaucratic advancement. He settled down in K Village and, acquiring a few acres of good land, decided to spend the remainder of his life as a farmer. At his home he had a detailed atlas of Taiwan. In the early days of the new government under Japan, which was quite uninformed about the affairs of Taiwan, he was prevailed upon several times to come out and offer his help. With stubbornness, he declined. In fact, he refused to have anything to do with politicians.

In all appearances Master Tou-wen was leading the life of a hermit. But in his heart he was not. His blood frequently boiled on behalf of his compatriots. Even though he did not participate in the practical activities when the Social Movement was reaching its heyday, he did contribute a lot to an affiliated activity of the movement, the cultural movement.[14] As more Taiwanese learned to speak Japanese, fewer of them were able to understand Chinese. He understood that Japanese was for the Taiwanese people a necessary tool for making a living. But it was also necessary for them to know Chinese, since the very identity of the Taiwanese people was involved with the Chinese language. As he decided to revive Chinese, he gathered some comrades and formed a poetry club, promoting the writing of classical Chinese poetry. The promotion had quite an impact on society: poetry clubs cropped up everywhere; poetry writing became a fad all over the island; the number of practicing poets at the time almost equalled that in the golden days of the T'ang dynasty. However, while he tried to make use of poetry to salvage the moribund Chinese language, shameless poets used it as a tool to socialize, to curry favor from those in power—they even composed poems in memorial of deceased Japanese politicians, with whom they were utterly unrelated.

As Master Tou-wen witnessed such a perverted phenomenon, he became remorseful about ever setting up a poetry club in the first place.

"Classical verse isn't poetry; only the mountain songs from the mouths of the common people are poetry," he often remarked with a sigh. He came to regard himself as a sinner in the Taiwanese literary circle because he was the first to establish a poetry club. In the spring of 19—[15] when all of the poetry clubs of the island gathered in Taipei to compose verses, he believed it was an opportunity to reform the ills of writing classical verse. Thus for the first time in his life he took a train. Maybe because he was not quite well, maybe because he was totally unprepared—anyway, just as the train's steam whistle sounded, Master Tou-wen was so frightened that he passed out.

Today, fifteen years later, he had come to Taipei.

On the street before the Taipei station, the crowd swarmed toward the museum like a wave. Master Tou-wen was like a rudderless boat without a sense of direction: the geography of Taipei was no longer what he had remembered. Somehow, while he was at a loss, he was pushed right to the entrance of Exhibit Hall No. 2. Without thinking, he followed the crowd into the first section for cultural displays. He glanced at a model of Chih-shan Cliff,[16] and then walked to the left. On a door were the characters: "Room No. 1: Education." As a learned man, he could not resist taking an interest in matters of education. He scrutinized a map of school distribution, but was very disappointed by the fact that since he did not know Japanese he could not fully understand it. He shook his head sullenly. He then stood before a picture in which there were three students standing in a row in a school yard, the two on the right each carrying a spade, the one on the left carrying an abacus—all of them swaggering. Master Tou-wen was puzzled, and when he looked at its caption, he was unable to read it. In his helplessness, he stopped someone and asked, "Please, what does the caption say?"

"'The Great Leap Forward of Taiwan's Productivity is initiated by us,'" the man explained to him, looking him over, and broke into a guffaw.

"Ha, ha! …"

"Ha, ha! …"

Another two explosions of laughter suddenly started at his back. He hastened to turn around, and met contemptuous looks from two Japanese students, standing with arms akimbo, muttering you didn't know what. He felt a crushing sadness at the insult. He thought, If I knew Japanese I would certainly debate with them to the bitter end.

"Runts! Bandits![17] Japanese barbarians!" He could not help but let it go, regardless of whether they could understand or not. "Even though the rise and fall of a nation is fated, and the Ch'ing dynasty has already ended, yet it doesn't necessarily mean that the Chinese people … All this fuss about the Exhibit—it's just meant to brag about … Forget it. … 'The Great Leap Forward of Taiwan's Productivity' indeed! Only you Japanese devils are able to have a 'great leap forward.' I'm afraid Taiwan's youth don't even have the chance to inch forward. All this talk about education, indeed!"

He lost all interest, and left in a huff. He felt a pang of regret: he considered his trip a big waste! Instead of seeing the exhibit it would be a better idea to visit the Taiwan Provincial Yamen![18] Upon the thought of the Taiwan Provincial Yamen he felt like going back to his former self of forty years ago, and all his pent-up frustration vanished in an instant.

"Sir, where are you going? Need a ride?" A rickshaw puller who had been squatting outside the exhibit hall noticed that Master Tou-wen was hesitating; he stood up to accost him.

"I don't need a ride. I'm going to take a look at the Taiwan Provincial Yamen."

"Taiwan Provincial Yamen? Huh! Do you know where it is, sir?"

"On Fu-Center Street."

"Oh, no! Not there."

"No? Not there? Then … ?"

"I don't think you're a local person, sir. No wonder you don't know they have built the Taipei Municipal Hall on the former site of the Taiwan Provincial Yamen."

"What? Municipal Hall … ? Then it … ?"

"Take it easy, sir. Now I can say I had a good reason to accost you. I've been sitting here all day long without making a penny. Please let me take you to the Taiwan Provincial Yamen for twenty cents."

Fifteen minutes later Master Tou-wen got off the rickshaw in front of the Taiwan Provincial Yamen in the Botanical Garden. After the rickshaw puller had left, the old man sat under a coconut palm and, facing the yamen, lost himself in meditation. Why is it so deserted when it used to bustle with life? Ah! The facade of the yamen retains its old look, but where did all the remembered things of the past go? Overwhelmed with a sense of the capricious turns of history, he slowly stood up and leaned against the coconut palm. He groped in his breast pocket for the letter he had received the other day. He took the letter from the envelope. His glance fell on the letter, but all he saw was the colophon at the margin of the letter paper: *Image of the Isle of the Immortals.*

It was late autumn. The garden was deserted as nightfall descended. Fallen leaves rustled in the breeze. He relaxed his grip, and the letter was wafted away in the wind, only to settle down on the paulownia leaves that strewed the ground.

NOTES

1. *Hsien-sheng,* here rendered as "Master," is a title of honor, which, when used in conjunction with a person's given name, suggests that the one referred to is a professional or someone with intellectual qualifications. It is not to be confused with the standard usage of "Master" to address a boy too young to be called "Mister."

2. Wen T'ien-hsiang (1236–82), the last prime minister of the Sung dynasty, was executed by the Mongols after a three-year imprisonment. When in prison, he wrote "The Song of Righteousness," which expressed his patriotic sentiment and his reconciliation to the thought of death.

3. An imaginative account of a pastoral utopia by T'ao Ch'ien (365?–427), one of China's greatest poets.

4. Also variously known as *ch'ung-yang mu* and *ch'iu-feng,* its botanical name is *Bischofia javenica.*

5. *Hsiu-ts'ai:* A successful candidate of the county or prefectural level in the feudal civil service examination system.

6. *Tang-chü-che,* in the Chinese original.

7. *Hai-wai shih-chou chi,* as in the Chinese original, most likely ought to be *Hai-nei shih-chou chi,* whose authorship has traditionally been attributed to Tung-fang Shuo (154–93 B.C.), even though it may have been composed after the third century A.D.

8. A *fu* in the Ch'ing dynasty was the approximate equivalent of a prefecture. "Fu-Front Street" obviously indicates the location of the street relative to the administrative building.

9. Mang-ka, here transcribed to approximate its Taiwanese pronunciation, is the old name for Taipei. In Mandarin, it is Meng-chia.

10. A Taiwanese proverbial saying with reference to the three most prosperous cities in the earlier days of Taiwan, namely, Tainan (seat of Taiwan *Fu*), Lu-kang, and Mang-ka—in that order.

11. From "Autumn Meditations: Eight Poems" by Tu Fu (712–770).

12. In 1887 Taiwan became a province of the Ch'ing Empire and had its own *hsün-fu* (governor).

13. In Chinese, *huan le chu.*

14. Under the Japanese rule, Taiwanese frequently tried to work within the system to demand their rights and raise their ethnic consciousness. The Taiwanese Cultural Association, established in 1921 by Chiang Wei-shui, was the most notable example of such an effort.

15. Ellipses in the original.

16. A small hill on the outskirts of Taipei.

17. A pejorative reference to the Japanese, stressing that they are short.

18. A government office.

PART III

SHADOWS OF THE COLD WAR

(1945 – 1999)

THE MAO REGIME

PART 1

Edited by William Theodore De Bary and Richard John Lufrano

ESTABLISHMENT OF THE PEOPLE'S REPUBLIC

In the early years of the People's Republic of China, the Communist Party unified the country militarily (except for Taiwan) and fought the United States to a standstill in Korea. Domestically, it distributed land to the peasants, accelerated industrialization, revamped education on the Soviet model, and passed a marriage law. After decades of war and chaos, peace reigned. Gangsters and drug pushers were executed; prostitutes and opium addicts were rehabilitated. Health care improved and some serious diseases were eradicated in the countryside. Infant mortality went down and life expectancy gradually rose. Patriotic Chinese educated abroad came home to participate in the reconstruction of the motherland. China became a nuclear power in 1964. In later years many people looked back nostalgically on the early days of the Mao regime, imagining it as a kind of Golden Age.

Yet there were a number of anomalies in the Communist success. Having operated for twenty years in the countryside, the Party, when it came to power, adopted the Soviet model rather than building a new order based upon peasant experience or the needs of Chinese agriculture. Although the party had ridden to power on the backs of a largely peasant army, it was the urban population that benefited the most from the policies of the new state. The term *iron rice bowl* described the cradle-to-grave support now enjoyed by a large percentage of the urban population. Many of the comrades who had sacrificed during the long years of struggle believed that now, in this new state, they were entitled to good positions and special privileges. At the same time, the party and government, now ruling the whole country, recruited new cadres on a massive scale. Many such recruits constituted a "new class," in a position to pass privileged educational, health care, and housing opportunities on to their children. Meanwhile, the party conducted one class-warfare campaign after another against landlords, reactionaries, traitors, and corrupt officials, creating an atmosphere of terror and intimidation. Much of the early goodwill and sense of security began to dissipate.

By the mid-fifties Mao had become increasingly dissatisfied, as agricultural production, counted on to support heavy industrialization, lagged. Peasants who had been glad to receive land of their own were much less eager to see it collectivized. Against the advice of fellow leaders who favored a more gradual approach, Mao pressed ahead, with the result that all farmland in China became collectivized in a remarkably short time.

Despite Mao's efforts to rein in intellectuals during the Rectification Campaign of the early forties, in the mid-fifties he still counted on them to play a role in the modernization of China. By 1957 he believed that the new regime was well established and that the majority of Chinese now accepted the socialist path. Intellectuals, he hoped, could serve as a check on corruption and privilege in the party, a concern that had originally arisen during the Rectification Campaign and now was vented again in the campaign to "Let a Hundred Flowers Bloom." Some leaders had approved the idea of opening up the party to criticism from the outside, but when criticism became vociferous and even turned anti-socialist, Mao turned on the intellectuals he had previously encouraged to speak out, purging at least 300,000 and sending them into internal exile.

Undeterred by either economic or political setbacks, Mao pressed ahead with the Great Leap Forward in order to jump-start more rapid industrialization. The movement promoted bootstrap efforts in the countryside, typified by "backyard furnaces" to boost steel production. Seeking to decentralize some of the power that had accumulated in Beijing but also to gain greater control over agricultural production, Mao began to turn the countryside into autarkic communes, declaring that China was on the verge of communism, a claim that had not even been made by the Soviet Union. As a result of this and other differences, China had a major falling-out with the Soviet Union by 1960, and the two sides almost went to war at the end of the decade. The Great Leap Forward, too, went awry; agricultural production declined further, distribution was uneven, and famine led to the deaths of tens of millions of peasants.

At this juncture new leadership under Liu Shaoqi and Deng Xiaoping came forward to espouse more-moderate policies: the expansion of private garden plots, the opening up of local markets, and the offering of material incentives for increased production. All notions of achieving full communism were shelved. Mao fumed against Liu and Deng, believing that their policies would lead to a restoration of capitalism in China. After much political maneuvering, Mao managed to launch his Great Proletarian Cultural Revolution of 1966 and called upon the students of China to lead it, bypassing and outflanking the party and state bureaucracies.

Ostensibly, the purpose of the Cultural Revolution was to destroy the remnants of past tradition (especially Confucianism) and bourgeois liberalism, but more directly it aimed at opponents in the Chinese Communist Party (CCP) who were accused of "economism" (i.e., favoring markets and incentives) and of "walking the capitalist road." Mao singled out individuals in the party who were said to have been corrupted by power

and privilege. Liu and Deng, considered the top two "capitalist roaders" in China, were eventually purged from the party, along with thousands of alleged "followers." No one was immune to attack as a rightist; children were even encouraged to accuse their parents. Students, organized as Red Guards, also attacked intellectuals who, unlike members of the party, had no organization to protect themselves. Liu's and Deng's policies were reversed. The struggle between contending factions led to mass chaos and the near collapse of China.

MAO ZEDONG: "LEANING TO ONE SIDE"

In *Dictatorship of the People's Democracy* (1949) (see chapter 34), besides making the case for Leninist "democratic centralism," Mao also stated that the Chinese Communist Revolution should be guided by the experience of the Soviet Union and, as an ally of the Soviets, should take part in the world revolutionary movement. Anticipating the objection that this meant "leaning to one side" in favor of the Soviets, he defended the policy as follows:

"You are leaning to one side." Exactly. The forty years' experience of Sun Yatsen and the twenty-eight years' experience of the Communist Party have taught us to lean to one side, and we are firmly convinced that in order to win victory and consolidate it we must lean to one side. In the light of the experiences accumulated in these forty years and these twenty-eight years, all Chinese without exception must lean either to the side of imperialism or to the side of socialism. Sitting on the fence will not do, nor is there a third road. ...

"Victory is possible even without international help." This is a mistaken idea. In the epoch in which imperialism exists, it is impossible for a genuine people's revolution to win victory in any country without various forms of help from the international revolutionary forces, and even if victory were won, it could not be consolidated. This was the case with the victory and consolidation of the Great October Revolution as Stalin told us long ago. This was also the case with the overthrow of the three imperialist powers in World War II and the establishment of the people's democracies. And this is also the case with the present and the future of People's China.

[From Selden, *The People's Republic of China*, pp. 176–177]

MAO ZEDONG:
"STALIN IS OUR COMMANDER"

This speech, actually given in 1939, was published in the *People's Daily*, the authoritative organ of the Chinese Communist Party, only after the founding of the People's Republic of China on October 1, 1949. It constituted a reaffirmation by Mao after the more-moderate "New Democracy" phase, of his earlier revolutionary commitments, and of his continuing faith in Stalin as the leader of the world revolution. Of particular significance here is Mao's assertion that all of Marxism is summed up in "the one sentence: To rebel is justified." This was later invoked repeatedly, at the launching of the Great Proletarian Cultural Revolution.

At the present time, the whole world is divided into two fronts struggling against one another. On the one side is imperialism, which represents the front of the oppressors. On the other is socialism, which represents the front of resistance to oppression. ... Who is in command of the revolutionary front? It is socialism, it is Stalin. Comrade Stalin is the leader of the world revolution. Because he is there, it is easier to get things done. As you know, Marx is dead, and Engels and Lenin too are dead. If we did not have a Stalin, who would give the orders? ...

There are innumerable principles of Marxism, but in the last analysis they can all be summed up in one sentence: "To rebel is justified." For thousands of years everyone said: "Oppression is justified, exploitation is justified, rebellion is not justified." From the time when Marxism appeared on the scene, this old judgment was turned upside down, and this is a great contribution. This principle was derived by the proletariat from its struggles, but Marx drew the conclusion. In accordance with this principle, there was then resistance, there was struggle, and socialism was realized. What is Comrade Stalin's contribution? He developed this principle, he developed Marxism-Leninism and produced a very clear, concrete, and living doctrine for the oppressed people of the whole world. This is the complete doctrine of establishing a revolutionary front, overthrowing imperialism, overthrowing capitalism, and establishing a socialist society.

The practical aspect consists in turning doctrine into reality. Neither Marx, Engels, nor Lenin carried to completion the cause of the establishment of socialism, but Stalin did so. This is a great and unprecedented exploit. Before the Soviet Union's two five-year plans, the capitalist newspapers of various countries proclaimed daily that the Soviet Union was in desperate straits, that socialism could not be relied upon, but what do we see today? Stalin has stopped Chamberlain's mouth,* and also the mouths of those Chinese diehards. They all recognize that the Soviet Union has triumphed.

Stalin has helped us from the doctrinal standpoint in our war of resistance against Japan. Apart from this, he has given us material and practical aid. Since the victory of Stalin's cause, he has aided us with many airplanes, cannons, aviators, and military advisers in every domain, as well as lending us money. What other country in the world has helped us in this way? What country in the world, led by what class, party, and individual, has helped us in this way? Who is there, apart from the Soviet Union, the proletariat, the Communist Party, and Stalin?

[From Schram, *The Political Thought of Mao Tse-tung*, pp. 426–429]

GUO MORUO:
ODE TO STALIN—"LONG LIVE STALIN"
ON HIS SEVENTIETH BIRTHDAY, 1949

This poem to Stalin was written by Guo Moruo (1897–1977), a major intellectual figurehead of the People's Republic, unofficial poet laureate, and president of the Chinese Academy of Sciences. Before 1949 he was prominent as a writer, historian, and left-wing activist, but not as an open Communist; after 1949 he was a supposedly "non-partisan" representative in the

---

* A reference to the pact in 1939 between Stalin and Hitler that left the latter free to deal with Chamberlain and Britain.

People's Republic Political Consultative Conference, and later vice president of the Standing Committee of the People's Congress. At his death it was revealed that he had long been a secret member of the Party, but this Ode leaves little doubt where his sentiments lay.

The "orders of nature" spoken of at the end of the ode is presumably a reference to the Lysenko theory of evolution approved by Stalin in those years.

LONG LIVE STALIN!

(Stalin, Banzai!)

The Great Stalin, our beloved "Steel," our everlasting sun!

Only because there is you among mankind, Marx-Leninism can reach its present heights!

Only because there is you, the Proletariat can have its present growth and strength!

Only because there is you, the task of liberation can be as glorious as it is!

It is you who are leading us to merge into the stream flowing into the ocean of utopia.

It is you who are instructing us that the West will never neglect the East.

It is you who are uniting us into a force never before seen in history.

There is the fortress of peace of the USSR, standing firm, with unparalleled strength.

There are the new republics of Asia and Europe, side by side, growing more and more prosperous.

There is the Chinese People's Republic, turning in a new direction, brightening the world.

The history of mankind is opening a new chapter.

The orders of nature will also follow the direction of revolution.

The name of Stalin will forever be the sun of mankind.

Long live Great Stalin!

Long live Our Beloved "Steel"!

[Trans. by Chaoying Fang]

JI YUN: "HOW CHINA PROCEEDS WITH THE TASK OF INDUSTRIALIZATION" (1953)

Citing Lenin, Stalin, and the Soviet Union as models for the CCP, this statement gives early priority to heavy industry and agricultural collectivization in a Soviet-style Five-Year Plan. The Communists saw large-scale projects and a planned economy as the key to the nearly century-old goal of wealth and power.

The five-year construction plan, to which we have long looked forward, has now commenced. Its basic object is the gradual realization of the industrialization of our state.

Industrialization has been the goal sought by the Chinese people during the past one hundred years. From the last days of the Manchu dynasty to the early years of the republic, some people had undertaken the establishment of a few factories in the country. But industry as a whole has never been developed in China. … It was just as Stalin said: "Because China did not have its own heavy industry and its own war industry, it was being trampled upon by all the reckless and unruly elements. …"

We are now in the midst of a period of important changes, in that period of transition, as described by Lenin, of changing "from the stallion of the peasant, the farm hand, and poverty, to the stallion of mechanized industry and electrification."

We must look upon this period of transition to the industrialization of the state as one equal in importance and significance to that period of transition of the revolution toward the fight for political power. …

It was through the implementation of the policies of the industrialization of the state and the collectivization of agriculture that the Soviet Union succeeded in building up, from an economic structure complicated with five component economies, a unified socialist economy; in turning a backward agricultural nation into a first-class industrial power of the world; in defeating German fascist aggression in World War II; and in constituting itself the strong bastion of world peace today.

We are looking upon the Soviet Union as our example in the building of our country. Soviet experiences in the realization of industrialization are of great value to us. …

The foundation of socialism is large industrial development. Lenin said, "There is only one real foundation for a socialist society, and it is large industry. If we do not possess factories of great size, if we do not possess a large industrial structure with the most advanced equipment, then we shall generally not be able to talk of socialism, much less in the case of an agricultural country."

Accordingly, in order to enable our state to progress victoriously toward socialism, we must construct large industries. ... Numerous facts have proved that it is futile to attempt the enforcement of socialism on the foundations of small agriculture or small handicrafts. Industry must first be developed to provide possibilities for the collectivization and mechanization of agriculture, for the socialist reform of agriculture.

At the same time, only with industrialization of the state may we guarantee our economic independence and nonreliance on imperialism.

[Ji Yun, in *People's Daily*, May 23, 1953; adapted from Selden, *The People's Republic of China*, pp. 290–292]

Li Fuqun: "Report on the First Five-Year Plan for Development of the National Economy of The People's Republic of China in 1953–1957, July 5 and 6, 1955"

Although called a "report," the following is more a restatement of the goals of the first five-year plan than an actual account of progress made. Nevertheless, these policies did succeed in establishing some industrial base by the mid-fifties. Note the heavy investment in major capital construction, reflecting a similar Soviet emphasis on large-scale state projects of great visibility.

The general task set by China's first five-year plan was determined in the light of the fundamental task of the state during the transition period.

It may be summarized as follows: We must center our main efforts on industrial construction; this comprises 694 above-norm construction projects, the core of which are the 156 projects that the Soviet Union is designing for us and on which we lay the preliminary groundwork for China's socialist industrialization; we must foster the growth of agricultural producers'

cooperatives, whose system of ownership is partially collective, and handicraft producers' cooperatives, thus laying the preliminary groundwork for the socialist transformation of agriculture and handicrafts; and in the main, we must incorporate capitalist industry and commerce into various forms of state capitalism, laying the groundwork for the socialist transformation of private industry and commerce. ...

The total outlay for the country's economic construction and cultural and educational development during the five-year period will be 76,640 million yuan, or the equivalent in value of more than 700 million taels [a little over an ounce] of gold. Such an enormous investment in national construction would have been absolutely inconceivable in the past. This is possible only for a government led by the working class and working wholeheartedly in the interests of the people.

Investments in capital construction will amount to 42,740 million yuan, or 55.8 percent of the total outlay for economic construction and cultural and educational development during the five-year period. Of the remaining 44.2 percent, or 33,900 million yuan, part will be spent on work occasioned by the needs of capital construction, such as prospecting resources, engineering surveying and designing, stockpiling of equipment and material, and so on. Part will be spent to develop industrial production, transport and posts and telecommunications, including such items as overhaul of equipment, technical and organizational improvements in production, trial manufacture of new products, purchase of miscellaneous fixed assets, and so on; another part will serve as circulating capital for the various economic departments; and still another part will go to funds allocated to all economic, cultural, and educational departments for operating expenses and for the training of specialized personnel. ...

The industrialization that our country is striving to achieve is socialist industrialization, modeled on Soviet experience and carried out with the direct assistance of the Soviet Union and the people's democracies. It is not capitalist industrialization. Therefore, our industry, particularly those branches producing means of production, is capable of rapid development.

[Adapted from Selden, *The People's Republic of China*, pp. 295–300]

MAO ZEDONG: "THE QUESTION OF AGRICULTURAL COOPERATION," JULY 31, 1955

Under the Soviet model, Chinese agriculture, through the sale of grain to the Soviet Union, was to provide the resources to fund an ambitious industrialization program. By the mid-fifties, however, the leadership realized that agricultural production was lagging and the surplus derived from it was insufficient. Collectivization of the land was seen as the solution to this problem. However, farmers, having received land in the early land reform movement, could be expected to resist subsequent moves for them to surrender it. The program thus was envisioned as a long-term project that would take decades and would be done on a voluntary basis. In the following, Mao spelled out the steps by which the people could be persuaded to join in the process: building small-scale cooperatives that would then be expanded into large production units. When the farmers saw the advantages of cooperative farming, he thought, they would join the cooperatives of their own accord.

When production, fell, in part on account of the farmers' noncooperation, however, Mao decided to press ahead, convinced that the masses would go along with the tide of revolutionary change, and that the eventual results would confirm the rightness of his policies. Instead of taking several decades, China's land collectivization was accomplished in a year or two. Though less violent than the Soviet collectivization of the thirties, it was not without resistance and loss of life.

The following passages reveal, in the way Mao expresses himself, how easily his own thoughts are put into the minds of others—how prone, he is to letting the strong conviction of his own rightness color his reading of a situation.

A new upsurge in the socialist mass movement is in sight throughout the Chinese countryside. But some of our comrades are tottering along like a woman with bound feet, always complaining that others are going too fast. They imagine that by picking on trifles, grumbling unnecessarily, worrying continuously, and putting up countless taboos and commandments, they will guide the socialist mass movement in the rural areas along sound lines.

No, this is not the right way at all; it is wrong.

The tide of social reform in the countryside—in the shape of cooperation—has already reached some places. Soon it will sweep the whole country. This is a huge socialist revolutionary movement, which involves a rural population more than five hundred million strong, one that has very great world significance. We should guide this movement vigorously, warmly, and systematically, and not act as a drag on it. ...

It is wrong to say that the present pace of development of the agricultural producers' cooperatives has "gone beyond practical possibilities" or "gone beyond the consciousness of the masses." The situation in China is like this: its population is enormous, there is a shortage of cultivated land (only three *mou* of land per head, taking the country as a whole; in many parts of the southern provinces, the average is only one *mou* or less), natural catastrophes occur from time to time—every year large numbers of farms suffer more or less from flood, drought, gales, frost, hail, or insect pests—and methods of farming are backward. As a result, many peasants are still having difficulties or are not well off. The well-off ones are comparatively few, although since land reform the standard of living, of the peasants as a whole has improved. For all these reasons there is an active desire among most peasants to take the socialist road. ...

We have been taking steps to bring about a gradual advance in the socialist transformation of agriculture. The first step in the countryside is to call on the peasants, in accordance with the principles of voluntariness and mutual benefit, to organize agricultural producers' mutual-aid teams. Such teams contain only the rudiments of socialism. Each one draws in a few households, though some have ten or more. The second step is to call on the peasants, on the basis of these mutual-aid teams and still in accordance with the principles of voluntariness and mutual benefit, to organize small agricultural producers' cooperatives semi-socialist in nature, characterized by the pooling of land as shares and by single management. Not until we take the third step will the peasants be called upon, on the basis of these small, semi-socialist cooperatives and in accordance with the same principles of voluntariness and mutual benefit, to unite on a larger scale and organize large agricultural producers' cooperatives completely socialist in nature. These steps are designed to raise steadily the socialist consciousness of the peasants through their personal experience, to change their mode of life step by step, and so minimize any feeling that their mode of life is being changed all of a sudden.

[Mao, *Guanyu nongye hezuohua wenti;* trans. adapted from Schram, *The Political Thought of Mao Tse-tung,* pp. 343–346]

MAO ZEDONG:
"ON THE CORRECT HANDLING OF CONTRADICTIONS AMONG THE PEOPLE"

This speech, popularly known by the catch-phrase "Let a Hundred Flowers Bloom," is one of Mao Zedong's most important theoretical statements after the consolidation of Communist power on the mainland of China and after the death of Stalin left Mao the senior Communist theoretician. It was occasioned in part by the shock of the uprising in Hungary late in 1956, which showed the degree of pent-up dissatisfaction possible under even a seemingly well-established Communist regime. If Mao's gesture was meant to encourage the "letting off of steam," those who took advantage of the offer found, after a brief period of forbearance by the Party, that they would be subjected to severe attack and penalized for their outspokenness.

In long-range terms the significance of this statement lay not in any liberalization or loosening of Communist ideological control but precisely in its reaffirmation of the importance that Mao attached to unity in matters of theory and doctrine. As we have seen, for Mao and for Liu Shaoqi, the principal means of preserving that unity as a dynamic force had been ideological struggle. Yet under conditions of Party dominance, the threat of stagnation was always present. Consequently for Mao, always concerned to keep his cohorts in battle-readiness, the question was how to stimulate the airing of contradictions without allowing them to become antagonistic.

Mao continued to wrestle with this problem, hoping to find a use for "nonantagonistic" criticism as an outlet for discontent. However, with the Party standing as sole judge of what was antagonistic or not, and making an object lesson of those who unknowingly overstepped the invisible line, this particular contradiction could not be easily resolved.

Mao's speech was originally delivered on February 27, 1957, before a large audience at the Supreme State Conference. When finally published at the end of June, it had been substantially revised and probably represented a much more guarded statement of policy than the original lecture. The purpose was now less to encourage "fragrant flowers" and more to identify "poisonous weeds."

Two Different Types of Contradictions

Never has our country been as united as it is today. The victories of the bourgeois-democratic revolution and the socialist revolution, coupled with our achievements in socialist construction, have rapidly changed the face of old China. Now we see before us an even brighter future. … Unification of the country, unity of the people, and unity among our various nationalities—these are the basic guarantees for the sure triumph of our cause. However, this does not mean that there are no longer any contradictions in our society. … We are confronted by two types of social contradictions—contradictions between ourselves and the enemy and contradictions among the people. These two types of contradictions are totally different in nature. [pp. 14–15]

The contradictions between ourselves and our enemies are antagonistic ones. Within the ranks of the people, contradictions among the working people are nonantagonistic, while those between the exploiters and the exploited classes have, apart from their antagonistic aspect, a nonantagonistic aspect. Contradictions among the people have always existed, but their content differs in each period of the revolution and during the building of socialism.

In the conditions existing in China today, what we call contradictions among the people include the following:

Contradictions within the working class, contradictions within the peasantry, contradictions within the intelligentsia, contradictions between the working class and the peasantry, contradictions between the working class and peasantry on the one hand and the intelligentsia on the other, contradictions between the working class and other, sections of the working people on the one hand and the national bourgeoisie on the other, contradictions within the national bourgeoisie, and so forth. Our People's Government is a government that truly represents the interests of the people and serves the people, yet certain contradictions do exist between the government and the masses. These include contradictions between the interests of the state, collective interests, and individual interests; between democracy and centralism; between those in positions of leadership and the led; and contradictions arising from the bureaucratic practices of certain state functionaries in their relations with the masses. All these are contradictions among the people; generally speaking, underlying the contradictions among the people is the basic identity of the interests of the people.

In our country, the contradiction between the working class and the national bourgeoisie is a contradiction among the people. … The contradiction between exploiter and exploited that exists between the national bourgeoisie and the working class is an antagonistic one. But, in the concrete conditions existing in China, such an antagonistic contradiction, if properly handled, can be transformed into a nonantagonistic one and resolved in a peaceful way. But if it is not properly handled—if, say, we do not follow a policy of unity, criticizing and educating the national bourgeoisie, or if the national bourgeoisie does not accept this policy—then the contradictions between the working class and the national bourgeoisie can turn into an antagonistic contradiction between ourselves and the enemy. [pp. 16–18]

There were other people in our country who took a wavering attitude toward the Hungarian events because they were ignorant about the actual world situation. They felt that there was too little freedom under our people's democracy and that there was more freedom under Western parliamentary democracy. They ask for the adoption of the two-party system of the West, where one party is in office and the other out of office. But this so-called two-party system is nothing but a means of maintaining the dictatorship of the bourgeoisie; under no circumstances can it safeguard the freedom of the working people. …

Those who demand freedom and democracy in the abstract regard democracy as an end and not a means. Democracy sometimes seems to be an end, but it is in fact only a means. Marxism teaches us that democracy is part of the superstructure and belongs to the category of politics. That is to say, in the last analysis it serves the economic base. The same is true of freedom. Both democracy and freedom are relative, not absolute, and they come into being and develop under specific historical circumstances.

Within the ranks of the people, democracy stands in relation to centralism, and freedom to discipline. They are two conflicting aspects of a single entity, contradictory as well as united, and we should not one-sidedly emphasize one to the denial of the other. Within the ranks of the people, we cannot do without democracy, nor can we do without centralism. Our democratic centralism means the unity of democracy and centralism and the unity of freedom and discipline. Under this system, the people enjoy a wide measure of democracy and freedom, but at the same time they have to keep themselves within the bounds of socialist discipline. All this is well understood by the people. [pp. 21–22]

Marxist philosophy holds that the law of the unity of opposites is a fundamental law of the universe. This law operates everywhere—in the natural world in human society, and in human thinking. Opposites in contradiction unite as well as struggle with each other, and thus impel all things to move and change. Contradictions exist everywhere, but as things differ in nature so do contradictions in any given phenomenon or thing; the unity of opposites is conditional temporary and transitory, and hence relative, whereas struggle between opposites is absolute. Lenin gave a very clear exposition of this law. In our country a growing number of people have come to understand it. For many people, however, acceptance of this law is one thing and its application, examining and dealing with problems, is quite another. … Many people refuse to admit that contradictions still exist in a socialist society, with the result that when confronted with social contradictions they become timid and helpless. They do not understand that socialist society grows more united and consolidated precisely through the ceaseless process of correctly dealing with and resolving contradictions. … [p. 26]

On "Letting a Hundred Flowers Blossom" and "Letting a Hundred Schools of Thought Contend"

The policy of letting a hundred flowers blossom and a hundred schools of thought contend is designed to promote the flourishing of the arts and the progress of science; it is designed to enable a socialist culture to thrive in our land. Different forms and styles in art can develop freely, and different schools in science can contend freely. We think that it is harmful to the growth of art and science if administrative measures are used to impose one particular style of art or school of thought and to ban another. … In the past, new and correct things often failed at the outset to win recognition from the majority of people and had to develop by twists and turns in struggle. Correct and good things have often at first been looked upon not as fragrant flowers but as poisonous weeds; Copernicus's theory of the solar system and Darwin's theory of evolution were once dismissed as erroneous and had to win out over bitter opposition. Chinese history offers many similar examples. …

Marxism has also developed through struggle. … It is true that in China socialist transformation, insofar as a change in the system of ownership is concerned, has in the main been completed, and the turbulent, large-scale, mass class struggles characteristic of the revolutionary periods have in the main concluded. But remnants of the overthrown landlord and comprador classes still exist, the bourgeoisie still exists, and the petty bourgeoisie has only just begun to remold itself. Class struggle is not yet over. … In this respect, the question of whether socialism or capitalism will win is still not really settled. Marxists are still a minority of the entire population as well as of the intellectuals. Marxism therefore must still develop through struggle. … As humankind in general rejects an untruth and accepts a truth, a new truth will begin struggling with new erroneous ideas. Such struggles will never end. This is the law of the development of truth, and it is certainly also the law of development in Marxism. [pp. 44–46]

People may ask: Since Marxism is accepted by the majority of the people in our country as the guiding ideology, can it be criticized? Certainly it can. As a scientific truth, Marxism fears no criticism. If it did and could be defeated in argument, it would be worthless. In fact, are not the idealists criticizing Marxism every day and in all sorts of ways? … Fighting against wrong ideas is like being vaccinated—a man develops greater immunity from disease after the vaccine takes effect. Plants raised in hothouses are not likely to be robust. Carrying out the policy of letting a hundred flowers bloom and a hundred schools of thought contend will not weaken but strengthen the leading position of Marxism in the ideological field.

What should our policy be toward non-Marxist ideas? As far as unmistakable counterrevolutionaries and wreckers of the socialist cause are concerned, the matter is easy; we simply deprive them of their freedom of speech. But it is quite a different matter when we are faced with incorrect ideas among the people. Will it do to ban such ideas and give them no opportunity to express themselves? Certainly not. … That is why it is only by employing methods of discussion, criticism, and reasoning that we can really foster correct ideas, overcome wrong ideas, and really settle issues. [pp. 47–48]

So what, from the point of view of the broad masses of the people, should be a criterion today for distinguishing between fragrant flowers and poisonous weeds? …

Basing ourselves on the principles of our constitution, the will of the overwhelming majority of our people, and the political programs jointly proclaimed on various occasions by our political parties and groups, we believe that, broadly speaking, words and actions can be judged right if they:

1. Help to unite the people of our various nationalities and do not divide them
2. Are beneficial, not harmful, to socialist transformation and socialist construction
3. Help to consolidate, not undermine or weaken, the people's democratic dictatorship
4. Help to consolidate, not undermine or weaken, democratic centralism
5. Tend to strengthen, not to cast off or weaken, the leadership of the Communist Party
6. Are beneficial, not harmful, to international socialist solidarity and the solidarity of the peace-loving peoples of the world

Of these six criteria, the most important are the socialist path and the leadership of the Party. ... When the majority of the people have clear-cut criteria to go by, criticism and self-criticism can be conducted along proper lines, and these criteria can be applied to people's words and actions to determine whether they are fragrant flowers or poisonous weeds. These are political criteria. Naturally, in judging the truthfulness of scientific theories or assessing the aesthetic value of works of art, other pertinent criteria are needed, but these six political criteria are also applicable to all activities in the arts or sciences. In a socialist country like ours, can there possibly be any useful scientific or artistic activity that runs counter to these political criteria? [pp. 49–50]

[Mao, *Let a Hundred Flowers Bloom*, pp. 14–26, 44–50]

LIU BINYAN: "A HIGHER KIND OF LOYALTY"

In this essay Liu Binyan, a prominent journalist who later became an outspoken critic of the Mao and Deng regimes, recalls how thrilled he was by Mao's original speech on the Hundred Flowers Campaign, but then how disillusioned he was by the repression that followed. Liu subsequently became convinced that the campaign was set by Mao deliberately to trap his opponents; today, not all historians are so convinced, but there is little disagreement about the chilling outcome.

I do not remember a moment in my life more exhilarating than when Mao Zedong's February 1957 speech to the State Council was released. My estimation of him soared to sublime heights. At *China Youth News* the response was equally enthusiastic; it seemed as if we were at the beginning of a new era in China.

In his speech, Mao distinguished between two basically different sets of "contradictions"—antagonistic and nonantagonistic. In so doing, he appeared to be announcing that the era of class struggle was over, that "internal contradictions" (including those between capitalists and the working class) were the main ones within our society, and the foremost among these were contradictions between the Party and the people. These were seen as nonantagonistic conflicts. This also meant that the Party must be placed under supervision of the people and that the fight against bureaucratism was a major task, requiring our full and constant attention. In that speech, Mao announced that dogmatism should not be mistaken for Marxism; he reiterated his policy of letting "a hundred flowers bloom and a hundred schools of thought contend"; he advocated open criticism and reiterated that senior party leaders should not be exempt from criticism. As for strikes by workers and students—unprecedented since the founding of the People's Republic and now taken seriously for the first time—he said the right way of dealing with them was not by force or coercion but by overcoming bureaucratism.

These issues were exactly the unspoken ones that had been weighing on me for the last few years—special privileges within Party ranks, bureaucratism, and dogmatic tendencies. Now my disquiet had been dispelled as if by magic. The political climate in Beijing cleared up; the mood of intellectuals brightened; everything seemed to take on a rosy hue. Mao was virtually advocating more democracy and liberalization in matters of ideology; as a journalist and writer, I now felt I had a free hand in pursuing my vocation.

In March I went to Harbin and Changchun, two big cities in northeast China, and I was shocked by the state of things I saw. The local Party Committee's attitude toward Mao's speech was diametrically opposed to that of the intellectuals; local officials just sat back, waiting for a change in the wind. The Party Committee in Harbin was conducting its own criticism of "bourgeois ideology." The municipal Party secretary had decided that bureaucratism was a form of bourgeois ideology, so opposing bourgeois ideology covered everything.

Another thing that shocked me was the diametrically opposed interpretations of Mao's intentions. Mao's talk was filtering down to Party cadres in these two cities, and among those who had heard and studied the talk, some felt that Mao was attacking dogmatism and leftist tendencies, while others felt differently. It is true, the latter conceded, Mao had criticized Chen Qitong's January letter in the *People's Daily* attacking liberal tendencies in art and literature. But that criticism, they argued, was leveled at Chen's ineptitude in timing and presentation, not at his basic stand.

Thirty years later, I reread Mao's speech (the original version, not the one revised for publication) and realized that at the time I had been too preoccupied with his main drift to detect hints of other tendencies hidden between the lines. For instance, he did not mince words over Stalin's dogmatism, but then insisted that Stalin must be assessed on the "three-seven" principle—that is, seven parts merit to three parts fault. Again Mao considered "democracy" as basically a tool to mobilize the people for the Party's own ends.

[Liu Binyan, A *Higher Kind of Loyalty*, pp. 69–70]

US Occupation Policy on Shinto in Post-Liberation Korea and Japan

By Motokazu Matsutani

INTRODUCTION

After the victory in the Asia-Pacific War, General Headquarters/the Supreme Commander for the Allied Powers (GHQ/SCAP) took immediate action in reforming the militaristic Japanese society through democratization and demilitarization. Among the various policies, GHQ/SCAP put priority on dismantling the intimate relationship between the state and Shinto. The U.S. government believed the state system, where Shinto was placed at the center of both political and religious administration (hereafter, "State Shinto"*) served as a breeding ground for Japanese militarism and thus sought to remove it to promote democracy.

The dismantling of State Shinto was also a key issue for the United States Army Forces in Korea (USAFIK) following the end to Japan's 36-year colonial rule on the Korean peninsula. Despite Japan's defeat, laws that guaranteed various exclusive advantages for State Shinto were still in effect in Korea and shrines were left all over the peninsula. Therefore, the United States had to achieve the same task of the abolishing of State Shinto in both Japan and Korea.

Although both USAFIK and GHQ shared the common task of abolishing State Shinto, their policies

differed. USAFIK banned Shinto and abolished shrines without exception whereas GHQ preserved all shrines and permitted the continuation of Shinto in Japan. Why did USAFIK and GHQ take such contrasting approaches to achieve the common goal of dismantling State Shinto in the two countries? Was not there any policy coordination between GHQ and USAFIK, both of which were under the direct command of SCAP, General Douglas MacArthur?

In this paper, I will attempt to answer the above questions by focusing on the development of policy on Shinto in the post-war Korea and Japan. I will examine changes to the environment that surrounded Shinto on the Korean peninsula following Japan's surrender, and illustrate how these changes affected USAFIK's decision-making. Then, I will compare the Korean case to the Japanese case under GHQ/SCAP, by which I seek to clarify the conditions that commonly restricted occupational forces in both countries in planning policies on Shinto and reveal the mechanism which led to the two differing approaches.

SHRINES AFTER JAPAN'S DEFEAT

When Japanese colonial rule ended with the defeat of Japan, there were 70 shrines (*jinja*: 神社) and nearly 1,000 minor shrines (*shinji*: 神祠)—see Diagram 1—in South Korea (hereafter, "shrines" includes both

---

* State Shinto is also referred to as "National Shinto." Both were used as interchangeably in the U.S. policy documents.

Motokazu Matsutani, "US Occupation Policy on Shinto in Post-Liberation Korea and Japan," *Korean Studies Graduate Student Conference (April 17, 2004, Harvard University)*, pp. 1-28. Copyright © 2004 by Motokazu Matsutani. Reprinted with permission.

jinji and *shinji*).[*] During the early period of colonization, Shinto shrines in Korea were voluntarily built by Japanese colonial settlers. However after the 1930's, the Japanese Government-General of Korea started to take the initiative in shrine building as it tried to assimilate Koreans by forcing them to worship State Shinto by paying homage to shrines.[†] As a result, most of these privately-built shrines became nationalized and incorporated into a hierarchial system of State Shinto shrines according to their official "shrine rank" (*shakaku*: 社格)—given by the state—which placed the Grand Shrine of Chōsen (*Chōsen Jingū*: 朝鮮神宮) at the top.

On August 15, 1945, Emperor Hirohito's statement announcing Japan's surrender was also aired in Korea as it was in Japan. The news of liberation spread throughout the whole Korean peninsula and the Korean people, hoping for immediate independence, began to seize Japanese assets such as companies and governmental institutions. Some groups even attacked and destroyed these Japanese-affiliated buildings. The most frequent targets of such violent attacks were police stations and Shinto shrines. According to historical records, 136 Shinto shrines were attacked or set on fire between August 15 and 22, while 149 police stations were attacked and seized during the same period (see Diagram 2). These data clearly show that Shinto shrines, as well as police stations, were symbols of repeated physical, mental and spiritual violence and suppression to the Korean people.

However, these attacks on Shinto shrines did not last long. After about one week from the surrender, violence ceased and as a result, destructions of shrines were limited to less than 15% of the total number of shrines on the peninsula. It is also worth noting that the attacked shrines were mostly located in northern Korea and those in southern areas did not suffer much damage.[‡] Hence, it is said that the majority of shrines in South Korea remained intact even after the war.

The Japanese Government-General and Shinto priests took immediate action to protect the shrines when the attacks began. Firstly, high-ranking priests of the Grand Shrine of Chosen decided to carry out *shoshin-shiki* (昇神式) as soon as they confirmed the Japanese defeat over the radio on August 15.[§] *Shōshin-shiki*, which literally means a "ritual of elevating gods," refers to a ceremony through which gods or goddesses dedicated at a shrine are extradited to their divine homelands such as in rocks, mountains and nearby rivers.[¶] Just a day after the surrender, the head priests of the Grand Shrine of Chōsen visited the Government-General and proposed that it give orders to all the shrines in Korea to carry out *shoshin-shiki*. On August 16 to 17, the Government-General, taking in the proposal, sent orders to all the chief magistrates of local governments in Korea to conduct *shōshin-shiki*. The Government-General also directed local governments to disassemble the shrines after finishing the *shoshin-shiki*. In other words, the Japanese government decided on the removal of shrines from Korea after making sure that the appropriate measures of *shoshin-shiki* were taken.

By carrying out this ritual, the Government-General and Shinto priests tried to preserve Japanese

---

[*] Morita Yoshio, *Chōsen shūsen no kiroku*, (Gennando, 1964), p. 108. (hereafter, *Kiroku*). *Shinji* was defined as a public place where Japanese deities are enshrined, but smaller than ordinary shrines. The legal regulations for building *Shinji* in Korea were set by the governmental law in 1917. Chōsen Sōtokufu, ed., Chōsen Hōrei Shūran, (Kukhak saryŏwon, Seoul: 1996), p. 32.

[†] Han Sokki, *Nihon no chōsen shihai to shūkyo seisaku*, (Miraisha, 1988), pp. 169–179. Yamaguchi Kōichi, "Senjiki chōsen sōtokufu no jinja seisaku" in *Chōsenshi kenkyūkai ronbunshū*, No. 36, (Ryokuin Shobō, 1998), pp. 197–205.

[‡] Morita, *Kiroku*, pp. 112–13. Probably the reason for this is that the North had as twice high Christian population rate as the South. Also Korean Christians fought against mandatory shrine worshipping under Japanese rule and had the strongest anti-Japanese, anti-Shinto sentiments.

[§] For the descriptions in regard to *shoshin-shiki* hereafter are cited from Morita, pp. 109–113, Takeshima Hideo, "Shusengo no chosen jingu" in Morita Yoshio, *Chōsen Shūsen no kiroku Shiryō-hen dai 2 kan* (Gennando, 1980), pp. 164–67 (hereafter, *2 kan*).

[¶] Kokugakuin Dagaiku Nihonbunka Kenkyūjo ed., *Shinto Daijiten* (Kōbundō, 1994), p. 236.

deities—including the Meiji Emperor and the Sun Goddess of Amaterasu—from the Korean attacks. Japanese officials believed that the sanctity of shrines—where the nation's divinity and emperor's authority were symbolically displayed—would be preserved if they removed the shrines, through these proper rituals. To Japanese authorities, protection of the shrines did not mean the preservation of their buildings but rather a process to remove them in their own hands before any damage was done by the Koreans. Following the governmental decision, *shōshin-shiki* was first held at the Grand Shrine of Chōsen on August 16 and at various shrines located in local provinces by the end of August.[*] In this way, the removal of Shinto shrines started in Korea in parallel with the "exodus" of Japanese deities immediately following the collapse of Japanese colonial rule, even before the U.S. occupation began.

However, this top-down decision to conduct *Shōshin-shiki* was not welcomed by all Japanese residents remaining in Korea. Some of those who wanted to stay in Korea strongly demanded that the shrines should be preserved even after the war. To them, Shinto shrines were the center of their community and an important worshipping place. Therefore, they could not agree to the one-sided governmental order to remove the shrines aimed solely at protecting the Emperor's authority and state pride, and ignoring the faith of the Shinto believers.

The Japanese people who were unsatisfied by the government's policies on Shinto shrines started a movement to preserve shrines in post-war South Korea. The members of Japanese Mutual Aid Society (Nihon-jin Sewakai : 日本人世話会) in Keijō drew up a proposal to run the National Keijō Shrine—which was run by the government—in the private sector with the support of voluntary donations from Shinto followers.[†]

This plan was eventually submitted to USAFIK, not the Government General, where it had a big impact on U.S. Shinto policy-making. On the other hand, a Korean Shinto priest, Hong To-jae, tried to preserve the shrine by changing its name to "Sacred Mausoleum of Tan'gun (檀君聖廟)," but finally it was recycled as a medical school.[‡] This episode suggests that there was an attempt, even if minor, to indigenize Shinto and preserve it as a Korean religion after the war, however, any further details are not know from the currently available sources.

In any case, it is clear that the environment surrounding shrines in Korea dramatically changed as soon as the war ended. The Government-General, Japanese colonial settlers and Korean people all started different movements for either the abolition or continuation of Shinto shrines. Though both the Government-General and the Korean majority were for the removal of Shinto shrines—for totally different reasons—it was still unclear whether all the shrines in Korea would be abolished since the representatives of the Japanese community strongly supported their preservation even after the end of the Japanese rule.

SHINTO POLICY OF USAFIK BEFORE THE OCCUPATION

When USAFIK started the occupation, they did not have any clear plans for State Shinto and its shrines. This was because the U.S. government, which did not expect such an early Japanese surrender, had dispatched USAFIK mainly to prevent a Russian invasion from the north. Therefore, the U.S. government did not have enough time to plan for the Korean occupation and thus allowed USAFIK to take matters into their own hands for the most part.[§]

The policy makers of USAFIK, though they had some knowledge about Korea,[¶] visited the headquarters

---

[*] Morita, *2 kan*, p. 111–13.

[†] Morita, *Kiroku*, p. 406. Japanese Mutual Aid Society was formed as voluntary association by Japanese residence in Korea just after the war. The major activities were to assist the repatriation of the Japanese to Japan proper and to share information among those who remain in Korea. For more details, see Morita, *Kiroku*, pp. 132–48.

[‡] Morita, *Kiroku*, p. 406.

[§] Bruce Cumings, *Origins of Korean War 1945–47*, (Princeton University Press, 1981), pp. 126–29.

[¶] Bruce Cumings says Joint Army-Navy Intelligence Study of Korea (JANIS-75) offered much knowledge USAFIK before occupation. However, the present author was in Japan when of the U.S. Army Forces in the Pacific (AFPAC—which later became a part of GHQ/SCAP) in Manila in late August 1945 to ask for advice on the occupation policies in Korea.* AFPAC advised USAFIK to use Japan's occupation plan as a working basis for drawing up a plan for Korea.† Thus, it is highly probable that USAFIK's first input on Shinto policies was from this interaction with AFPAC as well as from the occupation plan for Japan.‡

The first occupation plan for Korea by USAFIK was drafted on August 29, 1945, in a document titled "Field Order 55." This order shows that USAFIK had basic knowledge of Shintoism and believed something must be done about it during the occupation.

> Freedom of religion will be proclaimed … Dissemination of Japanese militaristic, national-shintoistic and ultra-nationalistic ideology and propaganda in any form will be prohibited and suppressed.§

It seems that USAFIK defined State Shinto as an ideology similar to Japanese militarism and ultra-nationalism,

rather than as a religion. They were determined to stop the dissemination of Shinto ideology because it symbolized Japanese militarism, but they lacked concrete or specific plans—such as closing down Shrines or ordering Shinto priests to leave Korea. However, at this point, it was highly probable that USAFIK would take any necessary suppressive measure against Shinto and its shrines.

However, there was a danger, though not recognized by USAFIK, that violent suppression on Shinto might be regarded as violation to the principle of freedom of religion. Historically speaking, State Shinto was developed through the integration of traditional Japanese religion Shinto, the dogma of Emperor worshiping and the aggressive militarism, putting all shrines under government control.¶ Thus, it was not appropriate to identify State Shinto with militaristic ideology. Shinto certainly had religious elements and shrines were, without doubt, worshipping places for Shinto believers at that time. This means that if USAFIK sought to "proclaim the freedom of religion," as shown on the Field Order 55, it had to avoid taking suppressive actions on Shinto and its shrines. It was the credo for both USAFIK and GHQ that "the rule of law must prevail after victory (over Japan) since the war itself was a struggle of against lawlessness."**

GHQ/SCAP, which started the Japanese occupation slightly before USAFIK's landing on Korea, seemed to have recognized this danger that abolition of shrines might collide with freedom of religion. Thus, when the occupation began in Japan, GHQ did not take any aggressive actions against shrines but rather held the status quo.†† Moreover, GHQ/SCAP, being a higher-command of USAFIK,‡‡ instructed the Korean occupational forces

---

he wrote this paper, and not able to find this original source material.

* Leonard Hoag, *American Military Government in Korea: War Policy and the First Year of Occupation*, 1945–46, Draft Manuscript produced under the auspices of the Office of the Chief of Military History, Dept. of the Army, Washington D.C., 1970 in Shin Pung-Nyong ed., *Hankuk pundan charyŏjip 2* (Wŏnju munhwa sa, 1993). pp. 97–100.

† United States Armed Forces in Korea, *History of the United States Armed Forces in Korea*, compiled under the super vision of Harold Larsen, chief historian. Tokyo and Seoul, 1947, 48. Manuscript in the Office of the Chief of Military History, Washington D.C., Part III, Ch. I, p. 11 in *Chuhan Migunsa*, (Tolbaege, 1988). Hereafter, *HUSAFIK*.

‡ This plan is AFPAC's order, titled "Annex No. 8 to Operation Instruction No. 4." Ibid., p. 12. However, the original document was not available in Japan and the author was not able to confirm if anything on Shinto was mentioned in the document.

§ Cited in Hoag, pp. 105–105

¶ William P. Woodard, *The Allied Occupation of Japan 1945–1952 and Japanese Religions* (Leiden: E.J. Brill, 1972), p. 10.

** Cumings, p. 126.

†† Woodard, p. 52.

‡‡ Among GHQ/SCAP, Government Section (GS) had a function to collect information on Korea as well as Japan and to advise SCAP for the policies to be taken in Korea. Civil Information and Education Section (CIE) particularly worked on researching religious situation in Korea and was also able to advise SCAP. For the details of the role of GS, see Political

"to take all means to avoid desecration" of shrines in South Korea before the occupational administration began in Korea.[*] Consequently, it became difficult for USAFIK to implement the initial plan to prohibit the militaristic and shintoistic ideology as it might be perceived as desecration by the Japanese residence.

SHINTO POLICY AFTER THE OCCUPATION

When the USAFIK officers landed on South Korea, they faced a totally unexpected situation and greatly confused. As they entered the capital city of Keijō on September 9, 1945, they saw the Grand Shrine of Chōsen being taken part by the Japanese. As mentioned earlier, this was due to the governmental order to remove shrines upon completing *shōshin-shiki*.

Prior to the landing on South Korea, the Commander of USAFIK, General John R. Hodge, had received the certain amount of information regarding the political and social situation of Keijō by the radio communications with the Japanese Government-General. However, he did not receive any information about the removal of shrines and the on-going *shōshin-shiki*.[†] In addition, when an advance team of USAFIK officers arrived in Keijō on September 6, they received a petition from the Government-General that "we (Government-General) strongly hope for you (USAFIK) to respect the dignity of shrines."[‡] USAFIK must have taken this word

as evidence to show that the Japanese still wanted to preserve the shrines in Korea, and thus it was beyond their expectation that the Japanese would be voluntarily dismantling shrines before their arrival.

USAFIK reacted to the unexpected circumstances flexibly. Firstly, after verifying that Government-General was taking the initiative in disassembling the shrines, USAFIK ordered stop the actions by saying "all public buildings shall be requisitioned by USAFIK and the status quo shall be maintained."[§] This notice was not only in line with GHQ/SCAP's policy on Shinto, but also with the Article II of the Proclamation No.1, (issued on September 9 by USAFIK under MacArthur's name) which stated "all government employees … shall preserve and safeguard all records and property."[¶] It would have been of a great advantage for USAFIK to let the Japanese remove the shrines by themselves as it sought for dismantling State Shinto. However, USAFIK consistently followed the directions of GHQ/SCAP and prohibited the removal of Shinto shrines by the Japanese so that they could be preserved.

After the dismantling of shrines was banned by USAFIK, the members of Japanese Mutual Aid Society in Keijo submitted a petition to USAFIK on September 12, which was mentioned in the previous chapter. The petition claimed that the Japanese residents in Keijō would like to run the shrines under the private initiative.[**] By this petition, USAFIK seemed to have realized that the removal of shrines was initiated by the Government-General against the Japanese residents' opinions.

Therefore, Major General Archibald Arnold of USAFIK, when he met with the Government-General officers and the high priests of Grand Shrine of Chōsen to discuss about the shrine problem, clearly stated that shrines should be preserved unless the believers agree to the abolishing them.

---

reorientation of Japan, September 1945 to September 1948: report of Government Section, Supreme Commander for the Allied Powers. Washington, D.C.: U.S. Govt. Print. Off., 1949. App. G.8a(1), p. 796, and for CIE, see Woodard, pp. 23–24.

[*] William C. Kerr, *Notes on Religious Situation in Korea*, 1946, p. 73 in GHQ/SCAP Records: Top Secret Records, compiled by National Diet Library, file no. CIE(A) 09083-85.

[†] For the details for this communication, see *Lee Gyu Tae, Beiso no chosen senryō seisakuto nanboku bundantaisei no keiseikatei*, (Shinzansha, 1997), pp. 111–119.

[‡] In this petition there were 13 items of requests by Goverment-General. The 12th item was about Shrine. Yamana Sakio, "Shūsen zengo ni okeru chōsen jijōu gaiyou" in Morita Yoshio ed., *Chōsen shūsen no kiroku; shiryō-hen dai 1 kan* (Gennando, 1980), p. 18 (hereafter, *1 kan*).

[§] Morita, *Kiroku*, p. 405.

[¶] *FRUS, 1945, VI*, p. 1043. Proclamation No. 1 was drafted by GHQ and handed to USAFIK just before the occupation around September 5–7. HUSAFIK, Part I, Ch. IV, p. 20.

[**] See page 5 of this paper.

General MacArthur's order guaranteed freedom of religion. Japanese government shall not disassemble shrines. Such action could be permitted only if Shinto believers themselves truly wished so.[*]

MacArthur's order, Proclamation No. 1, only mentioned the protection of religious rights of the Korean people: "the Koreans are assured the purpose of the occupation is ... to protect them in personal and religious rights." However, here, General Arnold declared USAFIK would also respect the same rights of the Japanese people and protect Japanese shrines by nullifying the Government-General's order to abolish the shrines.

In addition to McArthur's order, the International law at that time also requested USAFIK to protect freedom of religion. The Laws and Customs of War on Land, agreed at the Hague Convention in 1907, stipulated that "family honour and rights, the lives of persons, and private property, as well as religious convictions and practice, must be respected."[†] The U.S. Army and Navy were well aware of this statute and directed it to be upheld by incorporating it in their occupational manual.[‡] In short, guaranteeing Shinto believers' faith and protecting shrine properties were also legal obligations for the military occupiers.

COUNTER-ARGUMENT BY GOVERNMENT-GENERAL; "SHINTO AS NON-RELIGION"

However, USAFIK's determination to preserve Shinto as a religion was immediately challenged by the Japanese side. The Government-General and Shinto priests, who believed that leaving shrines would endanger the dignity of the Japanese Emperor and deities enshrined from any Korean attacks, tried to persuade USAFIK to alter the decision. Interestingly, it turned out that the guardian of shrines in South Korea was the U.S. force, not the Japanese government.

The Government-General tried to persuade the USAFIK by claiming that Shinto was not a religion. They argued that "Shinto shrines not regarded as religious beings in Japan ... Shinto priests are public officers employed by government," and "A shrine is nothing more than a place where national events and ceremonies are held."[§] Therefore, they emphasized that "shrines must be treated differently from other religious buildings and temples,"[¶] and its abolishment has nothing to do with freedom of religion.

It is true that the Japanese government at that time did not define Shinto as a religion—this official view is often referred to as "Shrine as non-religion theory."[**] The Japanese government categorized Shinto shrines as non-religious institutions and guaranteed privileged rights that were not given to other religions. Instead, Shinto was strictly controlled by the government. Their duties were regulated by law, their wages were paid by government, and their prayers also had to follow an official guideline authorized by the government.[††]

The "Shrine as non-religion" theory had been invented by the Japanese government to force Shinto ideology and rituals to the followers of other religions. The Japanese government intentionally ignored the religious aspects of Shinto and required the nation to accept Shinto rituals as national rites. However, in the eyes of those of different faith, Christians in particular, Shinto was apparently a religion to worship Japanese

---

[*] Morita, *Kiroku*, p. 405

[†] Article 46, Chap. III, "About military authority over the hostile state," Laws and Customs of War on Land (Hague IV); October 18, 1907.

[‡] *Army-Navy Manual of Military Government and Civil Affairs* (War Department Field Manual 27-5, Dec. 1943), Part I, paragraph m. "Respect for religious customs and organizations," paragraph r; "Preservation of shrines and art."

[§] Morita, *Kiroku*, p. 404.

[¶] Morita, *Kiroku*, p. 404.

[**] Haruta Tetsuyoshi, *Nihon no kaigai shokuminchi no shūen* (Hara shobō, 1999), pp. 21–22

[††] For the legal regulations on Shinto shrine in Korea, see chapter II, *Chōsen hōrei shūran*.

deities. Likewise, for the ardent Shinto believers also, a shrine is not a mere place of national rites but a place of religious worship. This is the reason why those faithful Shinto believers in Keijō petitioned to USAFIK to maintain their shrine in the post-war Korea. Given the two contradictory views over how to define or view Shinto, USAFIK had to face a dilemma whether to let the Japanese government disassemble the shrines based on "Shinto as non-religion" theory, or preserving them in consideration of its religious nature.

CHANGE IN USAFIK'S POLICY

The available sources little talks about what was discussed by the USAFIK officers over this Shinto shrine problem. What is clear is that USAFIK finally decided to regard State Shinto as non-religion,[*] and retracted its earlier decision to preserve shrines for the sake of freedom of religion. Accordingly, USAFIK gave permission to the Government-General for disassembling shrines.[†]

At first glance, this change in USAFIK's Shinto policy seem to have benefited the Government-General. The Japanese officials probably thought in the same way. However, they were proven wrong later, when USAFIK began to take very suppressive policies on Shinto.

On September 21, 1945, USAFIK issued "General Order 5" and repealed the Japanese colonial laws that discriminated the Koreans.[‡] By this order, the Act of Shrine (jinja-hō: 神社法) along with other oppressive laws such as the Act of Preserving Order (chianiji-hō: 治安維持法) and the Act of Preliminary Imprisonment (yobikensoku-hō: 予備検束法) were also annulled.[§]

---

[*] "Activities of the Section on Religions in the Bureau of Education since Military Government," 17 December, 1945, USAFIK, Bureau of Education, GHQ/Records, CIE(D)04749-04750. In paragraph III of this document, it says "National or Shrine Shinto-not considered religion."

[†] Morita, Kiroku, p. 405, Yamana in Morita, 1 kan, p. 18.

[‡] Moirta, Kiroku, p. 405

[§] General Order 5 was later amended by Ordinance 11. see Official Gazette, United States Army Military Government in Korea, Headquarters, United States Army Military Government in Korea in Migunjŏng kwanbo vol. 1 (Wŏnjumunhwasa, 1992), pp. 116–118.

The abolishment of the latter two laws was to liberate religious groups from the Japanese suppression and to revive freedom of religion. On the other hand, the repeal of the Act of Shrine aimed at stripping the legal rights of State Shinto and made it virtually impossible for the shrines to survive. In the next step, USAFIK ordered the shrines, now deprived of any legal status, to transfer their financial assets to the occupational administration. The Grand Shrine of Chosen handed over its liquid assets, namely cash and stocks, to the Local Affairs Section of USAFIK on September 22, and the real estate on October 23.[¶] Likewise, the confiscation of shrine properties was implemented in local provinces, too.[**] It was only after the confiscation that the Government-General was allowed to disassemble the shrine buildings.[††]

REASONS BEHIND THE POLICY CHANGE

What caused USAFIK to change its Shinto policy drastically, from preservation to abolishment? The key to answering this question lies in the two contradicting objectives that USAFIK had formulated before the occupation—establishing freedom of religion and prohibiting Japanese militarism represented by State Shinto. As diagram 3A shows, there was a trade-off between these two objectives. Protecting Shinto shrine as a religion helps to establish the freedom of religion but

---

[¶] Takeshima, "Shūsengo no chōsen jingū" in Morita, 2 kan, pp. 164–67. For the functions of Local Affairs Division, see The Military Governor, United States Army Military Government in Korea, History of United States Army Military Government in Korea, Period of September 1945–30 June 1946, prepared by the Statistical Research Division of the Office of Administration, Headquarters United States Army Military Government in Korea, Part II, pp. 49–52.

[**] Morita, Kiroku, p. 405.

[††] On Nov. 2, 1945, USAFIK issued a directive saying "The main shrine of Shinto shrines may be burned. Books and property are to be controlled by the Government. Officials are to be present at burning, and a report is to be made to some Occupation commander within ten miles." Kerr, p. 73.

fails to eradicate shrines that disseminates the Japanese militaristic ideology. On the other hand, prohibiting shrines would successfully abolish militarism but this would clearly violate the freedom of religion or religious rights of Shinto believers. In other words, USAFIK had

A: Dilemma over disposal of Shinto shrine

	Shrine = Religion	
	Freedom of Religion	Prohibition of Militarism
Continuation of Shrines	O	X
Abolishment of Shrines	X	O

B: Resolution for the dilemma

Shrine = Non-Religion	
Freedom of Religion	Prohibition of Militarism
O	X
X→O	O

no choice but to either protect shrines overlooking its dangerous militaristic potentials or to abolish them violating freedom of religion.

As above, USAFIK first decided to protect shrines as a religion. However, after they were informed of the "Shrine as non-religion" theory by the Japanese government, they realized that shrines could be abolished without violating of the freedom of religion (See Diagram 3B). Thus, they decided to use the theory as a strategic tool in order to achieve the abolishment of militarism and protection of freedom of religion simultaneously.

It is important to note here that it was not USAFIK who first came up with this idea of using "Shinto as non-religion" theory as a mean to abolish shrines. About a year earlier, in March 1944, the inter-territorial committee of Department of State drafted a policy on Shinto in the following terms.

> These (militaristic shrines) could be closed without any violation of the principle of freedom of religious worship, as the Japanese Government has repeatedly asserted that National Shinto is not a religion but rather a manifestation of patriotism.[*]

---

[*] "Japan: Freedom of Religious Worship," Memorandum prepared by the Inter-Divisional Area Committee on the Far East,

This evidence clearly shows us that the policy-makers in Washington had been fully aware that "Shinto as non-religion theory" would play a critical role when they abolish shrines by force. Though it is unknown precisely whether policy-makers of USAFIK had referred to this document or received such instruction directly from the Department of State, another evidence proves that USAFIK had come to view State Shinto as non-religion by December 17 at latest.[†]

PROTECTION OF OTHER RELIGIONS

While prohibiting State Shinto, USAFIK protected other religions. For example, USAFIK carefully distinguished State or National Shinto from Religious or Sectarian Shinto (*Kyōha-Shinto*: 教派神道) such as Tenrikyō—categorized as religion under the Japanese administration—and preserved them as religion.[‡] Tenrikyō's church buildings and Japanese Buddhist

---

Mar. 15, 1944, cited in Jinja Shinpōsha, *Kindai jinja Shinto shi*, (Jinjashinpōsha, 1976), pp. 186–89.

[†] Activities of the Section on Religions in the Bureau of Education since Military Government," 17 December, 1945, USAFIK. In paragraph III of this document, it said "National or Shrine Shinto—not considered religion."

[‡] Paragraph III, "Activities of the Section on Religions in the Bureau of Education since Military Government," 17 December, 1945.

temples were not confiscated by USAFIK but transferred into the hands of the Korean followers after the decision by the Japanese.* In short, any "religion" was protected even if it had a Japanese origin.

In the same way, USAFIK distinguished Shinto priests from other religious leaders. On November 11, 1945, USAFIK ordered the "undesirables" to be deported from Korea immediately.† While Shinto priests were included in the "undesirables," Religious Shinto missionaries, Buddhist monks and Christian pastors were excluded from that category.‡ Though USAFIK probably knew that Religious Shinto and Japanese Buddhism were more or less engaged in disseminating militarism during the war, but yet USAFIK did not interfere with these religions and carefully avoided violating the principle of freedom of religion. These Japanese religionists were later repatriated by the USAFIK in early 1946, when it ordered all the Japanese to leave South Korea.§

COMPARISON WITH GHQ'S SHINTO POLICY

Even after USAFIK changed its policy on Shinto Shrines to abolish them, GHQ/SCAP continued to keep the status quo of shrines in Japan. This was because GHQ had not received any clear instructions from Washington about how to deal with shrines. The only direction GHQ received from Washington before the occupation began in Japan was:

> Freedom of religious worship shall be proclaimed promptly on occupation. At the same time it should be plain to the Japanese that ultra-nationalistic and militaristic

organizations and movements will not be permitted to hide behind the cloak of religion.¶

Though the strong concern towards religion and its affiliation with militarism hinted something should be done on Shinto, there was no direct reference to "State Shinto" and "shrines." Therefore, GHQ had to wait additional direction from Washington, while maintaining the status quo on shrines.

In addition, shrines in Japan did not become victims of attacks or were they not disassembled as were the cases in Korea. Both the Japanese Government and the leaders of State Shinto followers also agreed to act in unison for the continuation of shrines under the occupation.** Therefore, when the occupation in Japan began, GHQ was not faced with any pressing decisions on Shinto and thus was able to keep status quo on them without any difficulties.

THE VINCENT STATEMENT

On October 8, 1945, the U.S. government first announced its policies on Shintoisim in public. John Carter Vincent, Chief of the Department State's Division of Far Eastern Affairs, said in a television program aired in the United States that Shinto in Japan would be respected on condition that it is a religion.

> Shinto, in so far as it is a religion of individual Japanese, is not to be interfered with … Shinto as a state religion—National Shinto, that is—will go.††

Before this statement, both the Japanese government and Shinto leaders had never imagined that shrines could be protected in the name of freedom of religion. According to a governmental plan as of October 9, 1945, the Japanese government was going to explain to

---

*   Some of those buildings were used for collecting stations for the Japanese refuges from north part of Korea or Manchuria. Morita, p. 324, 408.

†   William J. Gane, *Beigunseichō jisshi no nihonjin sōkan* in Morita *2 kan*, pp. 24–25, HUSAFIK, Part I, Ch. VIII, pp. 8–9.

‡   Mitsutomi Yahachi, Gunzan nihonjin no hikiage, in Moirta *2 kan*, pp. 274–275.

§   Morita, *Kiroku*, p. 382.

¶   "United States Initial Post-Surrender Policy for Japan," August 29, 1945, in *PR*, Appendix A:11, pp. 423–26.

**   Woodard, p. 57.

††   Woodard, pp. 54–55.

GHQ that "rituals at shrines were originally aimed at praying for peace" and "it was an exception … that such rituals expressed militaristic aggression at the time of war"* lest GHQ should abolish them by coercion. The government was still sticking with the idea that Shinto was non-religion.

However, after the Vincent Statement, the Japanese government reversed the official interpretation on Shinto completely. In the revised plan dated November 16, it was sated that "we (the government) should seek for the continuation and further enhancement of Shinto by making it the official theory that Shrine Shinto is genuinely a religion."[†]

Given Shinto was regarded as a religion, it was impossible for GHQ to abolish shrines by using "Shinto as non-religiontheory," as it was the case in Korea. However, if not abolishing shrines, how was GHQ able to suppress militarism sufficiently? Put in another way, what was the GHQ's measure to exterminate militarism while protecting Shinto as a religion?

DIRECTION FROM JOINT CHIEFS OF STAFF AND SHINTO DIRECTIVE

A clue to solve the Shinto problem was given by a Joint Chiefs of Staff (JCS) instruction to GHQ on November 3, 1945. This was the first official direction to GHQ from Washington that directly mentioned on the policies on Shinto.

> The dissemination of Japanese militaristic and ultra-nationalistic ideology and propaganda in any form will be prohibited and completely suppressed. You (SCAP) will require the Japanese Government to cease financial and other support of National Shinto establishments.[‡]

What this direction suggested was that separation of Shinto shrines from the state—banning any official and financial support to Shinto by the government—would help prevent shrines from being used as a governmental tool for disseminating Japanese militarism.

Nevertheless, the members of Religions Division of Civil Information and Education (CIE) Section of GHQ—among them especially the Chief of Religions Division, William K. Bunce—believed that the JCS order was not able to achieve both eradicate militarism out of Shinto and protecting freedom of religion sufficiently. Firstly, he felt that as long as Shinto's doctrine and dogmas were embedded with militarism, Shinto would be of potential danger even after the separation from state. Secondly, if the governmental support was forbidden only for Shinto, it could cause criticism from the Shinto followers that such acts were unequal treatment and violate the religious rights of Shinto.[§]

Therefore, when Bunce drafted "Shinto Directive"[¶]—the first comprehensive order to the Japanese government on reforming State Shinto—he obligated the exclusion of all militaristic elements as a condition to its continuity as a religion.

> Shrine (State) Shinto after having been divorced from the state and divested of its militaristic and ultra-nationalistic elements, will be recognized as a religion.[**]

At the same time, he obliged all other religions to do the same in order to maintain equality among religions.

> … the purpose of the Directive is to separate religion from state … and put all religions … upon exactly the same basis,

---

* Jinja shinpōsha, ed., *Shinto shirei to sengo no jinja Shinto*, (Jinjashimpōsha, 1971), p. 18.

† Ibid., p. 27

‡ Paragraph I, 9-a) of "Basic Directive for Post-Surrender Military Government in Japan proper," JCS Directive, 1380/15, November 3, 1945, see PR, Appendix A:13, pp. 428–439.

§ For the discussion over the JCS directive within CIE, see Woodard, pp. 62–69.

¶ The official title of this direction is "Abolition of Governmental Sponsorship, Support, Perpetuation, Control and Dissemination of State Shinto," SCAPIN 448, December 15, 1945, see PR, Appendix B:3a.

** Paragraph 2-e(2), "Shinto Directive."

entitled to precisely the same opportunities and protection.[*]

What GHQ aimed for through the Shinto Directive was the separation of all religions from the state and to eliminate any militaristic ideas not only from Shinto, but also from all religions. GHQ believed that this was the only way to accomplish the complete abolishment of militarism without violating any religious rights or discrimination.

This GHQ's policy on Shinto was totally different from that of USAFIK in South Korea, and the sharp contrast between the two policies is presented in the diagram 4.

The disposal of State Shinto in the post-war Japan and Korea appeared to be a complicated issue. Since it was the two faces as a popular religion and a breeding bed of militarism, U.S. occupational forces had to face a dilemma whether to preserve is as a religion or abolish it as non-religion. And it was the differing strategies of USAFIK and GHQ to resolve this dilemma that resulted in the two different policies on Shinto in South Korea and Japan.[†]

However, it is worth noting that the contrasting policies brought about a great confusion and conflicts between USAFIK and GHQ officers. In early 1946, the CIE of GHQ sent its staff, William C. Kerr, to

Diagram 4: Different Strategy to achieve the two occupation objectives

	Freedom of Religion	Abolishment of Militarism
USAFIK; Abolishment of Shrines upon "Shinto non-religion" theory	X→O	O
GHQ; Continuation of shrines upon strict separation of religions from state	O	X→O

USAFIK implemented policies to suppress militarism by abolishing shrines. For this reason, it was necessary for USAFIK to categorize Shinto as non-religion so that it would not violate the principle of freedom of religion. GHQ, in contrast, defined Shinto as a religion due to the directive from Washington and thus had to respect its religious right, while eliminating militarism. This became possible by the Shinto Directive which set the very strict separation of all religions, including Shinto, from state. It was the only and necessary measure to achieve the elimination of militarism and the protection of freedom of religion simultaneously.

USAFIK to investigate the religious situation in South Korea.[†] During his visit, Kerr explained GHQ's policies on Shinto in Japan but was surprised to receive strong objections from the officers of USAFIK. Kerr wrote in a report to his chief W. K Bunce that

> … the proposal to unite the various shrines of the former State Shinto in to a new religious sect has brought surprise to a number of Koreans and Americans … They one and all look on the proposal with disfavor, feeling that it contains a number of dangerous possibilities.[‡]

[†] For the communications between Kerr and Bunce, see the letters filed in *GHQ/SCAP records*, CIE(D)04749-50.

[‡] "W.C.Kerr to W.K.Bunce, 30 Jan. 46," GHQ/Records, CIE(D)04749.

[*] Paragraph 2-a, Ibid. 21

Since USAFIK had already abolished shrines in South Korea before Kerr's visit, it was a shock to them to know shrines in Japan were preserved as religion. USAFIK was concerned that the continuation of Shinto shrines could lead to the reactivation of militarism in future.

This concern expressed by USAFIK clearly points out the contradiction in the Shinto policies taken in the two countries. Thus, Bunce, probably realizing this contradiction, was unable to give a logical answer on this point. In his reply to Kerr, he could only state an optimistic prospect that shrines would never gain power.

> I can understand the perturbation of your Korean friends and Americans relative to the establishments of a Shrine Association* in Japan. Actually this is not the establishment of a new sect, although Shrine Shinto has the legal status of Sectarian Shinto. The diversity of practice in Shrine Shinto is so great that there is little likelihood that any great uniformity can be established.

It is unknown how USAFIK reacted to Kerr's explanation but there is no further evidence to show that any significant action was taken to coordinate the two contradicting policies. Henceforth, the differing Shinto policies continued to exist until the end of occupation. As a result, all shrines in South Korea were abolished during the occupation while those in Japan survived.

Lastly, the final point to note here is that the two differing Shinto policies consequently led to the establishment of two different church-state relations in the post-war Japan and Korea. In Japan, a strict separation of religion and the state was introduced to prevent the revival of Shinto. On the other hand, USAFIK was less motivated to establish such rigid church-state relations in South Korea, because Shinto and shrines were completely abolished there, and there was little danger that Japanese militarism would regain the predominant power. In fact, USAFIK did not issue any legal measure to restrict church-state relations, something equivalent to the Shinto Directive of GHQ.

Consequently, the two different church-state relations produced a number of different customs in terms of religious administration. For example, while employing a prison chaplain started during the occupation, and the army chaplain under Syngman Rhee government in South Korea, while public chaplain was prohibited by the Shinto Directive and the New Constitution in Japan. It was common for Syngman Rhee and other religious leaders to make Christian-style prayers in public events, but again in Japan, such action was never observed. Moreover, religious holidays such as Christmas, Buddha's birthday and mythical Emperor's birthday were excluded from national holidays in Japan, whereas they all became national holidays in Korea during Rhee's regime. Yet, it is far beyond the reach of this paper to investigate how these differences in church-state relations affected the post-war religious-political development of the two countries.

---

* Shintoist leaders and adherents established this association as a religious group on voluntary basis after Shinto Directive. Jinjashimpōsha, Shinto shirei, pp. 58–65

Diagram 1: The number of Shrine in Korea (June, 1945)

Province	Grand National Shines	National Shrines	Other Public Shrines	Minor Shrines	Total
Kyŏnggi-do	1	1	5	155	162
Ch'ungch'ŏng-pukdo	-	-	3	71	74
Ch'ungch'ŏng-namdo	1	-	8	30	39
Chŏlla-pukdo	-	1	10	23	34
Chŏlla-namdo	-	1	9	245	255
Kyŏngsang-pukdo	-	1	5	62	68
Kyŏngsang-namdo	-	1	5	41	47
Hwanghoe-do	-	-	3	182	185
P'yŏngang-pukdo	-	1	1	32	34
P'yŏngang-namdo	-	-	5	134	139
Kangwon-do	-	1	3	42	46
Hamgyŏng-pukdo	-	1	5	20	26
Hamgyŏng-namdo	-	-	7	25	32
Total	2	8	69	1062	1141

(Morita, *Kiroku*, p.108, partly arranged by the author)

Diagram 2 : Violence in Korea during Aug.16-25, 1945

Events	16th	17th	18th	19th	20th	21st	22nd	23rd	24th	25th	Total
Attack to police stations	12	38	39	17	34	4	3	2	0	0	149
Looting of firearms, ammunition	1	12	12	12	3	1	0	0	0	0	41
Violence to Japanese policemen	3	19	16	13	9	0	6	0	0	0	66
Violence to Korean policemen	4	21	26	32	24	2	1	1	0	0	111
Attack to public offices	4	26	23	12	10	6	4	1	0	0	86
Violence to Korean civil officers	3	28	44	7	12	13	2	0	0	0	109
Attack to shrines	21	25	27	14	45	3	1	0	0	0	136
Violence to Japanese residence	11	8	21	10	11	7	12	0	0	0	80
Violence to Korean residence	0	0	50	2	1	4	2	1	0	0	60
Others	5	12	20	16	16	2	2	2	0	0	75
	64	189	278	135	165	42	33	7	0	0	913

(Yamana Sakio, "Shūsen zengo ni okeru chōsen jijō gaiyō" in Morita, *2 kan,*(Gennando, 1980), pp.13-14, partly edited by the author)

REFERENCES

PRIMARY SOURCES

English:

Army-Navy Manual of Military Government and Civil Affairs, (War Department Field Manual 27-5, Dec. 1943).

The Military Governor, United States Army Military Government in Korea, *History of United States Army Military Government in Korea, Part I-III, Period of September 1945–30 June 1946*, prepared by the Statistical Research Division of the Office of Administration, Headquarters United States Army Military Government in Korea.

GHQ/SCAP Records: Top Secret Records, compiled by National Diet Library in Japan.

Official Gazette, United States Army Military Government in Korea, Headquarters, United States Army Military Government in Korea.

Political reorientation of Japan, September 1945 to September 1948: report of Government Section, Supreme Commander for the Allied Powers. Washington, D.C.: U.S. Govt. Print. Off., 1949.

United States Armed Forces in Korea, *History of the United States Armed Forces in Korea*, Compiled under the supervision of Harold Larsen, chief historian. Tokyo and Seoul, 1947, 1948. Manuscript in the Office of the Chief of Military History, Washington, D.C.

U.S. Department of State, *Foreign Relations of the United States: Diplomatic Papers*, Washington, D.C., U.S. Government Printing Office, (FRUS), 1945, Vol. VI.

Japanese:

Chōsen Sōtokufu, ed., *Chōsen Hōrei Shūran*, (Kukhak saryŏwŏn, Seoul: 1996).

Morita Yoshio, *Chōsen shūsen n-o kiroku*, (Gennando, 1964).

Morita Yoshio, *Chōsen Shūsen no kioku; shiryō-hen dai 2 kan* (Gennando, 1980).

Shinto Daijiten, (Kōbundō, 1994).

SECONDARY SOURCES

English:

Bruce Cumings, *Origins of Korean War 1945–47*, (Princeton University Press, 1981).

William P. Woodard, *The Allied Occupation of Japan 1945–1952 and Japanese Religions*, (Leiden: E.J. Brill, 1972).

Japanese:

Han Sokki, *Nihon no chōsen shihai to shūkyō seisaku*, (Miraisha, 1988).

Haruta Tetsuyoshi, *Nihon no kaigai shokuminchi no shuen*, (Hara shobō, 1999).

Jinja Shinpōsha, *Kindai jinja Shinto shi*, (Jinjashinposha, 1976) 28.

Jinja shinpōsha, *Shinto shirei to sengo no jinja Shinto*, (Jinja shimposha, 1971).

Yamaguchi Kōichi, "Senjiki chōsen soutokufu no jinja seisaku" in *Chōsenshi kenkyūkai ronbunshū, No. 36*, (Ryokuin Shobo, Oct. 1998).

Yi Kyu T'ae, *Beiso no chōsen senryō seisakuto nanboku bundantaisei no keiseikatei*, (Shinzansha, 1997).

"PAK CHŎNGHŬI AND ECONOMIC DEVELOPMENT IN SOUTH KOREA" AND "KIM CHIHA AND PROTEST AGAINST AUTHORITARIAN RULE"

Edited by Yongho Ch'oe, Peter H. Lee, and William Theodore De Bary

PAK CHŎNGHŬI AND ECONOMIC DEVELOPMENT IN SOUTH KOREA

In May 1961 a group of military officers led by General Pak Chŏnghŭi (Park Chung Hee, 1917–1979) seized power in South Korea through a near-bloodless coup d'état. The military junta that was set up accused the previous government of the Democratic Party, headed by Prime Minister Chang Myŏn, of corruption and ineptitude, leading the country to the brink of collapse and danger, of subversion by Communist North Korea. The junta insisted that the country needed a strong leadership to undergo "revolutionary changes." Having himself been impoverished in his youth, Pak Chŏnghŭi was determined to eradicate poverty in South Korea and build a new economy that could withstand the threat from North Korea. In the name of "revolution," Pak and his government put foremost emphasis on economic development, which was to be accomplished through a series of five-year plans, mobilizing all available resources to achieve the goal of economic growth.

To Pak's credit, it can be said that he had remarkable success in achieving rapid economic growth. At the same time, Pak left behind him a legacy of bitter resentment against authoritarian rule, political repression, and excessive concentration of economic power in the hands of an industrial/financial oligarchy (the

chaebŏl). The arguments pro and con are typical of the issues in the debate on "guided democracy" in Asia or the so-called Asian model of development, claiming that only strong authoritarian rule can provide the political stability needed for economic growth. In the case of Pak, however, as in that of Chiang Kai-shek in Taiwan, it must be noted that Pak and Chiang at least professed to aim at—and left the way open for—the gradual development of liberal democracy which did indeed occur later. This contrasts with the Communist regimes in North Korea and China that have insisted on a one-party dictatorship and ruled out any "peaceful evolution" to a multiparty democracy.

The statement excerpted below, written in 1971, offers a retrospective picture of the thinking behind Pak's first five-year plan, which started in 1962.

PAK CHŎNGHŬI: TO BUILD A NATION

[From Chung-Hee Park, *To Build a Nation*, pp. 101–114]

The successful revolutionaries of 16 May 1961 faced complex political, economic, and cultural problems in their country. All of them required immediate attention. But emphasis had to be placed on their plan to construct a self-reliant economy by revolutionizing industry. Korea was well aware that this was the key to attaining the revolutionary goal: national reform and reconstruction.

Both the April 19 student revolution [in 1960] and the May 16 military revolution [in 1961] grew out of the chronic poverty of the nation. They were passionate expressions of the people's desire to live better. If poverty had been allowed to weaken them, as had happened before, they would have faced national collapse. Food comes before politics. Only with a full stomach can one enjoy the arts and talk about social development.

Before May 16 the Korean economy was in disorder. Accumulated political blunders and misguided economic policy had utterly disarranged it. The postwar rehabilitation of the nation was at a near-standstill, while the amount of grant-type foreign aid was lessening. Economic stagnation aggravated poverty and unemployment. Farmers' debts rose sharply. … With growth at a standstill at the turn of the 1960s, Korea found itself one of the lowest income countries in the world. The industrial structure was not solid. Due to a huge gravitation toward them of a huge amount of foreign aid, the secondary and tertiary industries seemed excessively swollen in comparison with primary industry. …

U.S. grant-type aid had totaled $2,700 million since liberation. Yet the Liberal Party and Democratic Party regimes [under Syngman Rhee and Chang Myŏn, respectively] failed to develop such basic industries as electricity, coal fertilizer, and cement, and such social overhead capital as roads. They failed also to develop an economic infrastructure involving such sectors as transportation and communications. Private industry could not solve such pressing problems as insufficient facilities, lack of raw materials, and financial difficulties because of inadequate government assistance.

As a result, industrial production slowed and the supply of commodities fell far short of the demand. The deficit budget and the misdirected monetary policy increased the amount of money in circulation, stimulating a sharp rise in prices. The economy was faced with collapse.

The institutional and moral aspects of the society were no better. People fatalistically took poverty and reliance on foreign aid as unavoidable facts of life. Businessmen and industrialists failed to fulfill their important role in economic development. Many corrupt government officials and parvenus worked together to amass illegal fortunes. The market, suffering from its small scale and lack of vigorous competition, did not function normally. The underdeveloped agricultural system was unable to meet the demand for food—we were forced to rely on the farm products of advanced countries. The whole economy was afflicted by inexperience, inefficiency, and wasteful management.

When I took over power as the leader of the revolutionary group on 16 May 1961, I felt, honestly speaking, as if I had been given a pilfered household or a bankrupt firm to manage. Around me I could find little hope or encouragement. The outlook was bleak.

But I had to rise above this pessimism to rehabilitate the household. I had to break, once and for all, the vicious circle of poverty and economic stagnation. Only by curing the abnormal economic structure could we lay the foundation for decent living standards. But I soon came to realize the difficulty of simultaneously achieving our goals of social stability and economic development and the goal of efficient government. I was also aware of the fact that economic development in the capitalist manner requires not only an immense investment of money and materials but also a stable political situation and competent administrators.

To achieve this stability, the military revolutionary government temporarily suspended political activities of students, the press, labor unions, and other social and political organizations, which had caused political crises and social unrest during the rule of the Democratic Party regime. We also made it clear that civilian government would be restored in 1963.

Meanwhile, we organized a planning committee of college professors and experts with specialized knowledge in many fields. By mobilizing the maximum available expertise for government administration and policy making, we intended to hold in check the arbitrariness and rashness of the military officers. The establishment of this committee served as a turning point. Korean professors began to show positive interest in the realities of the country and to present policy recommendations on the basis of scientific analyses of the country's situation. Even though not all of these recommendations could be justified in terms of efficiency and rationality, their advice was of great help to the revolutionary government. Thus the Confucian tradition of Yi Korea, in which scholars played a positive part in government affairs, seems to have been revived.

The key to improving a backward economy is the way one uses human resources, for economic development is a human undertaking, impossible without combining the people's potential into a dynamic driving force. This task requires not only strong national willpower but also the ability to translate willpower into achievement. Blueprints must be drawn and explained. If people have a sympathetic understanding of a task, they will voluntarily participate in it.

In 1961 the revolutionary government announced the first Five-Year Economic Development Plan (to start in 1962), the first such overall development program ever prepared for Korea. To prepare it, the revolutionary government mobilized all the wisdom and knowledge available and set clear goals, the primary goal being to establish a self-supporting industrial economy. The principle of free enterprise and respect for the creativity of private industry was adopted, for in this way we believed that the private sector would be encouraged to act voluntarily. Under the plan, however, the economy was not entirely free, since development of basic industries was directed by the government.

Taking into consideration the structural characteristics of the Korean economy, the five-year plan gave priority to the following things:

1. Development of energy industries such as coal production and electric power;
2. Expansion of agricultural production aimed at increasing farm income and correcting the structural imbalance of the national economy;
3. Development of basic industries and the economic infrastructure;
4. Maximum utilization of idle resources; increased employment; conservation and utilization of land;
5. Improvement of the balance of payments through export promotion;
6. Promotion of science and technology.

In raising funds for these projects, we tried to draw on domestic resources as much as possible. Self-reliant financing was encouraged.

The five-year plan aimed at an annual economic growth of 7.1 percent and a 40.7 percent increase of GNP during the plan period. It would raise the GNP to $2.5 billion and per capita income to $112 by the target year of 1966, in comparison to $94 in 1960. Exports were to rise to $138 million in 1966, a 420 percent increase over the base year of 1960, improving the international balance of payments. The weight of secondary industry in the industrial structure would increase from 194 percent in 1962 to 26.1 percent in 1966.

The plan's goal of a 7.1 percent annual growth rate was then considered almost impossible—unprecedented not only in Korea but also in other developing countries. Some people criticized the plan as too ambitious, but in view of what we needed for future economic development, it was the minimum objective. …

Success in the first five-year plan could not immediately bring about a self-reliant economy. It would be only a landmark the people had to pass on their long, painful journey toward this goal. Indeed, a self-sufficient economy and a welfare society may not be satisfactorily attained during one five-year plan or even two or more. But what can be begun today must not be put off until tomorrow. This common but everlasting principle was the foundation of our determination. The economy sustained a rapid rate of growth, and the industrial structure improved.

We are living today in an era of change and competition. Looking back to the achievements of the past decade, we find that the courage with which we met the challenge of modernizing our country has become our primary motivating force. We met with many difficulties, however, in formulating our policies. Long-range policies in themselves were often thought radical by businessmen. Moreover, both the administration and the ruling party lacked knowledge and experience in preparing long-term economic policy, and so we failed to present a clear vision of our policies. Without this vision it is hard to instill confidence. Some policies were hard to execute. For instance, a set of drastic measures taken during the 1960s to raise interest rates, to improve taxation, to liberalize trade, to encourage the introduction of foreign capital, and to place the dollar-won exchange rate under a unitary floating system drew much criticism. Still these policies eventually contributed much to the rapid development of the economy.

Of course, the government has sometimes made mistakes, though these did not have any major effect on the plan as a whole. Because the government's efforts were designed to bring about policy reform, such enterprises as required adaptation to the new pattern of economic activities endured more than a little inconvenience.

One of our big problems was the shaky foundations of private industry, which was unable to carry its share of the development burden. Furthermore, the market structure was not modernized. Consequently, the government had to play the leading role in the development plan, though we knew well that such a plan must, in the long run, rely on the creativity and initiative of private industry.

In the meantime, the government tried to readjust existing systems to help accumulate private capital, with a view to laying the groundwork for an efficient market competition system. We hoped to encourage businessmen who could play leading roles in planning. On the other hand, rigid restrictions were put on such business activities as ran against these efforts.

The raising of interest rates on both deposits and loans brought a sevenfold increase in bank savings during the ensuing five-year period. Improved taxation enabled the government to formulate a balanced budget. The unitary floating exchange-rate system and trade liberalization sharply increased exports. These all contributed to an increased inflow of foreign capital, to financial stabilization, and to the strengthening of the nation's international trading power. We now realize how important these decisions of the past decade were to rapid economic development. Although hard at the time, they were based on objective reality.

To consolidate our past gains, we are now confidently moving forward under the second five-year plan. With this second plan, the economy has greatly expanded its infrastructure and has seen a great development of heavy and chemical industry. The economy is continuing to grow rapidly at this moment.

KIM CHIHA AND PROTEST AGAINST AUTHORITARIAN RULE

Various programs to revitalize the Korean economy initiated by President Pak Chŏnghŭi were spectacularly successful, transforming the country from a backward agrarian community into a high-tech industrial society.

The transformation of the Korean economy came about initially through export of products produced in Korea taking advantage of abundant cheap labor. Under the protection and encouragement of the government, a number of enterprises grew to become giant business conglomerates known as *chaebŏl*. In their attempts to amass fortunes, many resorted to shady deals and corrupt practices. One sure way to business success, for example, was to secure patronage from the government, which was often achieved by bribery and other illicit means. The government actively intervened to keep wages low in order to gain competitive advantage in international markets. When voices of criticism were raised, they were suppressed by various government agencies. The press was placed under strict censorship throughout President Pak's rule, and the dissidents—often college students—who criticized the government were arrested and frequently subjected to severe torture.

One of the most courageous and outspoken critics of the Pak regime was Kim Chiha (b. 1941), who tormented Pak's authoritarian government with his fiery verses. Born in the southwestern province of Chŏlla (whose people were often discriminated against under the Pak presidency), Kim Chiha was arrested several times for his participation in antigovernment activities while a student at the prestigious Seoul National University.

The interruption of his college education allowed him to reflect on the form of his poetry, leading him to rediscover *p'ansori*, traditional Korean verses whose oral narrative often lampooned social ills and hypocrisy. Written in an experimental *p'ansori* form, "Five Bandits" (Ojŏk) was first published in *Sasanggye* (World of thought), an intellectual monthly magazine, in May 1970.

In biting satire, the poem condemned the five core power groups of the Pak regime—business tycoons, members of the National Assembly (legislature), senior government officials, generals, and cabinet ministers—as "five bandits" who had brazenly acquired wealth by illicit means. For the publication of this poem, Kim Chiha was arrested on the charge of "abetting the propaganda lines" of North Korea. He was sentenced to prison, and the *Sasanggye* monthly was ordered to close.

Undaunted by physical torture and other punishments, Kim Chiha continued to publish verse in the *p'ansori* style, castigating the abuse of power and violation of human rights by the government. In 1974, he was charged with violating the infamous National Security Act and instigating internal rebellion and was sentenced to death.

To mollify the worldwide protest movement organized by the International Committee to Support Kim Chiha, which included Willy Brandt, Jean-Paul Sartre, and Ōe Kenzaburō, among others, the government commuted his sentence to life imprisonment. In 1979 he was released, following the death of Pak Chŏnghŭi.

Although much of the rhythm, rhyme, and melodic quality as well as humor that are unique to its Korean original is lost in the process of translation, the English version of "Five Bandits" does nevertheless give a good picture of what the poet intends to convey, comparing the five power groups to fearsome brutes, who are satirically depicted in a competition of skills in plundering the nation's wealth—in language true at least to the earthiness and downright vulgarity of the *p'ansori.*

KIM CHIHA: "FIVE BANDITS"

[Kim Chiha, *Cry of the People and Other Poems*, pp. 39–59]

I want to write a poem with candid and bold words and without any hesitation. It's been a long time since I was last beaten up for writing with an unruly pen. My body is itching to be beaten; my mouth is eager to speak, and my hands are dying to write. Since my urge to write is beyond my control, I have made up my mind to write a story concerning strange bandits. I am doing this knowing that it will invite serious punitive measures, including physical pain.

It's the best story you've ever seen with your navel or heard with your anus since the country was formed under Mount Paektu[*] on the third of October[†] long, long ago.

We are now enjoying times of great peace that are unprecedented since Tangun[‡] founded the nation. In such peaceful and prosperous times, could there be poverty or could there be any bandits? Farmers eat so much that they frequently die of ruptured stomachs! People go naked the year round because they are loath to wear silk garments anymore!

Ko Chaebong[§] might claim to be a great bandit, but there were greater ones during the time of Confucius in China. Corruption and irregularities are on the rampage throughout the country; but, then, there were social evils during the golden age in ancient China too. Regardless of one's position, once one has formed the habit of stealing, one is most likely to retain it for the rest of one's life. Five bandits live as neighbors in the heart of Seoul.

Human waste characterizes the scenery in the southern part of Seoul. To the east, Tongbinggo-dong's[¶] luxurious mansions border the dirty Han River. Barren mountains surround the capital on the north like the hairless rear ends of chickens. Spread below the naked mountains are Sŏngbuk-tong and Suyudong.[**] Between the north and south, wooden shacks dot the landscape.

Towering high above the decrepit shacks scattered far below like pockmarks, inside the arrogant, jarring, great gates at Changch'ung-dong and Yaksu-dong,[††]

---

[*]   Korea's highest mountain, located on the China-Korea border. It has long served as a symbol of Korea.

[†]   South Korea celebrates this as the national foundation day, when the legendary Tangun was said to have established Korea in 2333 B.C.E.

[‡]   The legendary forebear of the Korean people, said to have founded Korea on Mount Paektu in the year 2333 B.C.E.

[§]   A murderer who received wide news coverage in the 1960s after killing a great number of people in the outskirts of Seoul.

[¶]   A nouveau-riche district in Seoul, once nicknamed "a bandit's village."

[**]   New middle-class districts in the northern part of Seoul.

[††]   Wealthy districts in Seoul.

are five stately flowery palaces, glittering, sparkling, shooting up into the sky without restraint, filled day and night with music and the sounds of feasting. These are the dens of the five bandits, who are unsurpassed in craftiness and brutality, with bloated livers the size of South Mountain* and necks as tough as Tung Cho's† umbilical cord. They are called the Tycoon, the Assemblyman, the Government Official, the General, and the Minister.‡

Although everyone else has five internal organs and six entrails in his abdomen, these fellows, each endowed with a robber's sack as large as the testicles of a huge bull, have five internal organs and seven entrails. They originally learned robbery from the same master, but each of them developed his potential in a different way. Ceaselessly committing robbery day and night, they developed their skills until they were almost magical.

One day, when the five bandits had gathered together, one of them said: "Ten years ago today each of us, swearing on our blood, opened up in business. Since then we have improved our skills daily, and accumulated more and more gold. How about chipping in for a prize of 100,000 *kŭn*§ of gold to see which one of us has developed the best techniques over these months and years?" Thus they decided to hold a contest under the slogan "Banditry."

The spring sun was warm, the day pleasant, the wind gentle, the clouds floating by. The five bandits, each brandishing a golf club, each determined to win, set out to display their miraculous skills. The first bandit

stepped forth, the one called the business tycoon, wearing a custom-made suit tailored of banknotes, a hat made of banknotes, shoes made of banknotes and gloves knitted of banknotes, with a gold watch, gold rings, gold buttons, a gold necktie pin, gold cufflinks, a gold buckle, golden teeth, golden nails, golden toenails, and golden zippers, with a golden watch chain dangling from his wiggling ass.

Watch the tycoon demonstrate his skill!

Roasting the cabinet minister a beautiful brown, and boiling the vice minister red, sprinkling soy sauce, mustard, hot sauce, and MSG, together with red pepper, welsh onions, and garlic on them, he swallowed them up, together with banknotes collected from taxes, funds borrowed from foreign countries, and other privileges and benefits.

Pretty girls he lured to himself, made them his mistresses, and kept busy producing babies. A dozen daughters thus made were given as tribute to high officials as midnight snacks. Their tasks were to collect information on the pillow, thereby enabling him to win negotiated contracts, buy land cheaply, and make a fortune once a road was opened. He claimed in his bids a thousand *won*§ when five *won* were sufficient to do the work, pocketing the difference as well as withholding laborers' wages.

Even Sun Wu-k'ung** would be no match for his subtle techniques of appropriation, his superb skills of flattery.

Now the second bandit steps forth with his cronies from the National Assembly

Here come hunchbacks, alley foxes, angry dogs, and monkeys. Hunched at the waist, their eyes are as narrow and slanted as Ts'ao Ts'ao.†† Lumbering, rasp-

---

* The mountain situated at the center of Seoul.

† A man in China in the Later Han period, known for his ferocity and cruelty.

‡ The poet spells out the Korean words for tycoon (*chaebŏl*), assemblyman (*kukhoe ŭiwŏn*), senior government official (*kogŭp kongmuwŏn*), and minister and vice minister (*changch'agwan*) using old Chinese ideographs that are homophonic with the Korean pronunciation but denote "a pack of mad dogs," "hunchbacked foxes and dogs snarling at monkeys," "meritless pigs seated on mountaintops," "gorillas," and "mad dogs winking at the rising sun," respectively.

§ Somewhat more than 50 tons.

---

§ U.S.$1 = 396 *won*.

** The monkey in the Chinese fiction *Hsi-yu chi* (The journey to the west), known for its prodigious wit, intelligence, and magical powers.

†† Ts'ao Ts'ao (155–220), Emperor Wu of Wei. Generalissimo and chancellor during the declining years of the Later Han dynasty; he was known for ruthlessness.

ing, covering their hairy bodies with the empty oaths of revolution, coughing up mucus, raising their golf clubs high into the sky like flags, thunderously yelling slogans, rolling on viper-colored jagged floors:

Revolution, from old evil to new evil!

Renovation, from illegal profiteering to profiteering illegally!

Modernization, from unfair elections to elections unfair!

Physiocracy, from poor farms to abandoned farms!

Construction, all houses to be built in Wau* style!

Clean up society, follow Chŏng Insuk!† Rise up! Rise up! Bank of Korea notes! Korean rice wine! Fists! Ballots spoiled with numerous seals and pockmarks! Owls, weasels, blind men, ghosts—all put to use in the holy battle of stealing votes!

Sun Tzu, that old Chinese strategist, declared long ago that soldiers do not reject vice, that governors are bandits, that a public oath is an empty oath.

You foolish people, get out of the way!

You stink!

Let me play golf!

Now the third bandit emerges, looking like a rubber balloon with viperous pointed eyes, his lips firmly closed. Portraying a clean government official, when sweets are offered, he shows that he doesn't like them by shaking his head. "Indeed, it must be true. But look at this fellow's other face. He snoops here and smiles there, stout, impudent, sly; his teeth are crooked and black from an overindulgence in sweets, worn out until they could decay no more.

He sits in a wide chair as deep as the sea, before a desk as high as the sky, saying "no thank you" with one hand and "thank you" with the other. He cannot do possible things, but he can do impossible things; he has

_____

* The collapse of the Wau Apartments in April 1970 was attributed to cheap and faulty construction on the part of Seoul's Bureau of Construction. Seoul's mayor was relieved of his duties as a result of the accident, which claimed some 128 lives.

† One Chŏng Insuk was murdered allegedly by her brother early in 1970 because of her immorality. It was later discovered that she had been on intimate terms with various high government officials and was privy to a great many state secrets.

piles of documents on top of his desk and bundles of money under it. He acts like an obedient shaggy dog when flattering superiors, but like a snarling hunting dog to subordinates. He puts public funds into his left pocket and bribes for favors done into his right pocket. His face, a perpetual mask of innocence, conveys purity—the purity of a white cloud. His all-consuming passion is asking after the well-being of madams of deluxe restaurants.

The fourth bandit steps forth, a big gorilla. He is tall, reaching almost to the heavens. The marching column of soldiers under his command is as long as China's Great Wall. He has white tinted eyes, a tiger's mouth, a wide nose, and a shaggy beard; he must be an animal. His breast is adorned with colorful medals made of gold, silver, white copper, bronze, and brass. Black pistols cling to his body.

He sold the sacks of rice meant to feed the soldiers, and filled the sacks with sand. He stole the cows and pigs to be fed to the soldiers, and gave a hair to each man. No barracks for the poor enlisted men in a bitterly cold winter; instead, hard labor all day to keep them sweating. Lumber for the construction of barracks was used for building the general's quarters. Spare parts for vehicles, uniforms, anthracite briquettes, monthly allowances, all were stolen. In accordance with military law, soldiers who deserted their units because of hunger and desperation were arrested, beaten and thrown into the brig, and harassed under orders. University students summoned for military service were assigned to the general's quarters as living toys for his wanton wife. Meanwhile the general enjoyed his cleverly camouflaged life with an unending stream of concubines.

Now the last bandit and his cronies step out: ministers and vice ministers, who waddle from obesity, sediment seeping from every pore. With shifty mucus-lined eyes, they command the national defense with golf clubs in their left hands, while fondling the tits of their mistresses with their right. And, when they softly write "Increased Production, Increased Export and Construction" on a mistress's tits, the woman murmurs "Hee-hee-hee, don't tickle me!" And they jokingly reproach: "You ignorant woman, do national affairs make you laugh?" Let's export even though we starve, let's increase production even though products go unsold.

Let's construct a bridge across the Strait of Korea with the bones of those who have starved to death, so we can worship the god of Japan! Like slave-masters of olden times, they drive the people to work harder and longer, with the beating of burst drums and the sounds of broken trumpets, with one aim in mind: to increase their own wealth.

They buy a Mercedes in addition to their black sedans, but feign humility by riding in a Corona.* They make their fortune by cheating the budget and further fatten it by illegal biddings, but chew gum to rid themselves of the smell of corruption. They shout loudly not to deal in foreign goods, while lighting up a Kent. They hastily write decrees to ban foreign goods and are pleased with how nicely the law was written. They deny their dishonesty to an "ignorant" journalist who, hearing of a big scandal, rushes upon the scene. And for an answer they smugly whisper: "What is your golf handicap?"

Even the ghosts who watched the horrifying cunningness displayed in the contest grew alarmed and fled, for fear that they too would get caught and lose their bones.

The ripened pumpkins of September and October waiting to be harvested were rotting in the fields. From beyond the blue sky a stern voice was heard rolling like thunder, commanding: "Arrest those bandits who disgrace our national honor!" And an answer was heard, saying: "Yes, sir. They will be arrested at once."

And now look at the prosecutor general, with his bumpy pig-nose smeared white with wine sediment, his catfish nose slobbering saliva! His whiskers are as wild as those of Chang Fei;† his eyes are red with the blood of the dead; a dangling tumor as big as a fist grows on his forehead. With arms stretched out, roaring like a lion, he kicks and punches men around him at random, removing their skin, chaining them in dungeons.

But listen with me to what was happening.

The order coming from the stern voice behind the blue sky was not followed. The bandits were not arrested. Instead the keeper of the law of the land arrested in a different direction. Blowflies‡ in Chongno 3rd Street; big flies in Myŏng-dong; dirty flies in Yang-dong; nasty flies in Mugyo-dong and Ch'ŏnggye River; dung flies in Wangsim-ni.§ All were collected and assembled in one place where they were beaten, struck, kicked, stamped upon, burnt, pinched, bitten, thrown away, flattened, crashed, punctured, twisted, broken, knifed, bayoneted, infringed upon, and bent like the willow branches along the banks of the Nodŭl River.¶

With six-angled clubs, three-angled iron bars, hooks, long and short swords, large and small swords, large and small knives, ropes, handcuffs, sticks, clubs and whistles.

At hand were also dog-legged, cow-legged rifles, submachine guns, hand grenades, tear gas bombs, smoke bombs, dung bombs, urine bombs, dirty water bombs, and more of the latest sophisticated weapons.

All neatly arranged.

The prosecutor general roared arrest orders with a voice as loud as a tiger farting. People dragged out from all parts of the country bowed deep and trembled. Peasants from Chŏlla province trembled like the others, as if shivering from severe cold. And he began his questioning:

"You are the five bandits, aren't you?"

"No, sir, I am not."

"Then who are you?"

"I am a snatcher."

"Aah, good. Snatcher, pickpocket, robber, burglar, and swindler. They are the five bandits."

---

* A small Japanese-made car assembled in Korea.

† Chang Fei (166–221), a sworn brother of Liu Pei, is known for his tiger's whiskers in *The Romance of the Three Kingdoms*.

‡ A diminutive used to underscore the Korean people's helplessness.

§ Chongno 3rd Street and Yang-dong were centers of prostitution at one time. Myŏng-dong is a luxury center, Mugyo-dong is an entertainment center, Ch'ŏnggye River is a slum, and Wangsim-ni is a human-waste disposal area in Seoul.

¶ A river in a popular song along whose banks men are said to live happy lives.

"No, sir, I am not that kind of snatcher."

"What are you then?"

"I am a pimp."

"Aah, good. A pimp is better. Pimp, prostitute, madam, hoodlum, and informer. You're the five bandits, aren't you?"

"No, no, I am not a pimp."

"Then, what are you?"

"I am a peddler."

"Aah, peddler! Much better. Gum peddler, cigarette peddler, sock peddler, candy peddler, and chocolate peddler. They are the real bandits living on imported goods."

"No, no, sir, I am not that kind of peddler."

"Then, what are you?"

"I am a beggar, sir."

"Aah, if you are a beggar, it is even better. Beggar, leper, ragpicker, pauper, thief, all these together are the five delinquent bandits. Shut up, you dog: to the big house with you!"

"No, no, I don't want to go, I am not the five bandits, I am a peasant from Chŏlla province. I came to Seoul to earn my livelihood because I couldn't feed myself by farming. The only crime I committed was stealing a small piece of bread because I was hungry last night."

But nobody listens to him. The rope around him is tightened, left and right, up and down, and he twists hopelessly, listening to the squeaking noises. The tortures used are compressing, beating, water torture, fire torture, tanning, branding, hanging upside down, swinging in the air. Soapy water, to which red pepper and vinegar are added, is poured on him. But his answer remains the same: "No, sir. No. No, sir."* That is all he says.

The prosecutor general is at his wits' end. He needs a confession! Unable to wring one out in spite of infamous tortures, he decides to persuade the victim gently. He suggests that he make a guess as to who the five bandits might be, promising to spare his life. Hearing this, the countryman, more dead than alive, answers: "The five bandits are five animals called Tycoons, Assemblymen,

___

* The poet uses the dialect of Chŏlla province, thus indicating politeness and vulnerability.

Government Officials, Generals, and Ministers, who are now staging a banditry contest in Tongbinggo-dong."†

"Aah, those names sound familiar. Are they really animals?"

"Yes, they are very ferocious brutes!"

"I am glad to hear that, my boy! You should have told me before." The prosecutor general, overjoyed, slapped his knees so hard that he cracked one of the bones.

"Hey, boy! Get up! Take the lead! Let's find them and hack them to pieces. I will be a success! I will be famous!"

The young peasant in the lead, the prosecutor general sets out on his mission with dignity and determination, his eyes shining brightly like those of a tiger tensing for the kill. Shouting continuously: "All of you, stand aside! Out of my way! I am going to arrest the bandits!" he marches on:

Tarum tarum tarum-tum-tum, tarum tarum tarum-tum-tum, tarum tarum tarum-tum-tum.

Leaping over South Mountain, he overlooks Tongbinggo-dong. The large crowds who had followed him are clapping their hands. To them it seems that General Yi Wan‡ has been reborn. The prosecutor general rushes into the battlefield roaring: "Bandits, listen! You nasty beasts who live by sucking the people's blood.

"Your traitorous acts have defamed our national honor!

"People's complaints are heard everywhere! By the order of the king, you are under arrest."

The bandits stared at him without blinking an eye. Remember they were animals in appearance, luxurious, colorful animals.

The prosecutor general couldn't believe his eyes. He wasn't sure whether he was dreaming or awake. A paradise before his eyes! The clear blue swimming pool full of naked fairies. In the garden, trees and foreign dogs worth a million *won*, large and small rocks, stone lamps and Buddha statues worth ten million *won*, carp and bream swimming in the pond, and sparrows and quail

___

† See note 20

‡ A hero in the war against the Manchu in 1636, Yi Wan (1602–1674) was known for courage and integrity while serving as the police commissioner.

sitting in cages worth a hundred million *won*. The doors were automatic, the walls were automatic, drinking was automatic, cooking was automatic, women were performing automatic wanton acts, and everything was automatic, automatic, automatic. The housemaids were college girls, the accountants were doctors of economics, the gardeners were doctors of forestry the house managers were doctors of business administration, the tutors were doctors of philosophy, the secretaries were doctors of politics, the beauticians were doctors of aesthetics, doctors, doctors, and more doctors.

For fear that the grass might freeze, a steam heating system had been installed in the lawn and the ponds were temperature-controlled. Heaters were placed in the bird cages so that the birds would not feel cold, and a refrigerator was placed near the dog house so the dog food would not rot. Korean tiles covered the roof of the western-style, marble-walled residence. The columns were Corinthian and the center beam was Ionic. Truly a palace. The glass rooms had double doors. Artificial grass had been put on the stone walls. The second story had a tiled roof garden with folding windows decorated with the old Chinese graph for "bandit." The inner and outer gates were built in Persian style, the bath in Turkish style, and the pig sties in pure Japanese style.

A pond and an artificial mountain had been created nearby. Standing on this mountain, the prosecutor general peered into the house through the opened door and saw a cabinet decorated with pearls, a chest decorated with the carving of a Chinese phoenix, a larger chest decorated with carvings of dragons, and an enormous chest decorated with the carving of a carnation, a dish decorated with precious stones as large as an athletic field, candlesticks of gold and bronze as high as the ceiling, an electric clock, an electric rice bowl, an electric kettle, an electric bag, glass bottles, wooden wares, celadon, and white porcelain. A Picasso was hung upside down, and a Chagal was hung sideways. The picture of an orchid in a golden frame shone brightly. ...

Look at the women's accessories! Sapphire hairpins decorated with white precious stones, ornamented shoes, golden broaches, white gold false teeth, amber ear plugs, coral anus plugs, ruby navel plugs, golden buttons, pearl earrings, diamond nose rings, violet quartz

necklaces, sapphire bracelets, emerald anklets, diamond belts, and Turkish eyeglass frames made of stone.

And yet the five bandits wore brass rings worth a measly three *won* on their pudgy fingers, for didn't they shine like torches in the night!

The prosecutor general turned around, peering through another open door. And what did he see: great quantities of delicious foods piled high on large tables. Cow hair steaks, fried pig snouts, fried goat's whiskers, boiled deer antlers. ... Field-fruit wine, Suntory, cinnamon flavored distilled spirits, champagne, pine wine. ...

Forgetting to shut his mouth and with spittle drooling out the prosecutor general sighed: "Aah, such good fortunes are the rewards of banditry! If I had but known this, I would have joined them long before. My conscience has surely been my worst enemy."

One of the five bandits sidled up to the prosecutor general inviting him to eat and drink with them. Never had he tasted such delicious food! Never had he drunk such good-tasting wine! At first he ate and drank in moderation, but soon without control, like a pig. Becoming drunk, but still master over his tongue, he scrambled to his feet to make a speech.

Chewing, spitting, and making a lot of noise, he nevertheless spoke in a grave and dignified voice.

"Dear fortunate and honorable bandits! I believe that you should not be punished for your crimes. Instead our society should be blamed and held responsible for the deeds you have committed.

"You are not bandits, but respectable robbers who are the faithful servants of our society! It is my deepest desire that you should continue on your trodden way."

The bandits responded with shouts and laughter, slapping each other on the back. The prosecutor general ran out and arrested the young peasant, binding his hands behind his back and saying: "I arrest you for having falsely accused these five servants of the people."

Twilight had come. With the sun setting on the western hill, the lonely wild goose had found her partner and the waxing moon cast its light over the earth.

Pushing the helpless young peasant, who had starved in Chŏlla province,

who had come to Seoul to seek his fortune,

who had been oppressed by everyone,
who was ending up in jail,
the drunken prosecutor general returned to
his office with unsteady steps.

There was nobody who would help the young peasant.
There was nobody who could help the young peasant.
Good luck!
Good bye!

The five bandits thanked the prosecutor general for his courage. They rewarded him with a house guarded by dogs next to their own residences. With a deep sense of achievement, the prosecutor general had the most sophisticated weapons at his disposal to guard the bandits' properties, while enjoying his life in a grand style.

But one beautiful late morning, stretching himself out luxuriously in bed, he was struck dead by a lightning bolt.

The five bandits were struck down at the same time and bled from the six orifices of the body.*

Such incidents have been occurring for a long time and are on everyone's lips. I, a poor poet, merely attempt to pass the story on.

---

* A form of Heaven's retribution against heinous evil deeds, which may escape human punishment but not that of Heaven, according to popular Korean belief.

Kim Ilsŏng [Kim Il Sung] and Chuch'e (Juche) Thought in North Korea

Edited by Yongho Ch'oe, Peter H. Lee, and William Theodore De Bary

Born into a devout Christian family,[*] Kim Ilsŏng (1912–1994) was not highly educated but became active as a revolutionary from his youth, waging guerrilla warfare against the Japanese before 1945. Chosen by the Soviet authorities, Kim became the first premier when the Democratic People's Republic of Korea was proclaimed in North Korea in 1948, and he also became the chairman of the all-powerful Korean Labor Party. After the Korean War in 1950–1953, Kim successfully eliminated those who had threatened his power, including the so-called domestic Communist group headed by Pak Hŏnyŏng, the Yenan group, and the Soviet-Koreans, and established himself as the unrivaled ruler in North Korea by 1958. Once his supremacy was assured, North Korea began to build a personality cult around Kim Ilsŏng and rewrote much of the modern history of Korea to glorify "the heroic struggle" of the Kim family starting with his great grandfather, who is said to have fought against "the American imperialists" as early as 1866 by leading the attack that destroyed the American merchant ship *General Sherman*. Kim Ilsŏng was extolled as the supreme leader and "the sun" of all the people. The language North Korea used in glorifying Kim exceeded even that devoted to Stalin or Mao in their "cult of personality."

The single most important ideology that permeates all levels of North Korean society is the idea of *chuch'e* (an assertion of self-identity and self-reliance), which Kim developed as the guide and foundation of all conduct in North Korea. First presented in a speech delivered to "the party propaganda and agitation workers" in December 1955, the *chuch'e* idea called for creative application of Marxist-Leninist principles to the realization of the Korean revolution, whose unique conditions required a correct understanding of Korean tradition and history. After being pushed aside for nearly a decade, this idea was taken up again in 1963, when Kim spoke of the importance of *chuch'e* to the Korean People's Army. Thereafter, an all-out effort was devoted to promoting the idea of *chuch'e* in all things. Fiercely nationalistic, *chuch'e* emphasized independence in political work, self-sustenance in economic endeavors, and self-defense in national defense. So great is the importance attached to the life of Kim Ilsŏng and his *chuch'e* idea, that after the death of Kim in 1994, North Korea officially adopted a new calendar year, counting the birth year of Kim—1912—as the first year of *chuch'e*.

The following selection is taken from a speech Kim made in December 1955 in which he proposed for the

[*] See Yŏng-ho Ch'oe, "Christian Background in the Early Life of Kim Il-sŏng," *Asian Survey* 26, No. 10 (October 1986).

first time the application of the *chuch'e** spirit to the Korean revolution.

Kim Ilsŏng: "On Eliminating Dogmatism and Formalism and Establishing Juche [*Chuch'e*] in Ideological Work"

[From *Kim Il Sung's Works* 9:395–408]

Today I want to address a few remarks to you on the shortcomings in our Party's ideological work and on how to eliminate them in the future. As you learned at yesterday's session, there have been serious ideological errors on the literary front. It is obvious, then, that our propaganda work also cannot have been faultless. It is to be regretted that it suffers in many respects from dogmatism and formalism.

The principal shortcomings in ideological work are the failure to delve deeply into all matters and the lack of Juche. It may not be correct to say Juche is lacking, but, in fact, it has not yet been firmly established. This is a serious matter. We must thoroughly rectify this shortcoming. Unless this problem is solved, we cannot hope for good results in ideological work.

Why does our ideological work suffer from dogmatism and formalism? Why do our propaganda and agitation workers only embellish the facade and fail to go deeply into matters, and why do they merely copy and memorize things foreign, instead of working creatively? This offers us food for serious reflection.

What is Juche in our Party's ideological work? What are we doing? We are not engaged in any other country's revolution, but solely in the Korean revolution. This, the Korean revolution, determines the essence of Juche in the ideological work of our Party. Therefore, all ideological work must be subordinated to the interests of the Korean revolution. When we study the history of the Communist Party of the Soviet Union, the history of the Chinese revolution, or the universal truth of Marxism-Leninism, it is entirely for the purpose of correctly carrying out our own revolution.

By saying that the ideological work of our Party is lacking in Juche, I do not mean, of course, that we have not made the revolution and that our revolutionary work was undertaken by outsiders. Nonetheless, Juche has not been firmly established in ideological work, and this leads to dogmatic and formalistic errors and does much harm to our revolutionary cause.

To make revolution in Korea we must know Korean history and geography as well as the customs of the Korean people. Only then is it possible to educate our people in a way that suits them and to inspire in them an ardent love for their native place and their motherland.

It is of paramount importance to study and widely publicize among the working people the history of our country and of our people's struggle. ... Only when we educate our people in the history of their own struggle and its traditions can we stimulate their national pride and rouse the broad masses to revolutionary struggle. Yet, many of our functionaries are ignorant of our country's history and so do not strive to discover, inherit and carry forward our fine traditions. Unless this is corrected, it will lead, in the long run, to the negation of Korean history.

The mistakes made recently by Pak Ch'angok[†] and his kind are due to their negation of the history of the Korean literary movement. They closed their eyes to the struggle waged by the fine writers of the "KAPF"—Coréen Artiste Prolétarienne Fédération—and to the splendid works of our progressive scholars and writers. We urged them to make a profound study of excellent cultural heritages and give them wide publicity, but they did not do so. ...

The Kwangju Student Incident [in 1929], for example, was a mass struggle in which thousands of Korean students and other young people rose against Japanese imperialism. It played a big part in inspiring broad sections of Korean youth with the anti-Japanese

---

* *Chu* means "give primacy to" or "emphasize" and *ch'e* "substance" corresponds to the Neo-Confucian *t'i*, as in the Chinese *t'i yung* ("substance/function") or *tai* in the Japanese *kokutai* ("national substance or polity").

---

† Born and educated in the Soviet Union, Pak Ch'angok represented a faction that favored Soviet Russia. He was an editor of a party journal and a vice-premier in North Korea before he was purged in 1956.

spirit. Propaganda workers should have publicized this movement widely as a matter of course and educated our students and other young people in the brave fighting spirit displayed by their forerunners. While they have failed to do this, Syngman Rhee has been making use of this movement in his propaganda. This has created the false impression that the communists disregard national traditions. What a dangerous thing! If we go on working in this way, it will be impossible for us to win over the south Korean youth. ...

The same must be said of the June 10 Independence Movement [in 1926]. This was another mass struggle in which the Korean people rose up against Japanese imperialism. It is true that the struggle was greatly hampered by the factionalists who had wormed their way into it. Considering that even after liberation, the Pak Hŏnyŏng-Yi Sŭngyŏp spy clique* crept into our ranks and wrought mischief, it goes without saying that in those days the factionalists were able to carry on subversive activities more easily, But, even so, was the struggle itself wrong? No. Although it ended in failure because of a few bad elements who had wormed their way into the leadership of the organization, we cannot deny its revolutionary character. We should learn a lesson from that failure.

---

* A lifelong Communist active within Korea since the early 1920s, Pak Hŏnyŏng (1900–1955) headed the Korean Communist Party in South Korea before he was forced to flee to North Korea in 1946 when the United States Military Government issued an arrest warrant for him. When the Democratic People's Republic of Korea was inaugurated in North Korea in 1948, Pak was concurrently a vice-premier and minister of foreign affairs. Representing the mainstream of the Communist movement in Korea, Pak was a formidable rival to Kim Ilsŏng and was executed in 1955 on the charge of having been a spy of the United States—a charge few outside North Korea believed to be true. A lieutenant of Pak, Yi Sŭngyŏp (1905–1953), had been an active Communist in South Korea before moving to North Korea to avoid being arrested by the United States authorities in 1946. Yi and many other Communists who moved from South Korea were purged in 1953 on the charge of attempting to overthrow the North Korean government and of spying for the United States.

No publicity has been given either to the March First movement [in 1919]. If you work in this way, you cannot expect to lead progressive people with a national conscience along the right path. The lack of Communist Party leadership was the principal cause of the failure of the March First movement. But who can deny that it was a nationwide resistance movement against Japanese imperialism? We ought to explain the historic significance of this movement to the people and use its lessons to educate them. Many revolutionary movements in our country ended in failure because of the scoundrels who managed to get themselves into the leadership, but no one can deny the people's participation in those struggles. ... What assets do we have for carrying on the revolution if the history of our people's struggle is denied? If we cast aside all these things, it would mean that our people did nothing. There are many things to be proud of in our country's peasant movements of the past. In recent years, however, no articles dealing with them have appeared in our newspapers.

In schools, too, there is a tendency to neglect courses on Korean history. During the war, the curriculum of the Central Party School allotted 160 hours a year to the study of world history but only very few hours to Korean history. This is how things were done in the Party school, and so it is quite natural that our functionaries are ignorant of their own country's history. In our propaganda and agitation work, there are numerous examples where only things foreign are extolled while our own are slighted.

Once I visited a People's Army rest home, where there was a picture of the Siberian steppe on the wall. Russians probably like that landscape. But we Korean people like the beautiful scenery of our own country. There are beautiful mountains such as Kumgang and Myohyang in our country. There are clear streams, the blue sea with its rolling waves, and fields with their ripening crops. If we are to inspire in our People's Army men a love for their native place and their country, we must display more pictures of our own landscapes. ... I noticed in a primary school that all the portraits on the walls were of foreigners, such as Mayakovsky and Pushkin, but there were none of Koreans. If children are educated in this way, how can they be expected to have national pride? ...

We should study our own things in earnest and get to know them well. Otherwise, we shall be unable to solve new problems creatively in keeping with our actual conditions, problems that crop up one after another in practice.

As a matter of fact, the form of our government should also be suited to the specific conditions in our country. Does our people's power take exactly the same form as that in other socialist countries? No. They are alike in that they are based on Marxist-Leninist principles, but the forms they take are different. There is no doubt, too, that our platform is in keeping with the realities of our country. ...

Pak Yŏngbin,* on returning from the Soviet Union, said that as the Soviet Union was following the line of easing international tension, we should also drop our slogan against U.S. imperialism. Such an assertion has nothing to do with revolutionary initiative. It would dull our people's revolutionary vigilance. The U.S. imperialists scorched our land, massacred our innocent people, and are still occupying the southern half of our country. They are our sworn enemy, aren't they? It is utterly ridiculous to think that our people's struggle against the U.S. imperialists conflicts with the efforts of the Soviet people to ease international tension. Our people's condemnation of and struggle against the U.S. imperialists' policy of aggression against Korea are not in contradiction with but conducive to the struggle of the peoples of the world to lessen international tension and defend peace. At the same time, the struggle to ease tension on the part of the peace-loving people the world over, including the Soviet people, creates more favorable conditions for the anti-imperialist struggle of our people. ...

Some comrades working in the Propaganda Department of the Party tried to copy everything mechanically from the Soviet Union. This was also because they had no intention of studying our realities and lacked the true Marxist Leninist approach to educating the people in our own merits and revolutionary traditions. Many comrades swallow Marxism-Leninism raw,

---

* Pak Yŏngbin was a Soviet Korean, holding a key party post in North Korea before he was purged in the 1950s.

without digesting and assimilating it. It is self-evident, therefore, that they are unable to display revolutionary initiative.

Propaganda workers have so far failed to take proper measures to study our history and national culture systematically. Ten years have passed since liberation yet they have failed to tackle the matter energetically. They have conducted it only in a hit-or-miss way. We had few cadres before, but now we have scholars, foods, and material, and sufficient conditions for doing it. It is quite possible if only you make a good study and organize the work. Every effort should be made to discover and promote our national heritage. True, we should energetically learn from what is progressive internationally. But we should develop the fine things of our own while introducing advanced culture. Otherwise, our people will lose faith in their own ability and become a spineless people who only try to copy from others.

Hearing us say that it is necessary to establish Juche, some comrades might take it in a simple way and get the wrong idea that we need not learn from foreign countries. That would be quite wrong. We must learn from the positive experience of socialist countries. The important thing is to know what we are learning for. Our aim is to turn the advanced experience of the Soviet Union and other socialist countries to good account in our Korean revolution. ...

It does not matter whether you use the right hand or the left, whether you use a spoon or chopsticks at the table. No matter how you eat, it is all the same insofar as food is put into your mouth, isn't it? Why need one be fastidious about "fashion" in wartime? We do political work to strengthen our People's Army and win battles, and any method will do so long as our aim is achieved. ...

It is important in our work to grasp revolutionary truth, Marxist-Leninist truth, and apply it correctly to our actual conditions. There should be no set rule that we must follow the Soviet pattern. Some advocate the Soviet way and others the Chinese, but is it not high time to work out our own? The point is that we should not mechanically copy the forms and methods of the Soviet Union, but should learn from its experience in struggle and from the truth of Marxism-Leninism. So, while learning from the experience of the Soviet Union, we must put stress not on the form but on the essence of its experience. …

Merely copying the forms used by others instead of learning the truth of Marxism-Leninism does us no good, only harm. In both revolutionary struggle and construction, we should firmly adhere to Marxist-Leninist principles, applying them in a creative way to suit the specific conditions and national characteristics of our country. If we mechanically apply foreign experience, disregarding the history of our country and the traditions of our people and without taking account of our own realities and our people's political level, we will commit dogmatic errors and do much harm to the revolutionary cause. This is not fidelity to Marxism-Leninism nor to internationalism. It runs counter to them.

Marxism-Leninism is not a dogma, it is a guide to action and a creative theory. Thus, Marxism-Leninism can display its indestructible vitality only when it is applied creatively to suit the specific conditions of each country. The same applies to the experience of the fraternal parties. It will prove valuable to us only when we study it, grasp its essence, and properly apply it to our realities. But if we just gulp it down and spoil our work, it will not only harm our work but also lead to discrediting the valuable experience of the fraternal parties….

Our struggle for peaceful reunification boils down to two points—to carry out construction successfully in the northern half of the country and direct effective political work toward the southern half. If we strengthen the democratic base by promoting socialist construction in the north and rouse the people in the south to struggle for liberation through effective political work directed to the south, peaceful reunification can be realized.

Political work directed toward the south means strengthening the influence of the north on the people in the south and getting the broad masses there to support us. To this end, socialist construction in the north should be carried out successfully. The living standards of the people should be raised and the economic base strengthened in the north through successful economic construction, and the entire people should be rallied around our Party. Then, no matter how desperately Syngman Rhee may try, he will never be able to dampen the fighting spirit of the people in the south, who are constantly inspired by socialist construction in the north. …

Before liberation, merely to hear that in the Soviet Union the working class held power and was building socialism made us yearn greatly for that country where we had never been. How then can the people in the south not yearn to see the socialist construction in the north carried out by our people who are of the same stock as they are? That is why successful construction in the north is more important than anything else.

Thus, when the people in the south are roused to action against U.S. imperialism and the Syngman Rhee regime through successful socialist construction in the north and effective political work directed toward the south, peaceful reunification can be brought about.

MILITARY-FIRST POLITICS (SONGUN)
UNDERSTANDING KIM JONG-IL'S NORTH KOREA

*By Han S. Park**

INTRODUCTION

As one might say that, without a proper understanding of *juche,* Kim Il-sung's North Korea cannot be comprehended, one might also say that a proper understanding of Kim Jong-il's North Korea is impossible without a proper comprehension of *songun*. *Juche* and *songun* are inseparable in that *songun* is predicated on the principles of *juche.* The *songun* theoreticians claim that *songun* has advanced *juche* to a higher plane by providing it with a realistic perspective on the history and politics of the world. Just as in the case *of juche, songun* is said to be in a constant process of evolving toward its perfection. At present, there are limited written sources available in any language for a researcher to discern its definitive picture. Yet, by consulting available publications from North Korea and conducting a series of personal interviews with scholars who are the leading advancers and theoreticians of this system of ideas, one might be able to portray the essence of its philosophical and theoretical attributes. It is hoped that the following pages may be of some help to observers of North Korea in explaining the system

characteristics and policy behaviors of the Democratic People's Republic of Korea (DPRK) under Kim Jong-il.

CHARACTERISTICS OF *SONGUN*: WHAT IS MILITARY-FIRST POLITICS?

MILITARY THE CENTER OF THE POLITICAL SYSTEM

Since the death of Kim Il-sung in 1994, the concept of the center—*dang jungang*—of the Korean Workers' Party has been used in North Korea to refer specifically to Kim Jong-il. The center in this context means more than the locus of power. It means the central nervous system (as of the body). The military is the guardian for the body, which must be protected and never allowed to be vulnerable. When the military is theorized to be the center, it carries the same connotation. In this sense, the military is not just an institution designed to perform the function of defending the country from external hostility. Instead, it provides all of the other institutions of the government with legitimacy. All policy goals are articulated by the military and then disseminated to other organizations with specific strategic and tactical recommendations for implementation. After policies are implemented, their effectiveness will be evaluated by the military. In this way, the military serves as the brain in the nervous system of the body politic.

When the new (current) constitution was adopted in 1998, Korean observers around the world became

* **Han S. Park** is University Professor of Political Science, School of Public and International Affairs, and Director of the Center for the Study of Global Issues (GLOBIS), at the University of Georgia, in Athens, Georgia. An earlier version of this paper was presented at the Korea Economic Institute, Washington, D.C., on 23 May 2007.

puzzled by the fact that Kim Jong-il assumed only the chairmanship of the Military Commission, while he permitted the office of head of state to be assumed by the chairperson of the Standing Committee of the Supreme People's Assembly (the current occupant is Kim Yong-nam). This rather unconventional arrangement would not have been regarded as puzzling if viewed through the lens of *songun* doctrine, however, because the constitution itself specifies that the military and civilian sectors are one and indivisible (Article 61) and that the Military Commission makes decisions and issues directives and orders (Article 104).

MILITARY THE DELIVERER AND PROVIDER

To North Koreans, the military is not an abstract authority but a practical performer. It responds directly and effectively to people's needs and wants. It delivers in a way that no others can: it delivers services and goods to the people and provides security. When I asked a farmer about his understanding of the *songun* doctrine, he offered that "it is the military that makes farming possible as the soldiers come into the village to perform the complete range of farming tasks from toiling the soil to seeding, irrigating, and harvesting." He continued, "The military not only protects the people's lives from foreign hostility, but it also delivers food and services." It is common to notice in the streets of North Korea that soldiers carry bags of grain to civilian homes.

The concern commonly expressed by the foreign providers of food aid that the military may snatch the food away from the civilians is in fact rather speculative. The reality is that the military has food and other necessities in relatively ample supply because of its independent accounting system whereby the military retains the revenues it generates from exporting military equipment—including both missiles and conventional weapons. In this way, the military is in a position to share its resources with the public. This also allows the military to perform the service of delivering foreign aid food to the civilians in even the most remote villages. In fact, the delivery and provision functions of the military are not limited to services and food; they include virtually all commodity goods.

MILITARY THE PROBLEM SOLVER

Not only is the military regarded as the embodiment of legitimate power and authority, it is also considered the most able problem solver in practically all spheres of people's lives. Each unit of dwellers (called a *ban*) is assigned to a military post that is responsible for looking after all the occupants' needs, ranging from repairing household electrical appliances to fixing faucets and sewage systems. Under *songun* society, the people are supposed to trust that the military is equipped with the resources, knowledge, and skills necessary to solve such problems encountered in people's daily lives. In this way, the doctrine calls for the complete dependence of the people on the military. The popular belief being promoted under the banner of *songun* is that "no problem is too big or too small for the military to solve." In this way, the idea is promoted that, without the military, people cannot sustain their existence.

MILITARY THE ENGINE FOR SOCIAL ENGINEERING

The military is also the prime opinion leader. People trust that soldiers are the best educated in ideological preparedness. In fact, military education always places ideology and politics at the top. The soldiers are the ones who teach the common villagers. When soldiers are on leave from their military barracks, they are in essence assigned to their hometowns to teach the villagers in such a way that the commoners will be prepared to carry on the "revolution" just as effectively as the soldiers themselves. In my numerous trips to North Korea, I have consistently been amazed by the ability of soldiers to spell out in most specific terms their mission as soldiers and, hence, as leaders of the so-called revolutionary struggle. It might be appropriate to characterize the mission of the military in North Korea today as that of social engineering.

The concept of social engineering is one of future orientation. Social engineering requires designing society for the future and, thereby, directing the course of social change toward desired goals. People are expected to look up to the military for its visionary leadership; they supposedly need only follow its guidance. The norms and values desirable for the society will be created by the military, which is also designated to disseminate them to the people. In this sense, the military is society's greatest educator.

At the heart of military education is the Military University. This institution is central to developing the ideology of *songun,* training military officers, and disseminating the *songun* philosophy throughout the other educational institutions in the country.

MILITARY THE CREATOR AND ADVANCER OF NEW CULTURE

Cultural change occurs in every society, and North Korea is no exception. The fact that there seems to be no appreciable cultural generation gap in the country defies the common expectation that, as society becomes modernized, the youthful population should become disillusioned with the establishment and attracted to a consumerist lifestyle. There also seems to be little difference between the rural and urban areas in this regard. The country has maintained a remarkable degree of uniformity in the cultural orientation of its populace. This uniformity has been created and maintained largely through the institution of the military.

With a 10-year compulsory military service and a large portion of the population (in excess of one million) serving at any given time, virtually every family has at least one soldier in military service. In fact, there is hardly any separation at all between the military and civilian sectors. The military performs an extensive role in the civilian villages, and the military's role is further heightened by the fact that practically all physically functioning people in the country are mobilized in the People's Militia. It is no surprise that the military's culture is the North Korean culture. Thus, the country's cultural traits include uniformity, obedience to authority, a clear definition of a common enemy, and resolve and determination as the highest virtues.

The *songun* doctrine has created a belief system in which the public must follow the military because the military is always right. It is no longer the Korean Workers' Party that leads the way, neither is it the government that assumes the role of leadership.

One intriguing feature of the North Korean culture is the pervasive sense of equality. The participation of average citizens in decision-making processes provides a significant sense of self-worth and a morale boost to the population. Except for the office of the Supreme Leader, everyone is supposed to be equal in the sense that all are involved in making decisions that affect everyone. Life in North Korea, therefore, is one of successive meetings and deliberations at all levels of society, including the military itself. Typical meetings begin with self-criticisms (confessions) by every participant and conclude with remedial recommendations for any wrongdoing committed by any member, regardless of that person's standing in the social and political strata.

The principle of "one for all, and all for one" is not just a slogan anymore. It works and is felt in the country. This doctrine epitomizes the "military way." Thus, the same practice is emulated in civilian life. Every administrative unit, the *ban,* convenes a regular weekly meeting for the purpose of information dissemination from the center (the Supreme Leadership) and to stage the process of self-criticism.

MILITARY THE SYNTHESIZER OF BODY-MIND-SPIRIT

Unlike *juche,* which primarily emphasizes self-defense, *songun* is a much more comprehensive doctrine; its concern is not limited to the physical and material aspects of existence but rather extends just as importantly to the psychological and spiritual domains. In this way, *songun* has become the contemporary fountainhead of political and social philosophy, just as *juche* was during the Kim Il-sung era. One should remember that the doctrine of *juche* reached its height as it advanced the philosophical concept of the "political-social body" (PSB) in the late 1980s. With the PSB, *juche* attempted to articulate a theory of human development (maturation) by providing a progressive theory of personal development: one is said to become a social body as one undergoes the process of transformation from a biological being to a social being. The biological being is one full of instinctive desires for physical comfort. The social being, however, is charged with social and political consciousness (*eusiksong*). Hence, the concept of human development became an important feature of the *juche* philosophy.

Now the philosophy of *songun* is attempting to integrate the three components of human existence, the body-mind-spirit. Here, as before, the notion of an ideal personhood is being created, but this time with three elements: one becomes ideally developed through the attainment of martial art (body), education and training in the arts and sciences (mind), and devotion to a sense of mission for life (spirit). The curriculum for education, in both the military and civilian sectors, is designed to promote all three.

MILITARY THE EXEMPLAR

During my frequent travels in North Korea, my favorite question to pose to a single woman or girl is to ask what kind of man she would wish to marry. Of late, I have noticed that the most common answer is "a soldier." One has to appreciate this in the context of *songun,* for the military institution houses the best manifestations of all three components (body-mind-spirit) of human existence. For instance, military artists are revered, as their ranks include most of the accomplished artists in the country; the military houses the best scientists, as demonstrated by the advancement of nuclear physics and the engineering of the bomb; and, of course, the military shows resolve and unwavering loyalty to the cause of fighting the "most powerful enemy" in the world, the United States.

Even this cursory review of *songun* clearly suggests that it is a peculiar system of ideas that are not commonly found in world politics. If it is so unique, how has the pattern of thought culminating in this doctrine come about? What conditions or causes may have been responsible for the birth and development of such an ideology?

ORIGINS AND CAUSES OF *SONGUN*

REMOTE ORIGINS

Kim Il-sung as guerrilla fighter. Militarism in North Korea cannot be properly comprehended without an appreciation of the formation of Kim Il-sung's charisma as a young guerrilla fighter in Manchuria. When he returned home after the Japanese surrender, he was heralded as a military general although he never attained that rank. The most popular song about him, in fact, was promoted at the very time of his homecoming

and has since become deeply entrenched in the North Korean soul: its title is "General Kim Il-sung." This set the stage very early for a militarism whose development remains unimpeded even today.

Hiroshima-Nagasaki shock. When Kim Il-sung was active as a guerrilla fighter, he lamented the fact that he and his comrades did not have enough guns and grenades, and he was awed by the military might of the imperial army of Japan. He thought that the Japanese military, which was able to attack the United States at Pearl Harbor, was indeed invincible. But such a military power had to surrender almost instantly to the nuclear bombs dropped on Hiroshima and Nagasaki in 1945. Judging by Kim Il-sung's remarks in his writings, he must have been shocked by the force of the bombs. It is not far-fetched to infer from this that the North Korean nuclear program may have started as early as in the late 1950s, when Kim solidified his leadership, and that the program has been nurtured ever since. In fact, during the 1950s and 1970s, Pyongyang sent scores of scientists to Moscow for long periods of study and established Soviet scientists in residence in North Korea in order to contribute to the development of North Korea's indigenous nuclear science and technology.

Juche's **self-defense.** The ideology of *juche* was initially prompted by the passionate desire on the part of Kim Il-sung for keeping the country from repeating its experience under Japanese colonialism. When the Japanese colonial power was removed, it did not take much time for the Korean War (which began in 1950) to introduce yet another "imperialistic" power that occupied the southern half of the nation and posed a constant threat to the peninsula's security.

Juche was Kim Il-sung's response to this string of foreign ambitions and dominations. It was natural that *juche* started out as a doctrine of antiforeignism and self-defense. For self-defense, the ideological preparedness was not enough; as Kim Il-sung used to say, "a soldier without a gun is a straw man [puppet]." When he criticized South Korea, he always aimed his condemnation at Seoul's dependence on the U.S. security umbrella. Although *juche* developed a diverse set of ideological properties over time, the backbone of its philosophical premises has always been military self-defense: "You must have a nation before working on its prosperity." The much-used notion of a revolutionary struggle must also be seen in the ideological light of protecting the nation from imperial forces and achieving national unification as a sovereign and integrated nation-state rather than in terms of the realization of a Marxist proletarian classless society.

INTERMEDIATE ORIGINS

Demise of the Communist bloc as a support system. Until the early 1970s, North Korea maintained a level of economic development that was superior to that of South Korea. This was possible in part because of economic, technological, and military assistance from the Soviet Union, China, and, to a lesser degree, the Eastern European countries with which Pyongyang had maintained trade and diplomatic relations. The 1970s, though, marked the onset of a series of alarming changes for North Korea, beginning with the deepening rift between the two superpowers of China and the Soviet Union and the ensuing demise of the socialist countries in Europe, Eventually the fall of East Germany as it was absorbed into the West caused extreme alarm among the North Korean leadership. Kim Il-sung attributed this massive change in the world political landscape to the lack of solidarity and ideological cohesiveness on the part of the socialists, and he began to tighten up political education and accelerate his military buildup.

Encirclement by enemies. While North Korea was losing its international support system, South Korea was allied with the United States and Japan. By the end of 1980s, South Korea had become a formidable economic power in the region and the world and had staged a hugely successful Summer Olympic Games in 1988. Furthermore, the U.S.-South Korea joint military exercise (Team Spirit) that took place annually in South Korea was regarded by the North Korean leadership as a warning that the country could be attacked at any time. Reminding themselves of the devastation of the Korean War in which the U.S. air assault virtually flattened Pyongyang and other major cities, they began creating bomb shelters. The subway system in Pyongyang, which extends some 34 kilometers and is 100 meters in depth on average, was designed as a massive bomb shelter for the two million residents of that city. In addition, it is believed that virtually every town is equipped with similarly secure shelters. This sense of fear of the threat of a U.S.-backed South Korea accelerated the development of the nuclear weapons program.

Legitimacy war with the South. Since the inception of the political system in 1948 and especially since the Korean War (1950–53), the divided Koreas have constantly engaged in a competition over legitimacy for ruling the entire peninsula. An unmistakable reminder of this competition is the fact that each of the Koreas officially (constitutionally, in fact) claims to be the sole legitimate regime. As it became evident that the North could no longer compete with the South on economic terms, the North began to see a clear advantage in its ideas of national sovereignty and self-defense. In advocating nationalism vis-à-vis the South, nothing proved handier than the North's. *juche* and its doctrine of military self-preparedness.

IMMEDIATE ORIGINS

Death of Kim Il-sung and consolidation of military. The abrupt death of Kim Il-sung in July 1994 meant a profound turning point for North Korea in many ways, none more important than Kim Jong-il's succession to power. When the senior Kim held control, the young Kim was primarily responsible for the ideology and propaganda functions of the Korean Workers' Party. The military at that time was still in the hands of members of the "old guard," such as Marshall O Jin-u; but Marshall O died in February 1995, one year after Kim Il-sung.

The young Kim was left with the huge task of consolidating the military under his control. Upon assuming leadership, he never neglected to pay attention to the army, as his almost exclusive visits ("on-the-spot guidance") to the military barracks attest. At the same time, he worked on replacing the old guard with young soldiers loyal to him. In this process of leadership consolidation, Kim Jong-il devised a strategy, and that strategy came in the form of *songun*. This new doctrine gave him a new version of legitimacy and the rationale required for restructuring the military elite. Kim Jong-il's strategic move was also necessitated by his need to prevent the possibility of a military coup d'état.

Need for solidification of political power. Once the military was consolidated under his leadership, Kim Jong-il never overlooked the importance of solidifying political power. This prompted the promulgation of a new constitution in 1998, which was designed to accomplish two separate but related objectives. The first was the creation of Kim Jong-il's own basis of power legitimacy, not by denouncing his father but by deifying him as an eternal, soulful leader of the nation. In the real and unforgiving world of power politics, Kim Jong-il needed his own basis of legitimacy, and he found one in the doctrine of *songun*. This doctrine was embedded in the constitution, as well, because the chair of the Military Commission is elevated to the top of the authority structure. It was envisaged then (just as it is now) that *songun* was and would continue to be Kim Jong-il's legacy. One might note that the testing of the Taepo-dong 2, a multistage long-range missile, was conducted in the same year to tangibly demonstrate this development.

The Bush administration. The election of George W. Bush as president of the United States and his administration's hostile policy toward North Korea became the immediate stimulus that was exploited by Kim Jong-il to provide the rationale for further advancing *songun* politics. Following his inauguration in January 2001, President Bush announced no policy toward the North at all until after the events of 11 September 2001 (nearly eight full months after his inauguration). His administration then promptly dropped all policies that were premised on direct negotiation with North Korea. The Bush administration pronounced its principle of no negotiation with countries that are considered "evil," and Kim Jong-il's North Korea was included in the "axis of evil" along with Iraq and Iran.

Refusing to talk directly with Pyongyang, President Bush opted to pursue a multilateral framework, allowing China to take the leadership role in organizing and hosting the six-party talks to be convened in Beijing for

disarming North Korea. Amid all this, the Kim Jong-il government went ahead with missile tests in July 2006 and ultimately the underground nuclear test in October of the same year. Despite the Bush administration's success in moving the UN Security Council to adopt additional economic sanctions, Pyongyang has not shown any wavering with regard to its nuclear program. This incredible degree of persistence on the part of Pyongyang would not be possible without the pervasive authority and unquestionable legitimacy given the regime by its adoption and advancement of the *songun* doctrine.

Afghanistan and Iraq. When one asks any North Korean about the reason for the U.S. invasion of Afghanistan and Iraq, one will get one answer only: Those countries were invaded because they did not have the military capability to defend themselves. Every North Korean is also likely to offer the view that the United States would not have attempted either invasion if the target country had had nuclear weapons. Setting aside the issue of the credibility of such an answer, it is quite evident that North Koreans believe that it is only the nuclear and military capability of their country that prevents a U.S. invasion. When Bush declared three countries as the axis of evil in 2002 and invaded Iraq in 2003, North Korea did not yet have a nuclear bomb—but it was certainly pressured by the unfolding events to become a legitimate nuclear state at all costs in order to avoid the same fate as Afghanistan and Iraq. In the minds of the public in North Korea, the bomb itself is a product of *songun,* and *songun* will continue to deter U.S. aggression. North Koreans are thoroughly "realist" in that they believe that "the flesh of the weak is eaten by the strong" *(yakyuk kangsik).*

IMPLICATIONS AND RAMIFICATIONS OF *SONGUN*

The above discussion ascertained the nature and characteristic features (properties) of *songun*. It also specified the historical and political context in which *songun* has been articulated and promoted. Now I would like to explore how *songun* has been practiced in political behavior and social life.

3-3-4 PRINCIPLES

Professor K. P. Chon, one of the leading architects of *songun* in North Korea, spelled out clearly the common principles on which *songun* is based:[1]

Three functions of the military. First and foremost, the military must "live and die with *Soryong* to the end."[2] This implies that every soldier's commitment and devotion to the leader is absolute and unconditional. Second, the military will achieve its assigned goals at all costs. Third, the most admirable quality of a soldier lies in the spirit of sacrifice for the greater good, and nothing is greater than being with the leader to defend the nation.

Three objectives for education and training. First, the objective of organization must be followed; that is, individuals are meaningless and considered dead when they are not organized. In a collective system of the North Korean breed, individuals exist only for the group (although similarly, the group exists solely for its members). Second, in the core of behaviors and actions, discipline must find its place. In education and training, the virtue and practice of discipline occupies the center. It is only through this discipline that the "arduous marches" can be won. Third, once again it is unity and solidarity that should never be compromised.

Four virtues of the People's Army. Although this was discussed earlier in this paper, it is important to introduce the slogan of the "four virtues of the People's Army." The first is patriotism to the country; second, love of the nation; third, care for the people; and fourth, devotion to *Soryong*.

SONGUN IN OPERATION

New authority structure. As alluded to earlier, the 1998 constitution itself reflects this *songun* doctrine unambiguously: It places the National Defense Commission firmly at the very center of the government as the repository of all political authority and power. Kim Jong-il was advanced to its chairmanship under Kim Il-sung's leadership on 9 April 1993, some 15 months before the elder Kim's death. This suggests that the senior Kim was paving the way for the junior to have a firm grip on the military during his reign. Yet, the specific ideology of *songun* did not emerge until after the promulgation of the new constitution in 1998.

Economy. *Songun* makes the defense industry the core of the economic structure. In fact, the heavy-industry sector is regarded as the most essential and central to the national economy, followed by light industry and agriculture, which are considered coequally secondary. As a result, the military industry is the only one that brings in foreign revenue. This, Pyongyang's own policy choice, coupled with international economic sanctions and the North's inaccessibility to external investors render the economy in a state of chronic poverty. In this sense, *songun* may have been necessitated by a number of national imperatives, but it has not served the economy of the nation well.

Education. At all levels of education, military training is the backbone of the curriculum. Military education begins with *songun,* which is a required subject for all students. One of the peculiar features in education in the country is the fact that the military itself is referred to as a form of "university." This suggests that people learn in the military just as well as they do at institutions of higher education. This parallels the practice of the "factory-college," whereby workers attain college-level education. These extraordinary "universities" and "colleges" are staffed with commuting professors and experts from the ordinary institutions throughout the country.

The family. The tie between the family and the military is intimate. A family contributing to the military in an extraordinary way is praised by the public and rewarded by the government. When there is more than one member on active duty, the family is rewarded in a variety of tangible ways, such as a larger food ration and additional perquisites regarding other daily necessities. When all children are in the army, the government sends workers to the parents to help them with household chores. If daughters are in the military, the government sends female helpers to the parents. In this way, the family can relate to the military naturally and appreciatively. This is an important way for the government to mobilize grassroots support.

The arts. It is said in North Korea that any form of art lacking an ideological message is useless. The ideological message today is *songun*. New musical creations, including popular songs that herald the military and the *songun* philosophy, have been pouring out in recent years. The People's Army itself created its own musical group called the "*Songun* Chorus"; it is regarded as the very best in the country. The chorus performs regularly for radio and television broadcasts. In this way, even the tone of North Korean music has shifted to one of militarism and revolutionary consciousness, and not necessarily with artistic charm.

Culture. As pointed out earlier in this paper, *songun* is changing the popular culture in North Korea by promoting a set of specific values and norms. These include reverence for the military, military culture, and individual soldiers. Also included in these norms is the notion that it is noble to find pride and self-esteem despite economic hardships; the "arduous march" of life is precious; life in the midst of gunfire is the noblest; and we are living for tomorrow, not for today. In this cultural atmosphere, the leadership contends that there is no room for foreign "decadent" cultural values to slip into the society. During one recent visit to Pyongyang, I came across an anecdote involving a wounded and handicapped soldier who was seeking marriage. Upon learning of this story, hundreds of girls expressed their desire to become this soldier's bride. One can find this attitude only in *songun* North Korea!

Foreign policy. *Songun* politics advances a series of mythical or ideological doctrines. Whether these notions carry any objective credence is irrelevant because both the military leadership and the *songun* theoreticians appear to have great faith in them:

- Foreign policy works when it is accompanied by the barrel of gun. This notion is strikingly and intriguingly similar to the premise upon which current U.S. foreign policy is built.

- North Korea's defiance of U.S. force will popularize "progressive" ideologies and deepen the bonds of friendship among all the "progressive" peoples of the world.
- All those against U.S. "imperialism" must and will unite, and the days of imperialist hegemony are numbered.

Reunification of Korea. The common belief among *songun* followers is that national reunification will be brought about by the force of nationalism, and it is the North that will prevail over the South because its political system is one of nationalism. North Koreans see the South as richer, but not as a legitimate system. They believe that the past two administrations in the South (the administrations of Kim Dae-jung and Roh Moo-hyun) have tilted toward nationalism and, hence, toward the North Korean ideology.

CONCLUDING WORDS

This survey of North Korea's military-first politics suggests that *songun* is much more than a political slogan, and it is more than the simple practice that the military holds all the power and the civilian sector is thus undermined and neglected. It is, in a single phrase, a pervasive philosophical ideology that undergirds the very structure and function of North Korean society. Understanding that fact renders the society intelligible. It is a misconception, for example, that the leadership pushes for weapons programs despite people's dissatisfaction and discontent. It is equally mistaken to conclude that the regime persists only because of its oppressive and brutal military leadership that cracks down to silence any voices of dissent. On the contrary, *songun* is the product of historical and political circumstances unique to North Korea. To the extent that *songun* is pervasive throughout the population and deeply integrated into the mass belief system and the lives of the masses, it is highly improbable that the regime will collapse as a result of internal rebellion.

The analysis offered in this paper is largely based on personal, firsthand observations, and interviews and conversations with North Koreans during my own numerous and frequent trips to North Korea. Although limited references have been consulted, all are from North Korea. Much remains to be done to further document the arguments made herein. The doctrine of *songun* is still being formed, and it is therefore elusive.

REFERENCES CONSULTED

References used for this paper are numerous; most important among these are a number of firsthand interviews and conversations carried out in North Korea, particularly since 1998 when the current constitution was promulgated. The following books have also been consulted:

Kim Bong-ho. 2004. *Widaehan Songun Sidae* [The great *songun* era]. Pyongyang: Pyongyang Publishing House.

Kim Il-sung. 1992–98. *Segi wa Doburo* [With the century]. 8 vols. Pyongyang: Korean Workers' Party Publishing House.

Kim In-ok. 2003. *Kim Jong-il Jangkun:* Songun *Jongchi Yiron* [General Kim Jong-il: Theory of military-first politics]. Pyongyang: Pyongyang Publishing House.

Kim Jong-il. 2005. *Kim Jong-il Sonjip* [Selected works of Kim Jong-il]. Vol. 15. Pyongyang: Korean Workers' Party Publishing House.

Park, Han S. 2002. *North Korea: The Politics of Unconventional Wisdom.* Boulder Colo.: Lynne Rienner Pub.

ENDNOTES

1. K. P. Chon, interview with author, Pyongyang, 23 March 2007.
2. *Soryong* means "supreme commander," and this title is reserved for Kim Il-sung.

THE MAO REGIME

PART 2

By William Theodore De Bary and Richard John Lufrano

THE CULTURAL REVOLUTION

Despite its name, the "Great Proletarian Cultural Revolution" emerged not from the "proletariat" but from a power struggle at the top in which certain leaders, including Mao, sought to enlist the "masses" (especially students) in a campaign against moderate leaders then in control of the Party and state administration. The initial battle cry "To rebel is justified" was taken from an early speech by Mao (see p. 453), but "rebellion" came to mean almost anything, depending on whatever group was activated to engage in generalized "class struggle," and before long the movement deteriorated into an anarchy of cross-purposes and violent infighting.

The *Sixteen Points,* briefly excerpted here, are taken from a decision of the Party Central Committee, engineered by Mao, Lin Biao, and their cohorts in 1966. They are perhaps the closest thing to a coherent statement of Mao's original purposes in attacking "those in authority taking the capitalist road."

THE *SIXTEEN POINTS*: GUIDELINES FOR THE GREAT PROLETARIAN CULTURAL REVOLUTION

1. A New Stage in the Socialist Revolution

The Great Proletarian Cultural Revolution now unfolding is a great revolution that touches people to their very soul and constitutes a new stage in the development of the socialist revolution in our country, a deeper and more extensive stage. ...

Although the bourgeoisie has been overthrown, it is still trying to use the old ideas, culture and customs, and habits of the exploiting classes to corrupt the masses, capture their minds, and endeavor to stage a comeback. The proletariat must do just the opposite: it must meet head-on every challenge of the bourgeoisie in the ideological field and use the new ideas, culture, customs, and habits of the proletariat to change the mental outlook of the whole of society. At present our objective is to struggle against and crush those persons in authority who are taking the capitalist road, to criticize and repudiate the reactionary bourgeois academic "authorities" and the ideology of the bourgeoisie and all other exploiting classes, and transform education, literature, and art and all other parts of the superstructure that do not correspond to the socialist economic base, so as to facilitate the consolidation and development of the socialist system.

2. The Main Current and the Zigzags

The masses of the workers, peasants, soldiers, revolutionary intellectuals, and revolutionary cadres form the main force in this Great Cultural Revolution. Large numbers of revolutionary young people, previously unknown, have become courageous and daring pathbreakers. They are vigorous in action and intelligent.

Through the media of big character posters and great debates, they argue things out, expose and criticize thoroughly, and launch resolute attacks on the open and hidden representatives of the bourgeoisie. ...

Since the Cultural Revolution is a revolution, it inevitably meets with resistance. This resistance comes chiefly from those in authority who have wormed their way into the party and are taking the capitalist road. It also comes from the old force of habit in society. At present, this resistance is still fairly strong and stubborn. However, the Great Proletarian Cultural Revolution is, after all, an irresistible general trend. There is abundant evidence that such resistance will crumble fast once the masses become fully aroused. ...

9. Cultural Revolutionary Groups, Committees, and Congresses

Many new things have begun to emerge in the Great Proletarian Cultural Revolution. The cultural revolutionary groups, committees, and other organizational forms created by the masses in many schools and units are something new and of great historic importance.

These cultural revolutionary groups, committees, and congresses are excellent new forms of organization whereby under the leadership of the Communist Party the masses are educating themselves. They are an excellent bridge to keep our party in close contact with the masses. They are organs of power of the Proletarian Cultural Revolution.

The cultural revolutionary groups, committees, and congresses should not be temporary organizations but permanent, standing mass organizations. They are suitable not only for colleges, schools, government, and other organizations but generally also for factories, mines, and other enterprises, urban districts, and villages.

It is necessary to institute a system of general elections, like that of the Paris Commune, for electing members to the cultural revolutionary groups and committees and delegates to the cultural revolutionary congress.

[Adapted from Selden, *The People's Republic of China*, pp. 550–556]

QUOTATIONS FROM CHAIRMAN MAO ZEDONG

Mao replaced Peng Dehuai as defense minister with Lin Biao, another prominent general who had been with Mao since the early days of the revolution. Lin used his position to turn the army into a bastion of Mao loyalism, employing *Quotations from Chairman Mao*, or the *Little Red Book*, to inculcate the peasant recruits. When the Cultural Revolution started, the Red Guards adopted this book as their "bible," memorized it, and waved it in the air at huge rallies at Tiananmen Square.

—Be resolute, fear no sacrifice, and surmount every difficulty to win victory. [p. 102]

—Thousands upon thousands of martyrs have heroically laid down their lives for the people; let us hold their banner high and march ahead along the path crimson with their blood! [p. 102]

—Whoever wants to know a thing has no way of doing so except by coming into contact with it, that is, by living (practicing) in its environment. ... If you want knowledge, you must take part in the practice of changing reality. If you want to know the taste of a pear, you must change the pear by eating it your self. ... If you want to know the theory and methods of revolution, you must take part in revolution. All genuine knowledge originates in direct experience. [p. 118]

—Unquestionably, victory or defeat in war is determined mainly by the military, political, economic, and natural conditions on both sides. But not by these alone. It is also determined by each side's subjective ability in directing the war. In his endeavor to win a war, a military strategist cannot overstep the limitations imposed by the material conditions; within these limitations, however, he can and must strive for victory. The stage of action for a military strategist is built upon objective material conditions, but on that stage he can direct the performance of many a drama, full of sound and color, power and grandeur. [p. 49]

—Who are our enemies? Who are our friends? This is a question of the first importance for the revolution. The basic reason why all previous revolutionary struggles in China achieved so little was their failure to unite with real friends in order to attack real enemies. A revolutionary party is the guide of the masses, and no revolution ever succeeds when the revolutionary party leads them astray. To ensure that we will definitely achieve success in our revolution and will not lead the masses astray, we must pay attention to uniting with our real friends in order to attack our real enemies. To distinguish real friends from real enemies, we must make a general analysis of the economic status of the various classes in Chinese society and of their respective attitudes toward the revolution. [p. 7]

—Historically, all reactionary forces on the verge of extinction invariably conduct a last desperate struggle against the revolutionary forces, and some revolutionaries are apt to be deluded for a time by this phenomenon of outward strength but inner weakness, failing to grasp the essential fact that the enemy is nearing extinction while they themselves are approaching victory, [pp. 44–45]

[From Schram, *Quotations from Chairman Mao,* pp. 7, 44–45, 49, 102, 118]

WHAT HAVE SONG SHUO, LU PING, AND PENG PEIYUN DONE IN THE CULTURAL REVOLUTION?

The big character posters plastered over the walls of campuses, towns, and cities became a ubiquitous form of expression for those attacking the establishment. The most famous of these posters was put up on May 25, 1966, at Beijing University by Nie Yuanzi and six other philosophy instructors attacking the university authorities. Although the government tried to repress it, Mao had it broadcast on June 1 and the Beijing media carried it the next day. The poster's strident tone characterized writings during the Cultural Revolution.

At present, the people of the whole nation, in a soaring revolutionary spirit that manifests their boundless love for the Party and Chairman Mao and their inveterate hatred for the sinister anti-Party, anti-socialist gang, are making a vigorous and great cultural revolution; they are struggling to thoroughly smash the attacks of the reactionary sinister gang, in defense of the Party's Central Committee and Chairman Mao. But here in Beijing University the masses are being kept immobilized, the atmosphere is one of indifference and deadness, whereas the strong revolutionary desire of the vast number of the faculty members and students has been suppressed. What is the matter? What is the reason? There is something fishy going on. …

Why are you [top Beijing University officials cited in title] so afraid of big character posters and holding of big denunciation meetings? To counterattack the sinister gang that has frantically attacked the Party, socialism, and Mao Zedong's thought is a life-and-death class struggle. The revolutionary people must be fully aroused to denounce them vigorously, and angrily, and to hold big meetings and put up big character posters, is one of the best ways for the masses to do battle. By "guiding" the masses not to hold big meetings, not to put up big character posters, and by creating all kinds of taboos, aren't you suppressing the masses' revolution, not allowing them to make revolution, and opposing their revolution? We will never permit you to do this! …

All revolutionary intellectuals, now is the time to go into battle! Let us unite, holding high the great red banner of Mao Zedong Thought, unite around the Party's Central Committee and Chairman Mao and break down all the various controls and plots of the revisionists; resolutely, thoroughly, totally, and completely wipe out all ghosts and monsters and all Khrashchevian counterrevolutionary revisionists, and carry the socialist revolution through to the end.

Defend the Party's Central Committee!
Defend Mao Zedong Thought!
Defend the dictatorship of the proletariat!

[Adapted from Benton and Hunter, *Wild Lily, Prairie Fire,* pp. 105–108]

RED GUARD MEMOIRS

Although portrayed as a spontaneous movement among students, it is clear from the following account that the initiative came from above and surprised many middle-school and college students who were organized into units known as the Red Guards to form the vanguard of the Cultural Revolution. At massive rallies in Tiananmen Square in Beijing, Mao sanctioned their role in rooting out the "capitalist roaders" in party and government. These developments are reported by a student participant as recorded many years after the actual events.

At a school assembly the working group announced that we were now in revolution, the Cultural Revolution. We finally knew what was happening in our school. The working group then informed us about our new Revolutionary Committee, and asked each class to elect a Cultural Revolutionary Small Group to lead the campaign. … Thus the Cultural Revolution, which lasted ten years, entered my life. Important newspaper articles and Central Party documents were passed to our small group, and we in turn organized the students to study them. We learned that during the seventeen years of Communist Party control, China's culture, art, and education had been under the dictatorial command of "capitalist and revisionist black gangs." Later each student was issued a pamphlet, *Chairman Mao's Comments on Educational Revolution.* …I was astonished to learn that our country was in such bad shape. Until then I hadn't suspected that the songs I sang, the movies I watched, and the books I read were unhealthy. I had thought my school a revolutionary one, maybe too revolutionary. Nevertheless, I swallowed what I was told and didn't raise a single negative question, not even to myself. I had been chosen leader of this revolution in my class. If I had problems in understanding these documents, how could I expect the rest of the class to do so? Besides, what experience and qualifications did I have to judge what Chairman Mao and the Central Committee deemed right and wrong?

My classmates tried to comprehend too. We all considered ourselves progressive youth, and we were determined to follow Chairman Mao and the Party center. If they thought this Cultural Revolution to be necessary, if they wanted us to participate, we would.

[Adapted from Zhai, *Red Flower of China*, pp. 61–62]

The students quickly ignored the call to refrain from violence in the Sixteen Points, *and teachers and intellectuals became one of their main targets. Many were maimed or killed by the students, while others committed suicide rather than face further torture and humiliation. Like the above account, this one was recorded many years after the events described.*

The list of accusations grew longer by the day: hooligans and bad eggs, filthy rich peasants and son-of-a-bitch landlords, bloodsucking capitalists and neo-bourgeoisie, historical counterrevolutionaries and active counter-revolutionaries, rightists and ultra-rightists, alien class elements and degenerate elements, reactionaries and opportunists, counterrevolutionary revisionists, imperialist running dogs, and spies. Students stood in the roles of prosecutor, judge, and police. No defense was allowed. Any teacher who protested was certainly a liar.

The indignities escalated as well. Some students shaved or cut teachers' hair into curious patterns. The most popular style was the yin-yang cut, which featured a full head of hair on one side and a clean-shaven scalp on the other. Some said this style represented Chairman Mao's theory of the "unity of opposites." It made me think of the punishments of ancient China, which included shaving the head, tattooing the face, cutting off the nose or feet, castration, and dismemberment by five horse-drawn carts.

At struggle meetings, students often forced teachers into the "jet-plane" position. Two people would stand on each side of the accused, push him to his knees, pull his head back by the hair, and hold his arms out in back like airplane wings. We tried it on each other and found it caused great strain on the back and neck.

[Adapted from Gao Yuan, *Born Red*, pp. 53–54]

WANG XIZHE, LI ZHENGTIAN, CHEN YIYANG, GUO HONGZHI: "THE LI YI ZHE POSTER," NOVEMBER 1974

By 1968 it was clear that the Cultural Revolution had spun out of control, and Mao brought in the army to bring it to a halt. Thousands of young people whom Mao had a short time ago called upon to make revolution were now slaughtered by the military; millions more were sent down to the countryside to "learn from the peasants." Yet in the midst of the chaos of the Cultural Revolution what came to be known as the Thinking Generation had been born. Unable to find reliable guidance in the vague sayings of Mao, some Red Guards turned toward the works of Marx, Engels, and Lenin to discover the true nature of socialism. The wall poster put up in Guangzhou in 1974 and excerpted below reflects Marx's ideas about the role of democracy in a socialist society as well as the original goals of the Cultural Revolution as stated in the Sixteen Points. Notions of the party's responsibilities to the people expressed here would blossom in the "Democracy Wall" or "Beijing Spring" movement of the late seventies and early eighties. "Li Yi Zhe" is a composite pen name consisting of characters from three of four joint authors, one of whom, Wang Xizhe, went on to play a prominent role in that movement.

Expectations for the Fourth National People's Congress

How is the soon-to-be-convoked Fourth National People's Congress going to reflect the Great Cultural Revolution, which people call China's "second revolution"? Law is the expression of the will of the ruling class. So how is the country's basic legal system that is to be promulgated—the new constitution—to express the will of the proletariat and the broad masses in China who have experienced the Great Cultural Revolution?

What are the popular masses thinking now? What are their demands? What sort of expectations do they have for the representative congress of the "people of the whole country"?

Legal System, Yes! A "System of Rites," No!

Our country was born from a semi-feudal, semi-colonial society into socialism. The traditions formed by several thousands of years of feudal despotism stubbornly maintain their strong hold over thought, culture, education, law, and virtually every other sphere of the superstructure. ...

Under the conditions of proletarian dictatorship, how can the people's rights, under the centralized leadership of the Party, be protected in the struggle against the capitalist roaders and incorrect lines in the Party? This is the big topic facing the Fourth National People's Congress.

Needless to say, the Party's leadership should carefully listen to the masses' opinions, and it should be needless to note the people's own rights to implement revolutionary supervision over all levels of the Party's leadership. It is even more unnecessary to say that rebelling against the capitalist roaders is justified. Even

though the masses' opinion might be incorrect or excessive, or even if they become discontented because of misunderstanding certain Party policies, is it justified to implement a policy of "suppress if persuasion fails and arrest if suppression fails"? Moreover, the fragrant flower and the poisonous weed, correct and incorrect, and revolutionary and counterrevolutionary, are not always easy to distinguish. It takes a long process and has to stand the test of time. Therefore, we should not be frightened by an open and honorable opposition so long as it observes discipline and plays no tricks and engages in no conspiracy.

The Fourth National People's Congress should enact regulations clearly in black and white that ... will ... protect all the democratic rights rightfully belonging to the masses.

Limitation of Special Privileges

We are not Utopian socialists. We recognize that in the present stage of our society there exist various types of differences, which cannot be completely destroyed by a decree alone. However, the law of the development of a socialist revolutionary movement should not itself widen these differences but eliminate them, above all prohibit such differences from expanding into economic and political privileges. Special privilege itself is fundamentally in opposition to the interests of the people. Why should we avoid condemning such privileges? ... The Fourth National People's Congress should enact, in black and white, clauses limiting special privileges.

Guaranteeing the People's Right to Manage the Country and Society

"Who has given us our power?" The people have. Our cadres should not become officials and behave like lords, but should be servants of the people. But power can corrupt people most easily. When a person's status changes, it is most effective to test whether he is working for the interests of the majority or the minority. Whether he can maintain his spirit to serve the people depends, apart from his own diligence, mainly on the revolutionary supervision of the masses. And the mass movement is the richest source of the maintenance of the revolutionary spirit of the revolutionaries.

How should the masses' right of revolutionary supervision over the Party's and country's various levels of leadership be determined? And how should it be clearly established that when certain cadres (especially high-level cadres of the central organs) lose the trust of the broad masses of people, the people "can replace them any time"?

The Fourth National People's Congress should answer these questions.

[Adapted from Chan, Rosen, and Unger, *On Socialist Democracy*, pp. 74–80]

Excerpts from *Voices from the Whirlwind*

By Feng Jicai

FOREWORD

What follows are heart-breaking, yet ever so instructive declarations, memories, avowals; narrative presentations of life as it was lived in a great nation going through a terrible moral and political crisis. What follows, too, is history as it can be evoked and portrayed from the bottom up, so to speak—not the history of big-shot politicians and generals, not the history of historians either, but rather the history of ordinary men and women who suddenly, out of nowhere it seemed, did indeed feel the anxiety and pain, the continual terror that arrived in the name of a "Cultural Revolution;" a "whirlwind" for sure; so much swept away, so much shaken and buffeted, tossed about and torn apart.

As one reads these remembrances, one yet again realizes that our lives are not given shape only by the early childhood we happen to live, or even the particular social and economic world we inherit from our parents and grandparents. A nation's ups and downs, its political history, can become the ruling force upon the lives of thousands, millions of men, women, children—and, in some cases, can become instruments of terror and genocide. Because a "Cultural Revolution" took place, all sorts of human beings joined the ranks of the insulted and the injured, the scorned and the rebuked, their lives significantly changed—in some cases irreparably changed, and alas, in some cases, ended.

Those who speak in the pages that follow survived, though with minds that surely struggle hard, day and night, to put aside one central evil: what leaders who abuse power can do to their own people in the name of ideology. Here was a nightmare not unique to any country or continent; here was meanness and abusiveness become a national craziness: hysterical and cruel accusations and intimidations, lies and more lies, rumors turned into the clubs of vilification and even murder. Whole families, we get to know, were wrongfully arraigned or hunted down, and often enough, convicted of imaginary crimes, victims of a spell of out-and-out political madness that got turned into the everyday, wanton persecution of the innocent by the all too self-serving and self-aggrandizing—a nation's scandal and its shame.

Yet, amid such awful circumstances, amid so much wrongdoing and evil, amid a kind of panic and wickedness of vast proportions, and for a while, of seemingly endless duration, any number of vulnerable men and women and children managed to survive—not only survive in body, but in mind and soul. The "Cultural Revolution" was at heart a crazed, wanton assault on one part of a country's people by another part—an effort of some to frighten and intimidate others, to drive them into a land of fear and trembling, to use accusation in hopes that endless self-accusation would follow. The blind attempted to blind others (ideology run amok results in a loss of vision, a descent into the hell of slogans, clichés, rituals, rote exercises in surrender to anyone and everyone). Still, some kept their vision, saw clearly the lunatic excesses of their countrymen, whether in high or low places, and kept their eyes on what mattered, on a future they could only hope would come sooner rather than later. These "oral histories" are testimony to that kind of visionary survival: a moral and psychological triumph of enormous significance.

As I read these personal stories, each with its own losses and hurts to report, its own endurance and courage and resourcefulness to chronicle, I realized what totalitarianism can come to mean in the life of a nation, a people: the loss of all respect for the personal dignity of the individual; the constant hectoring through state-owned radio and television; the use of rumor, innuendo, gossip, and lies of all sorts as a means of scaring people, destroying their sense of their worth, their rights as human beings; and finally, the hounding of those people, the arrests and arraignments, the threats and beatings and denunciations and jailings.

Here is the social and political reality that writers such as Kafka only imagined: stories of a world gone cruelly wild; but stories, too, of resiliency, of endurance, of extraordinary courage demonstrated against the worst odds imaginable. We are lucky to know the people who appear in this book; their stories have much to teach us, not only about them, but about us; their unlucky fate and our enormous good fortune to be spared, so far, such a fate.

—Robert Coles Cambridge, Massachusetts 1990

KEY FIGURES DURING THE CULTURAL REVOLUTION

CHEN YUN Member of the Standing Committee of the Communist Party (CCP) Politburo (1956–1966); Vice-Chairman of the Central Committee of the CCP (1978).

DENG XIAOPING Secretary General of the CCP (1956–1966); Vice-Premier of the State Council (1973); Vice-Chairman of the Central Committee (1975, 1977).

THE GANG OF FOUR Jiang Qing, the wife of Mao Zedong and Politburo member (1973–1976); **Wang**

Hongwen, former textile mill worker who became Vice-Chairman of the CCP in 1973; **Yao Wenyuan**, editor at the Shanghai *Liberation Daily*, who became a Politburo member in 1973; and **Zhang Qunqiao**, secretary of CCP Shanghai Municipal Committee who became a Politburo member in 1973, then Vice-Premier of the State Council in 1975.

LIN BIAO Vice-Chairman of the Military Commission of the Central Committee of the CCP, and minister of defense (1959–1971).

LIU SHAOQI Chairman of the People's Republic of China (1959–1966).

MAO ZEDONG Chairman of the Central Committee of the CCP.

PENG ZHEN Mayor of Beijing.

ZHOU ENLAI Premier of the State Council.

CHRONOLOGY OF EVENTS

1957

- *February–April:* Mao Zedong advocates rapprochement with non-Party intellectuals and invites them to criticize the "bureaucracy, sectarianism, and subjectivism" plaguing the CCP.

- *May–June:* In the face of strident criticism and challenges to the CCP's authority by intellectuals, Mao and the Central Committee call for a crackdown, resulting in the "Antirightist" movement.

- *Winter:* The "Antirightist" movement climaxes when more than 550,000 intellectuals are labeled "Rightists"; many are forced to leave their positions in the cities to work on farms in the country.

1958

- *August:* The Great Leap Forward. The CCP initiates a plan to increase the nation's industrial and agricultural production by abolishing private plots and organizing people's communes throughout rural China.

1959–1962

- Agricultural production falls short of exaggerated estimates, and a nationwide famine hits China. An estimated 30 million people die of famine-related causes.

1965

- *November:* In a newspaper article generally regarded as the spark that sets off the Cultural Revolution, Yao Wenyuan criticizes *The Dismissal of Hai Rui from Office*, a play by Wu Han, vice-mayor of Beijing. Despite Mao's endorsement of Yao's essay, Beijing newspapers decline to publish it.

1966

- The Cultural Revolution begins. Mao decries the bureaucratization and stagnation in the CCP, blaming officials who are taking the "capitalist road." Lin Biao, in an attempt to improve his own position in the CCP hierarchy, incites blind idolization of Mao among the people.
- *June 1:* An editorial, "Sweep Away All Monsters," appears in *The People's Daily*, urging people to purge bourgeois ideology from the cultural sphere. Beijing's mayor, Peng Zhen, is ousted, along with Luo Ruiqing, vice-premier and Army chief of staff; Lu Dingyi, Politburo member and director of propaganda; and Yang Shangkun, member of the Central Committee.
- *August 8:* The Party Central Committee issues a sixteen-point directive calling on the people to guard against counterrevolutionary subversion. The Red Guards—radical students devoted to Mao—are organized to safeguard the revolution, resulting in widespread violence. Intellectuals are persecuted and tortured; some commit suicide. Millions are sent to rural areas to be reformed through labor.
- Lin Biao is designated Mao's heir apparent.

1967

- *January:* "The January Storm." Rebels in Shanghai seize power from Party organs. Red Guard organizations throughout China follow suit, ousting Party and government officials. A New Year's Day editorial in *The People's Daily* calls for a coalition of workers and peasants to overthrow the heads of factories, mines, and rural areas. In the ensuing months, revolutionary committees are established, replacing Party committees and government agencies at all levels.
- The CCP Central Committee, Military Committee, and State Council call on the People's Liberation Army (PLA) to support "Left workers and peasants," and institute military control and training.
- *Summer:* The PLA is ordered to disband all "counterrevolutionary organizations." Scores of civilians and soldiers are killed.

1968

- *December 22:* *The People's Daily* publishes Mao's directive for educated young people to "go to the countryside" for reeducation by "the poor and lower-middle peasants." Thousands of students respond to the call.

1968–1969

- According to Mao's directive of 7 May 1968, farm schools—the May Seventh Cadre Schools—are established throughout the country, where Red Guard cadres, government officials, as well as suspected "bad elements" are sent for ideological reeducation through manual labor. Liu Shaoqi, the deposed chairman of the People's Republic, is among those sent away. He dies in prison in 1969.

1971

- *September 13:* Suspected of plotting an attempt on Mao's life, Lin Biao flees China with his wife and son. All three are reportedly killed in an airplane crash in Mongolia.

1972

- *February:* Richard Nixon visits China, signaling the beginning of normalized Sino-U.S. relations.

1976

- *January 8:* Premier Zhou Enlai dies.
- *April 5:* During the Qingming Festival (a memorial festival for the dead) in Tiananmen Square, spontaneous mass demonstrations honoring the memory of Zhou Enlai and denouncing the Gang of Four are violently suppressed.
- *April 7:* The Tiananmen Square incident is declared "a counterrevolutionary political incident." Deng Xiaoping is denounced as the instigator and stripped of power.
- *September 9:* Mao Zedong dies.
- *October 6:* The Gang of Four is arrested, marking the end of the Cultural Revolution.
- *December 5:* Those persecuted for their opposition to the Gang of Four are declared "rehabilitated" by the CCP Central Committee.

THEY WHO HAVE SUFFERED GREATLY

- TIME: 1969
- AGE: 17
- SEX: Male
- OCCUPATION: *Deputy company commander of a state farm in H Province*[1]

I'm thirty-four years old. I was fourteen when the Cultural Revolution began and twenty-four when it ended. You're probably thinking I'm not like the people whose hair had turned completely gray by the end of the Cultural Revolution, or the ones who, even though they were just past fifty, had lost the best years of their lives and just threw in the towel. I seem to be doing OK, right? But even if I live to be seventy, I'll still feel I packed a whole lifetime's worth of living into those ten years.

If I told you everything, it would take days, so I'll give you a very condensed account, OK?

I'll focus on my experience in Heilongjiang.[2] Before then I was in school, and though I had plenty of thoughts and feelings there, they were nothing compared to the ones I had in Heilongjiang, out in the real world. I like literature because it's taught me how to understand myself and others, and informed me about society and life. But I hate literature too, because it makes me understand things too well, and that makes my mental burden even heavier.

I often wonder why going down to the countryside back then means so much to me and my generation. It wasn't just the physical labor, it was the way our fates became tied up with society, politics, economics, and culture during the Going to the Countryside Movement,[3] all set against the specific historical background of the Cultural Revolution. While each of us went through completely different experiences, each of us also represents the process of growing up in that time. Is it OK to say that? It's not overstating things, right? That's my feeling, anyway.

I was class of '68. The Cultural Revolution came in my first year of junior high school. You could say I knew what was what then, and you could also say I didn't know a thing. I was born into an ordinary workers' family. My father got TB before Liberation[4] and was going to die, and the boss fired him. Fortunately, Liberation came, and the state paid to send him to the hospital and cure him. It's no lie to say that the new society gave him a new lease on life. My mother's family was relatively well-off. Her first husband had gotten sick and died. After Liberation my father and mother both worked in a tailoring cooperative run by the neighborhood committee. My father could read, and taught classes. My mother taught tailoring to women just starting to work outside the home. They fell in love. My mother's brother was a capitalist who violently opposed my mother's second marriage because my father was poor. She followed her heart and married him anyway. First they had me, then my little sister. Our lives were hard. My uncle lived in a house with a courtyard just north of us. Whenever my mother went over, they were always on guard, in case she was coming to borrow money. In all those years, they never helped us out once. Whenever we kids went there to play, they always thought we were going to steal something because we were poor, and managed to find an excuse to get rid of us.

When the Cultural Revolution started, my uncle the capitalist was a "monster,"[5] of course, and his house was ransacked and all his property taken away. Life was hard for him, since he was used to living comfortably. Every month my mother managed to scrape together some money to give them. Though I was young at the time, I had a deep understanding of life. Nowadays you'd say I knew the way things were. That's why I had great respect for my parents. They were honest and kind people.

Considering my circumstances, would you think I'd have any problems loving the Party, the new society, or Chairman Mao? But it wasn't nearly that simple. When the Cultural Revolution began, all the students wanted to join the Red Guards.[6] However, it seemed there was a problem with my grandfather. What was it? Before Liberation, he had been a tax collector in a small town in Yunnan. When he and his boss were on their way to the provincial capital on business he was shot in the leg by some arms smugglers and bled to death. After Liberation, in response to my father's application to join the Party, they went to my grandfather's mother to investigate the situation. The old lady still thought in the old way and, because she was afraid people would look down on our family for being poor, she said, "My son made hundreds of yuan a month, he was a bureau chief there, rolling in money!" The Party man didn't believe her and said, "If your son made so much money, then, before Liberation, why did your grandson [my father] get so sick he almost died?" The old lady couldn't answer. So there was no way to settle my grandfather's status and the Party didn't have the money to go down to Yunnan and conduct an investigation on behalf of an ordinary guy like my dad, so the case was never resolved. And it continued to have an impact right up to my joining the Red Guards and the Party.

Looking back now, you'll think it's funny. But at the time I could only join the Mao Zedong Thought Outer Red Guards. At that time, Red Guards were divided into three classes. First-class citizens, the children of high-ranking cadres,[7] became Maoist Red Guards. Second-class citizens, the children of workers or poor and lower middle-class peasants, became Mao Zedong Thought Red Guards. The third group was made up of those who weren't from the five black categories[8] but weren't very pure either: They joined the Mao Zedong Thought Outer Red Guards, who weren't the objects of attack but of efforts to integrate them into the revolution. My sense of self-respect was hurt; I felt my enthusiasm for Mao and the Party was equal to anyone else's. But because of our different status, we weren't allowed to take part in certain activities, such as struggle sessions,[9] searching homes and confiscating things, and other important political actions. There was no way I could go along, and this really upset me. Originally I was class monitor, then overnight I was out. I was bursting to prove my devotion to the cause.

In 1969, when the call came to go to the countryside, I was the first to sign up and the first to put up a big-character poster,[10] asking to go to Inner Mongolia where living conditions were the hardest. At that time there were two options: In Heilongjiang you'd be sent to a state farm[11] and have the wages and benefits of a worker; in Inner Mongolia you'd be part of a production team[12] and treated as a peasant. I wanted to show that although I was an Outer Red Guard, I had just as much political consciousness as the rest of them. My family was behind me too. At that time, there wasn't a bit of coercion involved. The Chairman said youth should unite with workers, peasants, and soldiers! The thinking back then was that clear-cut and resolute. Now, though, it would probably be called ludicrously simple.

That move of mine set things in motion and got lots of people to sign up. But the school did something odd, and assigned me, who had signed up so eagerly, to Heilongjiang instead. Maybe it was a kind of reward, or maybe it was a tactic to get others to rush to sign up voluntarily instead of being ordered to go. Our three junior high classes and three high school classes, some 120 students in all, were organized into one company and sent to a state farm. I won't mention its name. They made me deputy company commander because, aside from the fact that I'd been the first to sign up, I'd been a class monitor and had some organizational ability. For instance, I wrote well and could speak in public. We were going to set out on August 16, but on the night of the fifteenth I suddenly developed a fever. Even the doctor never imagined that I would have an allergic reaction to the penicillin skin test he gave me. The safety coefficient of the test should be very high—probably not even one out of several ten thousands are at risk, and it had to be me. I immediately went into shock; my blood pressure dropped to twenty. That was a close call. They struggled frantically to save me, and I made it. When people from my school and others who had come from the state farm asked me if I could go, I said of course I could, even if I had to be carried on a stretcher. That's what my attitude was like then. The next afternoon, August 16, when I was helped onto the train by my family, my head was burning. I'd had a shot and packed some medicine and that's how I went.

Going to the Countryside then was completely different from what it was like later. It was voluntary then, and only later were people forced to go. Very few cried. I remember the scene perfectly: The station was filled with people seeing everybody off with drums and gongs. Of course some people did shed tears. But there was no sense of banishment, just the natural feelings when family members parted. The students on the train all helped each other out—everybody was chummy. By then there was no more distinction among Maoist Red Guards, Mao Zedong Thought Red Guards, and Mao Zedong Thought Outer Red Guards. We sang or recited quotes from Mao and shouted slogans all the way. The train was really alive with singing and dancing. For the great majority of us, it was the first time we'd ridden on a train in our lives. It was refreshing to watch the beauty of the landscape of our motherland along the way. It made us feel even more strongly that this was the only road for educated youth to take. That's the way we thought.

When we got to the Great Northern Wilderness, the first problem we faced was that working conditions were too harsh. The first real, direct challenge was survival itself. We very seldom ate flour or rice. Mostly we got so-called cornmeal and stuff, and every now and then they'd give us a little white flour, but very, very seldom. And the food was rationed. Every month we got thirty jin of meal,[13] but the work was so strenuous it wasn't nearly enough. Sometimes we were so hungry we couldn't stand it. We'd run over to the stables and steal the bean cakes they used for fodder. Strong guys like us could eat two jin in one meal when we were working. Working with empty stomachs, we got tired easily. The more tired we got, the hungrier we'd be, and the hungrier we were, the harder it was to get full—it was a vicious cycle. We had to get up every morning at three or four, and we worked till dark.

The farm had paddy fields, and its levels of mechanization was extremely low. All the tilling, sowing, and reaping had to be done manually. People were the machines. In the northwest, you prepare for planting in May, and first you have to till the land. For that you had to wear shorts, and on top you wore a cotton-padded jacket. Although the ice on top was completely melted and the water was only just over ten centimeters deep, the ground beneath was all mud and ice, and your feet got all cut up. I don't know if it was the ice or the cold water, but with the wind on top of that, your legs froze and the skin was covered with little cuts. One year I went home after spring planting. When my mother saw that the whole lower half of my body was covered with cuts, she felt so bad she cried. We didn't let the girls go into the water. When we boys did the planting we weren't allowed to wear boots for fear we'd trample the ground, so we had to go barefoot. At that time nobody was crazy about the idea, so we platoon leaders and company commanders had to take the lead. We'd work for a while and when we couldn't stand it any longer, we'd climb out, take a few swigs of "white lightning," and go back in.

Now, I don't even know what the hell we were thinking of back then. The day before yesterday I found a letter I wrote at the time. As soon as you read it you'll understand what it was all about in those days. This was a letter to my father, and of course it was a personal family letter.[14]

September 15, 1969

LONG LIVE CHAIRMAN MAO

Hi Dad!

I got your letter and have read it carefully. I'd like to share a few of my own thoughts with you below, and hope you'll criticize and correct my errors.

At the Tenth Plenary Session of the Eighth Central Committee of the Communist Party, our great leader Chairman Mao brilliantly pointed out that on the basis of Marxist-Leninist theory on class and class struggle, the "four existences"[15] would remain during the entire transition period in a socialist society. He stressed that we must discuss the "two-line struggle"[16] every year, every month, every day.

What you mentioned in your letter was a reflection of "two-line struggle." It's the uninterrupted pursuit of this kind of struggle that keeps our Party vigorous, for it strengthens the Party and promotes the progress of history. Chairman Mao said, "A momentary setback does not represent universal laws of history." Dad, you must not only struggle resolutely against certain bourgeois ill winds, but also be mentally prepared for long-term struggle, and stand a little higher, look a little farther.

Chairman Mao teaches us that we should believe in the masses and the Party, and I think you should completely rely on the Party, and accept the Party's guidance and teachings and truthfully report any problems you encounter in daily life to the next level of Party organization, without watering them down at all. Dad, we should be willing to sacrifice everything to defend Chairman Mao's revolutionary line. Chairman Mao's revolutionary line will surely prevail!

Also, a new revolutionary committee has been established in my province. The Central Committee was directly in charge of Heilongjiang and ferreted out X, exposed and criticized his terrible crimes, and launched an antirevisionism and rectification movement. Revolution is in full swing, X was guilty of four major crimes. He was:

1. A shameless traitor
2. A loyal running dog[17] of the KMT[18]
3. A counterrevolutionary revisionist
4. A chief culprit in opposing the Party and trying to take over the military

They've now begun a political examination of my application to join the Party. The branch secretary and other officials have come to talk with me and help me several times. I'm now in the process of intensifying my study to have a better understanding of the Party and truly join the Party in my heart. There are many intellectuals in the company, and hence many problems. I want to constantly strengthen my ideological reform and endeavor to season myself so that I will become a person who will give Chairman Mao no worries.

Take care of your health, Dad!

Long live the success of Chairman Mao's revolutionary line!

Your son,

XX

P.S. I received the things you asked my classmate to bring. P.P.S. It's harvest time already and we're busy again. And it's beginning to get cold here.

Don't you think that letter's weird? That's how we students wrote back then. Every last one of us. And those things weren't written for outsiders, but for our own families. Revolution became part of everything.

Then something I'd never expected happened. Damn it—my little sister was raped.

It was the worst blow of my life. To this day my mother doesn't even know about it. My sister's husband—when you write about this be as vague as you can. Whatever you do, don't let them figure it out. If my mother learned about it now it would kill her. This is the biggest secret weighing on my heart.

It was the winter of 1970. Company members started taking turns to go back and visit their families. I didn't go—I had to take care of a whole pile of stuff involving the whole company, I was a cadre, so I had to be extra strict with myself when it came to my own needs and let others go first. It was at that time that I suddenly got a letter from my father. My little sister went to the countryside in 1969. She was too young, and she was sent to Hebei Province so she'd be closer to home and easier to look after. … Don't mention which county or farm. My father's letter was really a bolt from the blue. He said my sister had been raped by one of the production brigade's bookkeepers. At that time my sister was very active politically; she'd been named a county-level activist for the study of Mao's works and we often exchanged letters and encouragement. The news literally tore me up. My thoughts turned at once to how my sister was, how desperate, how sad! I didn't want anyone else to know, and I didn't dare cry out loud, I just muffled my sobs in my blankets at night, I was really afraid she would commit suicide. To tell the truth, she was just a girl, not yet sixteen. Though at the time I only had a vague idea of the facts of life, I could imagine that it must have destroyed her. I decided to ask for leave to go home, to see my parents, but mainly to rush to see my sister. I knew how much she needed me!

At that time, I decided to have my sister transfer to where I was. Just before I left I talked the matter with the head of the farm's revolutionary committee and gave him the letter to read. That leader was a pretty good guy. He expressed his sympathy on the spot, and said that as long as they would let her go, we could take care of it. But if they said no, it would be difficult. It seemed I had someone I could count on.

When I got home, my father and I went to see my sister. Of course we kept my mother in the dark about it. My mother's health wasn't good, and if she'd found out, it would definitely have made her worse.

My father told me the details of my sister's situation. What had happened? She lived in a small room all by herself, very close to the bookkeeper's house. That bookkeeper was in his thirties, and had a wife and kids. The first time he forced his way in at night, my sister fought him, but how could she fight against such a big, strong man? Afterward she didn't dare tell anyone. I understand. She was so young, all alone, without a single relative there with her. How was she to know what to do? She thought about dying, but didn't want to if her family would be in the dark about why. She was torn. But a few days later he came again, that bookkeeper. After the second time, my sister truly couldn't take it anymore, and she went and told a commune leader. The commune notified my father, who didn't know what to do either, so he wrote and told me.

When I saw my sister—to tell the truth, even now it makes me very sad to talk about it, and it was even sadder then. So I tried my best to convince my sister, whatever you do, don't kill yourself, it's not your fault.

My sister was staying with the chairwoman of the Women's Federation then. She was just lying there when we came in, and as soon as she saw me she buried her head and started crying. She was too young, just turned fifteen. I wanted to go and have it out with the man, one on one. So what if we both died? My father held me back. I ran over to the commune leaders and demanded that they punish him severely, and they agreed.

I took my sister home, and of course I told her, "Whatever you do, don't let Mom find out." I said, "I'll definitely get you out of there. As soon as I get back, I'll fix it up for you. Our leaders have all agreed. While you're at home, don't you dare think of doing anything foolish, because if anything happens you've got me to answer to."

A few days later I went back to my sister's commune to ask about the procedure for her transfer, and to demand again that they deal with that bookkeeper. Actually, they never touched him, even afterward. In the countryside, the bookkeepers control the finances, and they're tight with the production brigade cadres, local tyrants, every one of them! As far as I know, they haven't dealt with him to this day. You think I should go back again now? It'd be even more useless than it was then! It's been over ten years; too much time has passed.

That trip home I stayed over ten days in all, but not one of them was spent sitting idle. On a broken-down bicycle, I visited the homes of over a hundred boys and girls in our company. Sometimes I would find the house, but everyone would be at work, so I'd have to go back later. I was a company leader, wasn't I? I just wanted to let the parents know what was going on with their children, keep them from worrying. We were all so young and so far away from home, so what parents wouldn't worry? My mother was very concerned about me and complained that she never saw me. But it was my responsibility to do those things, especially when I looked at my sister and was reminded of other people's families.

My sister couldn't eat, and every night she screamed and cried in her sleep. She lost a lot of weight and became extremely skinny, and her face lost all its color. My mother could tell something was wrong, but she never imagined, what was really going on. Later I transferred my sister to where I was. I was sure that once she was with me she'd be fine. But somehow rumors started spreading. It went all around that my sister was a girl of questionable morals who had only moved there because she couldn't stay any longer where she had been. I can't say whether the rumors were started by the person who handled her transfer. It would have been all right if people had known what really happened, but the rumors had reached the point where I couldn't very well have explained the truth—that would have ended up just digging her in deeper. The girls in particular looked askance at my sister, and she gradually sensed it. She couldn't explain; all she could do was work harder and make strict demands on herself in every area. She rose to the top in both work and study—she cut a mu[19] and a half of wheat for every mu others cut and still couldn't make advanced worker. She tried time after time to get into the Youth League[20] but never made it; the girl comrades wouldn't vote for her because they always had the nagging suspicion that she was a bad girl who wouldn't have moved there unless she'd done something wrong. Somebody even asked the Party organization to investigate her history. The Party knew perfectly well what her situation was but didn't dare tell anyone. They were afraid it would be too shameful for my sister. Life is full of contradictions. People toss off cutting remarks over the littlest things, saying things like "you dirty so-and-so," "tramp," "slut," stuff like that. Sometimes my sister would come find me at night. We'd go walking in the bumpy, overgrown fields and she'd always cry. I never imagined that the move would be so hard for her. I felt like crying too, but I held back my tears. Away from our parents, I had a responsibility to her, and wouldn't my crying just hurt her? So I tried to give her some encouragement. I told her how our father was orphaned in his teens and how hard it had been for him to bring up his younger brother and sister, how our aunt had nearly been tricked into the whorehouse. "Anything can happen in life," I said, "but we have to go on living! What's more, we're better off than so many others, far better off than those living among the peasants in the production teams. And gradually, as the people here get

to know you, their impression of you will change." I kept working on her like that, and it seemed to help—she gradually grew stronger.

Since I'm a very conscientious person and I stand up for my principles, I often offend people. Like everyone else, I'm not perfect either. So some people were always saying nasty things. Because of our particular circumstances, my sister and I were especially sensitive. I never gave my sister special consideration when it came to work—I've always felt that a little hardship never hurt anyone, and I couldn't do that, if only because I was a cadre. I had my sister work more than the others. She understood, and did everything I asked. I'm very grateful to her, really.

Some of the high school girls gradually came to appreciate what kind of people my sister and I were and stopped believing the rumors floating around. They told me that my sister often woke them all up in the middle of the night with her screams. They didn't know what had really happened, but they sensed that something was wrong, so they made allowances for her without being asked.

My sister's problems went on for two or three years. Fortunately, we made it through. Our work was outstanding, and we both made it into the Party. Later we were chosen to do office work.

I believe that what happened to my sister didn't happen to just a handful of the girls who went to the countryside at that time; it happened to thousands and thousands. Later, as those days were drawing to a close, when I worked in a Department of Organization[21] at the farm and was responsible for discipline and policy implementation, I came across many such cases. I discovered that many state farm cadres—they had the power—bullied the girls, and I read lots of briefs and documents on how these cases were handled. The head of the sixteenth regiment was executed because he alone had raped dozens of educated girls who'd been sent down. It wasn't just two or three at each state farm, and Heilongjiang had over a hundred farms. Nationwide, 20 million educated youths were sent to the countryside in those days, half of them girls—10 million. And a good many of them wouldn't talk about it even if it had happened to them. I'm not jumping to conclusions. In 1977, when cases were being reinvestigated, a veteran cadre at the farm asked for his to be. What was the is-sue? He'd been expelled from the Party for raping an educated girl who'd been sent to the countryside. The girl in question had gone off to college by then. The Department of Organization sent someone to find her and look into the matter, never imagining that she would refuse to admit it had ever happened. In fact, according to many details in the interrogation transcripts and case records, it really had. She just didn't want to have anything to do with it once she'd gotten a fresh start in life at college. That cadre probably figured she'd feel that way, and that's why he tried to get his conviction overturned. There was no proof, so there wasn't much we could do ... and that's why I say there were thousands and thousands.

Of course there's nothing unusual about that sort of thing happening anywhere, anytime. But if we hadn't made such policy errors—if it hadn't been for political and economic factors that came about as a result of the Cultural Revolution—and sent so many educated youths off to the country, thus giving those horny bastards opportunities, I think the tragic misfortunes of many, many girls could have been avoided. I met so many girls like that back then—I really don't want to talk about it.

Our generation has paid too great a price. But I still think that "Going to the Countryside" had its positive aspect too. It's just that the price was too high, wouldn't you say?

Why do I still have such a positive outlook on life today? Because my life back then, despite its harshness, still had rewards, real, true rewards.

A lot of the Great Northern Wilderness was cultivated by us. Yes, and I'm proud of it. It was a new farm with nothing on it, just virgin land as far as the eye could see. Eighty percent of the farm was young people, and the rest consisted of a few army veterans from the fifties and their families. We were the mainstay. Naturally, the older generation had laid a foundation for us. Really, no matter how exhausted we were in spring, we were still elated when autumn came and the wheat was ripe and the grain went to market and the watermelons were in season and the pigs were fattened up, because we had done it all! That's why I say our youth wasn't totally lost. It had its value. Right?

Many of my comrades-in-arms never came back; they lost their lives. There were many reasons—some died fighting fires, some were murdered. These things happened to people I worked side by side with. An educated youth from Shanghai and I got an order at the same time, saying there was a subversive trying to sabotage the state farm and we had to catch him. It was a dark night. We were the ones to find him, and we chased him to the river. The young man from Shanghai had him cornered, and when the suspect saw he had no way out, he jumped into the water. It was April, and the river had just melted, though pieces of ice were still floating on the surface. This guy from Shanghai jumped in too, but he hadn't had a chance to take off his cotton-padded jacket. He swam and swam and then sank, and I watched him go under. The subversive drowned too. I'll never forget that battle. Can you say that this educated youth died a meaningless death? He was defending our country!

There's a huge forest in the Great Northern Wilderness, bigger than most of the ones in the central plains: It's got a circumference of several hundred li.[22] Every year in spring and autumn, fires break out easily there. What with the dried branches and rotten leaves, fires just start. Most of them were caused by carelessness—with campfires, cigarettes, or sparks from truck exhaust—and some started naturally. At the first sign of a fire, we would run out to fight it. People were badly burned and some were burned to death. Once a dormitory caught fire, and an educated youth died trying to put the fire out. The night before we'd bunked together, talking and laughing. A girder came crashing down and killed him instantly.

Some died of rabies after being bitten by mad dogs, and of various other illnesses. Their ashes are there to stay and, of course, so is the impact of their lives.

Thinking of them makes me realize that there are things about our generation that are really worth eulogizing. They're not fiction; they're all facts, facts close to home. Things I saw with my own eyes. Some writers come up with stuff like "Testimony of the Wilderness" or "Testimony of the White Birch Forest," but they needn't bother, there's no need; I'm a witness.

Another thing I'll mention is my joining the Party then. I had to file three applications before one was finally approved. Many ordinary soldiers had already succeeded in joining the Party. The reason for the delay in my case was the problem with my grandfather that I mentioned earlier. In the beginning, my father was so grateful to the Party for saving his life that he worked harder at his job to repay them, but when he tried to join the Party, his application was turned down for this same reason.

When I went to the farm Party committee to ask what the problem with my grandfather was, they answered, "You say your grandfather was killed by an arms smuggler. What if that arms smuggler was part of a Red Army guerrilla detachment under the Communist Party? We have to be responsible to the Party!" To tell the truth, I never even laid eyes on my grandfather. He died when my father was fifteen.

Whether or not they let me into the Party, I worked hard just the same.

Some educated youths were always wavering in their commitment; they were always thinking about returning to the city. In fact, in the first year of "going to the countryside," children of high-ranking cadres relied on the influence of their parents to get them into the People's Liberation Army;[23] this was the first group. The second group had all kinds of ways out—a certain number were chosen to transfer to jobs or universities in the cities, some claimed special handicaps, some even managed to get transferred from farm work to factories in remote areas—sooner or later many, many of them left. I was determined to put down roots on the farm; I bit my finger and wrote an oath in blood to stay. I've got a document here from back then, take a look—"Work Team Brief." Back then certain outstanding youths were called "XX-style outstanding team members." XX was my name. In the end, the secretary of the Party Committee made the final decision; he said he'd take responsibility for any further problems with the business about my grandfather. So I joined the Party. I'll never forget that secretary. After I left there, he transferred to a government bureau and became bureau chief. He really knew what he was doing. He had three ribs broken in struggle sessions during the Cultural Revolution.

It was really hard for educated youths to transfer to the cities, especially the ones who had no way out. Watching everybody else leave one after another, they had to think of their own ways. What did the girls come up with? They resorted to marriage. They got engaged to somebody from a big city and then arranged their city residence cards;[24] love didn't enter into it at all. The boys were more desperate; there's no way to describe how they felt. With no way out, they manufactured illnesses, swallowed nails, or ate coins, which then showed up as shadows in the fluoroscopy. Or they cut their hands and dripped blood into their stools, or put a little egg white in their urine, so the tests came out positive. To tell the truth, it reached the point where they'd stop at nothing.

I remember a girl who was engaged to a worker in Beidagang. It was all arranged for her to go back and meet him over the May Day holiday. Most of the 100 or so members of the company went home for Spring Festival. I stayed. There were over a thousand pigs, several hundred sheep, and dozens of horses and cows, as well as many facilities that needed looking after. That girl stayed too, to save up a few more days of leave to use over May Day. She loved things to be clean. She was washing blankets in the dormitory. The room was quite warm and she was wearing thin clothes. Going outside a few times to fetch water, she caught a cold. Even several days of antibiotics did nothing to bring her fever down. We were worried, and took her to the hospital. Back then, the farm headquarters was miles away, and the electricity was out when they needed to do lab tests. So we carried her to the county hospital. A week had passed before she got proper treatment. By then she could no longer produce blood; she had aplastic anemia. I took along two boys and two girls and the five of us looked after her. She needed constant blood transfusions. I decided that the girls shouldn't give blood, and when we three boys had our blood tested, we found that one boy and I had type O. But he looked a little reluctant about it, so I said I'd give blood. I gave 400 cc, and the color came back into her face where it had been a yellowish green before. She perked up in no time. I spent the whole day squatting in the hallway. The doctor said to her, "That boyfriend of yours is really something." She replied, "He's our political instructor, not my boyfriend." The doctor was really moved, and insisted on giving me a bed so I could get some sleep. We didn't close our eyes for nine days and nine nights.

Despite all our efforts, we couldn't save her. After she died she was cremated in Harbin. When I returned after taking care of the funeral, people told me, "You look like hell." I looked as if I'd just come out of jail. On her deathbed, that girl held onto my hand and wouldn't let me leave. By then, her older sister and her brother-in-law had been contacted by telegram and rushed to see her, but they weren't allowed into the room during treatment. She had had a bit of a falling-out with them. She wouldn't let go of me. Her eyes stayed fixed on me and there were tears streaming down her face. By that point she could no longer speak, but she was still conscious. I was crying too. Our relationship wasn't one of lovers at all; we were like brother and sister. At that time my only thought was how to keep her alive. I felt we had suffered enough. She had fallen ill and couldn't even get to see her parents. With my own eyes, I watched her stop breathing. In Harbin, I carried the urn that held her ashes—it was still warm—and I thought, I would give any amount of blood if only she could live.

Thousands and thousands of girl comrades took that route. For those who had sacrificed love and dignity and the rights people ought to have for a way out, things weren't necessarily good. Because there was no love in that way out and that kind of seed was bound to produce bad fruit. And that was another tragedy for the girls. Their worth lay only in the fact that they were female. All we rough-and-tumble boys could do was destroy ourselves, swallow nails, and so on. I always yelled at people who did that: "We can't do that! If you can't stand the hardship, you don't deserve to live."

Almost all the educated youths had returned to the cities in 1979. I was the last of the company to go. When I left I felt guilty. I felt that even though I was the last to leave I was still a deserter, that in the end I had fought a losing battle, or that I hadn't been able to conquer myself, that I still had to follow the crowd. My family wanted me to come back. The place was nearly empty, and the dormitory was lonely as hell. At the time, the greatest pressure was loneliness. When a big group of hoods from Shandong, Hebei, and Henan came to take jobs as temporary workers, I was in charge of them, but it didn't feel right I thought, I've got to go.

I'll never forget my last day there. Dozens of veteran farm workers saw me off. I was carrying one bag—all it had in it were some worn-out clothes and a few old books and such. As we left the barracks and crossed that little bridge, it was like a funeral procession—they followed behind me, crying. Some buried their faces in their hands and sobbed. Even though they were ignorant and uncultured, if you compared the way they related to each other with the way city people did, these people were wonderful! They saw me off a long, long way, and I could still hear them crying after I had left them behind.

When I got back, for a long time I couldn't eat and didn't sleep well—everything was like a dream. In theory, you should eat and sleep better at home, but I just felt empty, as if I had lost many, many things. Later I felt I shouldn't be that way, that I should start over from the beginning. People have to start from wherever they are. And that's how I gradually regained my positive attitude toward life. Didn't I tell you I like literature? Besides working hard at my job, in 1980 I took lit classes at the Cultural Palace[25] in my spare time. In 1982, I started studying at a TV college.[26] I graduated last year. I don't want to boast, but I have to admit my academic record was satisfactory. I worked so hard because I was afraid of losing my identity. I'm studying literature for a reason. I think I have a responsibility to express myself and my generation. I'll never be a millionaire, and I'll never leave my son any property to speak of. But if while I'm alive I can leave behind a book, then I won't have lived my life in vain.

Those years left me in bad health. My arthritis often acts up, and my stomach too, and when they hurt I just … put up with it. Those aches and pains will probably be with me for the rest of my life.

My sister got married a long time ago, but has never been able to tell her husband about what happened back then. If she hasn't told him by now, it's better not to. There's much more buried in our hearts than that pain. But I think our generation is a great one. And I'm not just trying to console myself. Back then, the Cultural Revolution made such a mess of the national economy that it nearly collapsed, and if we hadn't gone to the countryside, 20 million people would have been an awful burden on the cities. Even if we were duped, even if we suffered, we still supported a part of the national structure that was on the verge of collapse; wouldn't you say? It should be said that our generation bore the brunt of the Cultural Revolution. We were the ones. But to this day, there has never been a correct appraisal of the Going to the Countryside Movement. I wrote a poem once; the manuscript's long gone. But I remember some lines; they went something like this:

When it should have been lush with leaves They fell too soon;
It supports a corner of the falling sky Though its trunk is covered with scars.

I know that poem's immature. But it expresses what I really think, my beliefs, my strength. And so I say that what our generation has lost and gained are equally important. Our lives weren't wasted. We'll never forget the Great Northern Wilderness. We left so many things there, and we brought so many things back. Wouldn't you say?

It has always been the people, not the sages, who rescued the country from disaster. — F. J.

FOOTNOTES

1. During the early part of the Cultural Revolution, all schools, universities, and work units were organized along military lines, i.e., team, platoon, company, battalion, regiment, and division.
2. Heilongjiang is a province of northeast China bordering the Soviet Union at the Amur River. The farm referred to was an undeveloped area of the Great Northern Wilderness—mostly wasteland and swamps.
3. On May 7, 1968, at the beginning of the Cultural Revolution, Chairman Mao issued a directive calling on all educated urban youths to go to the countryside to settle, unite with the peasants, and be reeducated by them.
4. In 1949, the People's Liberation Army, led by Mao Zedong, defeated the Nationalist Army led by Chiang Kai-shek, and founded the People's Republic of China.

5. "Monster" was a common epithet used during the Cultural Revolution for those considered extreme enemies of the working class.
6. Red Guards were members of a mass organization initiated at Chairman Mao's behest, which consisted of young people—mostly of high school and college age—and was dedicated to safeguarding the dictatorship of the proletariat and "Mao Zedong thought." They would take action against those they regarded as enemies of these things, and played a major role in turning the Cultural Revolution into a nationwide mass movement.
7. Cadres means leaders.
8. The five black categories consisted of landlords, rich peasants, counterrevolutionaries, Rightists, and "bad elements."
9. Struggle sessions were meetings held in public to denounce someone, and enumerate his or her crimes. These meetings usually involved physical punishment and humiliation.
10. A poster written in bold characters with ink and brush used during the Cultural Revolution for purposes of denouncing someone, airing complaints, and urging the masses to do likewise.
11. A farm owned and operated by the state.
12. An organization composed of farmers who worked together under the jurisdiction of the commune.
13. One jin equals half a kilogram, or a little more than one pound.
14. During the early phases of the Cultural Revolution, Chinese citizens, at the urging of Lin Biao, praised Chairman Mao and quoted him when writing letters, greeting one another, and the like.
15. Defined in a speech given by Chairman Mao in 1962 as consisting of *(a)* classes, class contradictions, and class struggles, *(b)* the struggle between the socialist and capitalist paths, *(c)* the danger of the restoration of capitalism, and *(d)* the danger of invasion or sabotage by imperialists.
16. "Two-line struggle" refers to the conflict between differing political and ideological viewpoints within the Party.
17. Negative term for devoted and blind follower.
18. The Kuomintang (often abbreviated as KMT) was founded by Dr. Sun Yat-sen and later headed by

Chiang Kai-shek. This was the party Mao ousted from power in 1949.

19. 1 mu equals 0.1647 acres.

20. The Communist Youth League is an organization affiliated with the Communist Party for young people who aspire to further the cause of communism but are not yet old enough to join the Party.

21. A Department of Organization oversees the performance, discipline, punishment, and rehabilitation of those under its supervision.

22. One li equals half a kilometer.

23. The army of the Communist Party, which, since defeating the Kuomintang in 1949, has been the only official army of the People's Republic of China; the name is often abbreviated as PLA.

24. A residence card is a document that both allows a Chinese citizen to live in a particular place and restricts him or her to living in that place.

25. An organization offering spare-time recreational and educational activities.

26. A college in which the courses are given by television to students working toward a college degree.

WAS I REALLY GUILTY?

- TIME: 1966
- AGE: 30
- SEX: *Female*
- OCCUPATION: *Doctor in the Children's Hospital of T city*

I killed my father with my own hands. You already know this.

I was planning to talk with you a couple of days ago. I had to get it out. But last night I didn't have a wink of sleep, so I decided not to say anything today. Just the thought of recalling what happened and the way my parents looked on that day brings everything back too clearly. It's too painful. I'm hypertensive and was afraid that I wouldn't be able to handle this interview. But as soon as I met you, I knew I just had to talk. I've got to say something. Perhaps it's better this way.

My wounds can never be healed. Even after twenty years I still can't figure out whether I was right to kill my father. My initial sentence was life imprisonment.

However, when the Gang of Four fell, I was declared innocent and released. But was I really guilty or not? My family, my brothers and sisters-in-law, all told me they understood. But after all, I was the one who ended my father's life. If not for me, he certainly would have lived until now. He had been very healthy. Did I rescue him or destroy him? One moment I feel as though I did the right thing, but the next I'm bitterly remorseful. Why is it like that? At the time it all happened, I was not in my right mind. I had a complete nervous breakdown. Everything seemed unreal, chaotic, totally confused.

Back then, my two older brothers lived on the ground floor and my parents had the upstairs floor. I was working as a doctor in the Children's Hospital. I was also an active member of the Communist Youth League. I was diligent in my profession and had even received awards as a model worker. When all this happened I was staying with my parents on sick leave after contracting hepatitis while working in the countryside with my medical team.

It was on the morning of the twenty-sixth of August, 1966. Oh no, it was the twenty-eighth. The twenty-sixth was the beginning of the ransacking of my home. It was also the climax of the ransacking in the city. Our door was suddenly forced open by a group of middle-school Red Guards armed with clubs. They declared that my father was a capitalist. In fact, it was a misnomer. My father had inherited a house from his parents and rented out a vacant room on the ground floor. At most he could be called a householder. But in those days renting was synonymous with exploitation, that is, profiting without labor. Within minutes the Red Guards had smashed everything in my home to bits. My whole family was forced to kneel down in the hallway. We were all very naive and had no experience of such violent abuse. We were scared out of our wits. My father was a painter and had had one of his paintings displayed in America before 1949. The Red Guards examined the certificate from the American exhibition and said, "Aha! So you've got imperialist connections! You must be a dirty spy!" We were frightened to death. Only schoolchildren, you might think. Why were we so frightened? Well, during the Cultural Revolution almost all the families in our neighborhood were molested and had their houses ransacked. If those Red Guards felt like it, they could execute you on the spot. Everyone was terrified. One bunch after another would raid the houses. They'd smash everything. Books, paintings, anything that struck them as bourgeois would be taken out and burned. Then they would seal up your house. So many, many of them. Their bonfires were everywhere.

From the twenty-sixth to the twenty-eighth, from dawn to dusk, my parents and I were locked up and beaten with belts. Our hair was shorn to the roots. We were dragged out to the street again and again to be denounced and humiliated before the neighborhood. We never had a moment's peace. They tormented us ceaselessly until we no longer even felt a semblance of humanity. Suddenly we had somehow become enemies of our country. Just cringing there. No idea of what our monstrous crimes must be. Oh, how we longed to find a refuge, but where? The whole city was like this. Red Guards everywhere parading people in the streets to the sounds of gongs and drums. Tension was mounting rapidly and we had reached our breaking point. Even death seemed preferable to this.

Until the twenty-eighth, for three entire days, my parents and I had nothing to eat. Even our bowls had been smashed. It was only when the Red Guards left to eat that we were able to hurriedly make some noodle soup to feed my brother's children—straight out of the wok. That night my parents and I were filled with terror and despair. At daybreak the Red Guards would show up again. More denunciations, more humiliating parades, more physical torture. Too much to face. There was no way out. So the three of us made up our minds to die together.

It was pitch black. The power had been cut off—perhaps to prevent us from electrocuting ourselves. We were sitting on the foyer floor, racking our brains for a way to kill ourselves. It was raining outside. Already past midnight. Day would soon break; no time to waste. I felt a pocket knife on the floor attached to a key chain. The Red Guards must have missed it in their search. The knife seemed to be a godsend. I'm a doctor. I know that if you puncture the carotid artery in the neck, the embolism produced will result in immediate death. This was the fastest and most effective way. My father asked whether it would really work and I assured him it would. My mother said how lucky they were to

have a doctor daughter to help them die. Since I was the doctor, we decided that I'd kill them first and then do it to myself. But things didn't turn out as we expected.

Before going through with it, we sat there hand in hand for God knows how long. The thought of parting forever was almost too much. I'd always been so close to my parents. They wanted me to help them die but to stay alive myself. That wouldn't do, I said. I'd be accused of murder and put to death anyway. The pass we had come to is unbearable to recall. As soon as I close my eyes, even the tiniest details come back to me. It was getting too late, already dawn. My parents both insisted that I go ahead with it. I had never thought myself capable of killing anyone, let alone my parents. But under these circumstances I was capable of it, and I had no other choice. My father encouraged me. He told me, "What you must do is something good. You will relieve our sufferings. Mother and I can't stand any more torturing when the Red Guards come again." My mind was too shattered. I felt compelled to do it.

I scrabbled about and found a crayon and two pieces of paper. In the lifting darkness I somehow managed to write out two suicide notes for the sake of my remaining family:

> We are the common enemy of the people. In order not to poison others surrounding us, we are determined to be liquidated from society. Long live the Great Proletarian Cultural Revolution!
>
> To XXX (my husband who was working in another city) and the Mu families (the families of my brothers who I didn't dare to identify as brothers for their own protection): You are resolutely following the revolutionary road. We are the sole cause of your trouble.

My father asked my mother to be first and she asked him the same, for whoever was first to die would be spared at least one grief. Finally father agreed to listen to mother one last time. He'd be the first to die.

I felt for my father's strong artery and pierced it. Immediately the hot blood spurted out. He even asked me to see if his pulse had stopped. I said that as far as I knew, it would be over in a minute. He said he wished it could be faster. Then my mother asked me if I was sure I could do it to myself. She knew I had to die with them; I couldn't be left behind. I reassured her that when they were finished, I'd die too. She waited there patiently as though I was about to give her medical treatment. We'd tried to be very quiet, not to alarm others. But suddenly one of my brothers ran upstairs yelling like a madman. It sounded as if the Red Guards were coming. He came and held me tight. All of a sudden I realized that I couldn't go on with this. I nearly fainted, but managed to struggle free. I ran to the third floor balcony and jumped. If I had hit headfirst, I'd have died. But there was no time even to think about how to jump or what would happen to my mother. I only remember hearing all the sounds of hell and then nothing.

It's like I told you. We were really being driven out of our minds. Mother and I hadn't planned to jump out the window. It just happened. When you reach the end, you close your eyes and do the obvious thing like we did. We jumped.

When I finally came to, I was still only half conscious. I thought I heard some voices. Maybe Red Guards. I don't know. When I opened my eyes for a second time, I was already in a hospital. I saw my mother and father lying beside me. But no, I was hallucinating. I shut my eyes, very scared, trying to think. This can't be. What happens if my father was saved? Faintly I could make out the babble of denunciation meetings and parades outside. In desperation I tried to concentrate. This was a women's ward. My father couldn't be here. My eyes were playing tricks on me. I didn't want to look again. My head was full of a cacophony of sounds. I think that it must have been a symptom of my mental disorder. I even tried to cry out, but somehow no sound came out of me. Afterward, the next time I came to, someone was questioning me about my case. I forget what he said.

When I fully regained consciousness, I was told that my mother had jumped off the balcony right after me. Later when I was being interrogated, I was told Father had died on the spot but Mother had been saved. How I cried for my dead father and also for my mother. I was badly injured and she was so old. She would be paralyzed or worse if she really had survived. It was only after the Cultural Revolution had ended and I was finally released that my sister-in-law told me the

truth. My mother hadn't died right away. Instead they took her to the hospital, but she was refused treatment. You probably know that at that time people without a socially acceptable family background weren't admitted. Sometimes the hospitals even organized the "respectable" patients to denounce and criticize those "bad elements" who had earlier gained admission. I was admitted only because I had to face legal proceedings. My mother died a few days later at home. My father had died as they said and was cremated a week later.

The hospital didn't want to treat a patient like me. Very soon I was transferred to a prison hospital called New Life Hospital. Both of my legs were broken—the left tibia and the right femur. The right leg was more seriously injured, with a compression fracture. The bone had splintered and compressed so that the fragments overlapped, shortening the leg. The first hospital had applied skeletal traction, using a ten kilo sandbag to pull the bone back into position. But when I was moved to the prison, the hospital insisted I leave the bag behind. So the doctor put the bone fragments back into the wrong position: Just like breaking it again. It was only a sandbag. They could at least have let me use it, but no, they refused. That hospital didn't give a damn about me. Neither did the doctor who treated me. I don't know where he is now, but I hope he's no longer practicing medicine. What treatment I did get I was given only so that I could face my legal responsibility. It's strange to think about it now. My broken bones were pulled this way and that. But I felt no pain, not even a little. Didn't cry either. It was as if I was dead.

It was eleven o'clock when we arrived at the prison. The prison hospital staff didn't start working until two in the afternoon. When they finally came, on, they separated my bone again and put in a steel pin. Then they manipulated the leg back and forth in the splint they made. My leg is still deformed. Only about a fifth of the bone has knitted. It aches a lot. I don't want to dwell on it. You can see I'm crippled for life.

I was formally arrested ten days later and hand-cuffed. That was September 7, 1966. In 1968 when the Military Control Commission[1] took over, I was charged with "committing the crime of murder in opposition to the Great Proletarian Cultural Revolution." Murder was a criminal offense and opposition to the Cultural

Revolution was a political crime. A very serious combination. I was sentenced to life imprisonment. I thought then that I'd rather get the death penalty. Life imprisonment meant continuing to suffer. Here, you have a look at my sentence:

It is verified that the accused Y, of a bourgeois family background, has failed to be reformed after Liberation. During the Great Proletarian Cultural Revolution, she has masterminded a scheme to resist the Great Proletarian Cultural Revolution through collective suicide and the murder of YY and furthermore has attempted personal suicide as a means of escaping punishment. The accused has both alienated herself from society and become an enemy of the people, thus committing the crime of murder in opposition to the Great Proletarian Cultural Revolution. In view of the seriousness of this offense, the vile manner in which it was committed, and the irrefutable evidence presented, this court, in solidarity with the proletarian dictatorship and the resolute defense of the Great Proletarian Cultural Revolution's continuing progress, hereby finds the accused guilty of murder in opposition to the Great Proletarian Cultural Revolution. The accused is sentenced to life imprisonment.

Someone from the commission said to me that if I had been just an ordinary housewife, my sentence wouldn't have been so severe. Obviously, however, I knew what I was doing. My father's case was considered very serious. He said I killed my father to save him from just punishment. That's the real reason I was sentenced to the crime of opposition to the Cultural Revolution.

Well, they said I killed my father to protect him. It's true. I did. This has been a great weight on my mind. What they meant is not the way I look at it. I saved my father from more torture, but they said I was guilty because I prevented them from torturing him anymore. Am I making myself clear? It's all very muddled. I've never been able to make any sense of it.

I was in prison for twelve and a half years. The only reason I didn't kill myself was that I always believed my mother was still alive. I tried to imagine how she was living. The three of us had planned to die together. My father, dead. Me, imprisoned for life. My mother—well, I'd never see her again. Every time my nephews came to visit me they'd tell me that Grandma was at home. Grandma wanted me to reform myself, they said, so that my sentence might be reduced. Sometimes even the prison guards would ask me to tell them about my mother. Of course, they knew my mother was dead, but they too tried to hide it from me. In fact I really had wished that my mother would have died. To live on was only more misery and suffering. If only I had been told the truth, I would have been at peace.

Once you've been in prison, you get a different perspective on things. I wouldn't have believed that so many good people could be so unjustly imprisoned until I saw them myself. My case, though, was different. I did kill my father with my own hands. I really wanted to atone for my sin, but I also hoped to get an early release so I could see my mother. I felt extremely guilty too toward my brothers. We have the same father but different mothers. However, we were so close that no one ever suspected. They never showed any hatred to me after Father died. They would often come to see me and send me food. Ah, each time I saw them I cried until I ran out of tears. I didn't know what to say. I felt I had betrayed them. But my brothers reassured me that they understood and that as long as they and my sisters-in-law lived, they'd never stop caring about me. For my brothers' sake, also I really had to redeem myself. I worked as hard as I could to reform.

At first I was given sewing to do, I didn't even know how to use a sewing machine, so I started from square one. Pretty soon I got skilled at it. To sew collars was the hardest. Since I had become the best worker, I was given the difficult and important tasks. I even managed to exceed the quotas. We also did things like produce slogan posters, propaganda articles, and political drawings. I tried to lend a hand at everything. For production I was sometimes awarded a Red Flag or Chairman Mao's "Little Red Book."[2] Hey, have a look at my glasses. Can you guess how strong they are? I got nearsighted from looking at my sewing in those days.

I was also called upon to use my medical skills. It wasn't only to treat fellow prisoners, but also the chief warden and his children. If the ordinary prison workers, along with their relatives and cadre friends, called upon me, I'd go at a moment's notice too. To feel trusted by others, not regarded as an enemy—that was a great consolation. In the middle of the night I'd often be awakened to treat someone's fever, stomachache, or convulsions. It always took at least a few hours, but the next day I'd be off to work as usual. I was working like mad both day and night. The prison workers showed their appreciation. Even today they still sometimes come to see me at the hospital to have me treat their children. Back then, not being treated too harshly was the best I could ask for. Please don't laugh at me. At the slightest praise I'd be overjoyed for days.

There's one thing I want to mention. When I was officially arrested on the seventh of September, 1966 in the prison hospital, I was still married. My husband was working in Beijing. The weather was getting cold, I thought, and his clothes and belongings had already been taken away when our apartment was ransacked. He shouldn't suffer anymore because of me. So I wrote a letter asking him to arrange a divorce. By the end of September, it came through. Not long after that his sister suddenly came to the prison. She left me some tonic and 20 yuan, a lot of money in those days. I asked the guards to pass on my request that she not bring any more money again or anything else. But I was penniless in prison, so I kept 5 yuan and begged one of my wardens to send the rest to my mother. Of course I didn't know she was dead. This warden was a retired army officer. At first he refused, but I pleaded with him and he finally agreed. Later that sister-in-law sent another 30 yuan. She came five or six times altogether gave me about 120 yuan. Each time I asked the warden to send it on to my mother. Strangely, though, my family never wrote me even once about this. I thought maybe they just hated me too much. A year later, when I was sentenced, I was finally allowed to see them. Whenever they visited, wishing Chairman Mao longevity and studying his quotations would take up half of the time while the rest was filled with my sobbing. Not much chance to talk. My family didn't say anything about the money and it was too awkward for me to ask. It wasn't until 1979 when I was released that I discovered the money hadn't reached them. All those years I had regarded that warden as my benefactor. I still don't understand what was going on. Maybe the post office had refused to deliver the money since the postal service often refused to handle mail for families in disgrace. But even if that was the case, the money should have been returned to me.

Believe it or not, there were some decent prison workers. I had been quite healthy before, but now my weight had dropped to about forty kilos. A warden, seeing how thin I'd become, stealthily slipped my sister-in-law a health certificate.[3] The next time she came to visit, she was allowed to bring in a kilo of cakes. I was upset. I thought that it would be much better if the cakes had been given to my mother and nephews. Life outside was hard too. In prison I was given 1.50 yuan pocket money each month. I didn't buy anything except soap, toilet paper, and toothpaste, which would last me for months. I tried hard to save as much as possible. When I had saved 5 or 10 yuan, I'd send it home. For without my family's warmth, what did I have to live for? I tried my best under the circumstances to do something good for them. It was a kind of atonement.

In prison we also had to do political study and practice criticism. Very often I was called upon to denounce my crime of resisting the Cultural Revolution. Those in charge asked me to set an example of self-criticism at many meetings, both large and small. Self-criticism was really not so bad. Sometimes I'd be feeling very down. When it was my turn to self-criticize, I'd talk about the many years of education I'd received from the Party and how I should have believed in the Party and its policy. If I had followed the Party's policy, everything would have been all right. After each self-criticism session, my confidence in the Party would be reinforced and I'd feel better about going on living. I'd think about how to perform even better to get an early release and be able to pay back the Party. Believe it or not, good behavior did work. In 1972 my sentence was reduced from life to an additional ten years—the most lenient treatment I could have expected. I could get out in 1982. So I had something to hope for.

Not long after the Gang of Four was ousted in 1976, the courts reexamined my case. They decided that I had been persecuted during the Cultural Revolution. I was not a murderer, but rather a participant in a group suicide. Thus I was declared innocent and released. I got out in 1979, two and a half years earlier than I had expected. The new verdict went like this:

The original sentence that Y committed the crime of murder in resistance to the Cultural Revolution is hereby declared invalid. Therefore the conviction is withdrawn and Y is declared innocent and is to be released.

I was released on the second of March, 1979. When I entered prison I only had on the hospital pajamas—the kind with blue and white stripes. Later, my brothers sent me a small suitcase of old clothes that I'd left with the rural medical team before the Cultural Revolution. I'd been wearing them for ten years. I was in rags when I came out. It was a heavy blow to learn that my mother had passed away a long time ago. It was my thoughts of her that had kept me going all those years. Now, with not only my father dead, but mother too, everything was finished. I was close to a nervous breakdown.

I came back home in March and started working in the Children's Hospital in May. I had had only two months rest. Lots of relatives and friends came to visit me. I couldn't sleep peacefully for all sorts of reasons. My mind kept going nonstop. I just couldn't relax. Three of us had planned to die together, but only I was alive. I felt terrible. People tried to comfort me, telling me how lucky I was even to be alive. So many higher-ups had followed Chairman Mao through hellish conditions on the Long March,[4] braving snow-covered mountains and impassable swamps. They too had been persecuted. Many had died; their families had been ruined. Their lot was worse than mine. But those who have survived are trying to make the best of things, aren't they?

My work unit was very considerate. When I was released, my family's houses were still occupied by others and hadn't been returned to us. So I just lived in the hospital dormitory. I'm a Muslim and my meals presented a bit of a problem. My nephew sent me suitable food every day by bicycle. He did this without fail for several years. As for my work, the hospital required me to work as a resident first. According to hospital regulations, you have to do a residency before getting an appointment as a staff doctor. I didn't have a home of my own to worry about, so I made full use of my time studying. In prison we weren't allowed to read professional books

and journals so I had to double my efforts to make up for lost time. Before long, I got up to date.

I was put in charge of eight wards scattered between the first and fifth floors. Every day I ran up and down, fourteen hours a day. One night when I was on duty, I suddenly felt as though I was walking on clouds. I got someone to take my blood pressure. It was 180 over 100. Too high. I immediately asked for an injection. The one I got was supposed to be effective, but half an hour later it still hadn't worked. The systole was up to 200. The nurses decided among themselves to stop calling me for emergencies and let me rest. They were afraid I was exhausted. But I just continued my rounds. They were very sympathetic and showed their respect. What can I say? Well, I just doubled my efforts. Normally residency takes a full year, but in only six months I was promoted to staff.

Around this, time I made a new acquaintance. He was a graduate from the East China Textile Institute. When he was young, he had shown great promise and had been highly recommended by one of his colleagues, a chief engineer. During the "Antirightist" movement,[5] his mentor was denounced as a Rightist. My friend was asked to expose him. He refused. Instead he tipped off the engineer. To act against his conscience was not part of his character. He was treated as a Rightist and he himself believed that he was one. When the Rightists were delabeled, he was told that it had never been recorded in his files that he was one. The mistake was his own. But for twenty years he had believed this. He'd never gotten a promotion or raise. He hadn't even married for fear of the label. How could such an absurd thing have happened? When I met him he was over fifty and still single. Well, we got married. We have a lot in common and can communicate well. He's very considerate to me. We're a comfort to each other.

I adopted one of my brother's sons. He's studying a foreign language now in Beijing University. My husband was recently promoted to director of his factory. At last I have a real home and family.

Even today, though, I still can't rid myself of thoughts of the past. I don't think about it every day, but there's no escaping from my memories. In my mind my father's image appears again and again. My colleagues have asked me, "You couldn't even step on an ant, how could you have done it?" In the Cultural Revolution people were deprived of their basic humanity. Who in their right mind could stab their own father to death? Under normal circumstances no one would even consider it. And what about my mother? How can I make up for that? If I hadn't done what I did, my parents would perhaps be enjoying life today. If I'm not to blame, then who is? No matter how hard I try to justify my actions, I still fail. I can't decide whether I saved my father or destroyed him. In the beginning I felt that I had saved him but I feel more and more now that I destroyed him. Other things I can make sense of, but not this. My mind just goes round and round. All those bad things were caused by the Gang of Four. Why then did all those others survive until now and not my parents? It must be my fault alone. Whenever I think this way, I feel that I must have been guilty. It's too depressing. And yet my friends tell me that only when I enjoy life will my parents be able to rest in peace. They're right perhaps, aren't they?

I can't say any more. Please don't ask me to go on.

In dehumanizing times, the highest expression of human nature is destroying oneself. — F. J.

FOOTNOTES

1. The Military Control Commission of the People's Liberation Army replaced the police, the legal apparatus, and the People's Courts during the Cultural Revolution. It was given power to create laws and to put itself above laws.

2. A pocket-sized collection of Mao Zedong's best-known quotations. It has sold more copies than any book in history but the Bible. During the Cultural Revolution, every Chinese was supposed to have one, and often did.

3. A document showing that the carrier was in poor health and in need of extra nutrition.

4. The Long March was a major strategic movement of the Chinese Workers' and Peasants' Red Army, led by Mao Zedong, which succeeded in reaching the revolutionary base in northern Shaanxi after traversing eleven provinces and covering roughly 7,500 miles in 1934–1935.

5. In 1957 people who criticized the Party line were labeled Rightists. They were mostly intellectuals and were considered antisocialist reactionary elements.

GROWTH VERSUS SUCCESS

JAPAN'S ECONOMIC POLICY IN HISTORICAL PERSPECTIVE

By Laura E. Hein
Edited by Andrew Gordon

Japan is internationally renowned for its stunning economic performance. This achievement excites foreign envy and Japanese pride, partly because it seems so painlessly achieved. Japan appears to offer a model for economic success without suffering, contention, or even much effort. Unfortunately, this is an illusion. Over the course of the postwar decades the Japanese struggled not only to devise a strategy for economic development but also to define their economic goals. Moreover, the strategies chosen have had significant costs to some Japanese. Elites and nonelites agreed on the importance of rebuilding the economy by 1946, but their economic policies evolved only slowly past that initial and hard-won consensus as new problems regularly emerged. The evolution of postwar Japanese history is a tale less of solutions than of debates, some of which began long before 1945 and some of which are unlikely ever to be resolved.

"ECONOMIC SUCCESS" AND "ECONOMIC GROWTH"

There has been very little exploration of economic debate in the many studies of the postwar Japanese economy or of the precise ways in which the postwar Japanese approached economic problems. Rather, this question has been obscured by a different one: how to explain Japan's unusually high rate of economic growth. This is not the logical place to begin an analysis of the postwar Japanese economy, but unveiling the mechanisms of growth has been in fact the problem that has engrossed most researchers. Finding the "secrets" of Japanese economic success has driven nearly all work done on the economy since the 1960s.

This focus has biased the analysis of postwar Japan in a number of specific ways. First, it has obscured all those aspects of Japanese economic history that have not directly contributed to Japanese success. Second, it has imparted false prescience to the Japanese, persistently giving the impression that successes were anticipated and planned, and so has minimized the extent to which luck and international developments outside of Japanese control were crucial to economic growth. Third, it has implanted the idea that there is a national "Japanese model" that is broadly characteristic of and accepted by all Japanese society, ignoring much conflict and tension.

It is not surprising that many outside observers of Japanese economic policy assume that these achievements were the result of a carefully planned, consistent national economic strategy, for Japanese leaders have not hesitated to take credit for them. This myth is both internationally constructed and "made in Japan." For example, Ojimi Yoshihisa, vice minister of the Ministry of International Trade and Industry (MITI), proclaimed in a 1970 speech that

> the Ministry of International Trade and Industry decided to establish in Japan industries which require intensive employment

Laura E. Hein, "Growth Versus Success: Japan's Economic Policy in Historical Perspective," *Postwar Japan as History*, ed. Andrew Gordon, pp. 99-122. Copyright © 1993 by University of California Press. Reprinted with permission.

of capital and technology, ... industries such as steel, oil refining, petro-chemicals, automobiles, aircraft, industrial machinery of all sorts, and electronics including electronic computers. ... According to Napoleon and Clausewitz, the secret of a successful strategy is the concentration of fighting power on the main battle grounds; fortunately, owing to good luck and wisdom spawned by necessity, Japan has been able to concentrate its scant capital in strategic industries.[*]

This bureaucrat presented a glowing but incorrect description of the development of Japanese industrial policy. He falsely left the impression that postwar Japanese officials knew which were "strategic industries" and that they agreed on where lay the "main battle ground" of economic policy. He also lumped together industries that were targeted early (steel) with ones that were adopted only later (petrochemicals), while glossing over one of MITI's worst embarrassments, its failure to see promise in Sony's new product, the transistor. In what later proved to be the right decision, Sony ignored government suggestions that the company use its resources for other projects. The military analogy also misleadingly suggested that a unified Japan had a clear, external enemy against which it could deploy its biddable economic forces. Success has a way of creating its own illusions, even for individuals who were involved in decision making.

But perhaps the greatest problem is that this approach confuses economic growth and economic success. Probably, if pressed, most people would define economic success by combining some measure of economic growth together with some measure of economic justice. However, in practice, economic growth alone is often the proxy for economic success, although these are not the same. Economic growth certainly can make tasks such as raising the general standard of living easier,

but it does not ensure that any such redistribution will take place. In fact, a number of years ago John W. Bennett and Solomon B. Levine argued that industrialization inherently generates what they called "social deprivation." In their formulation, economic success in Japan, as everywhere else, not only does not mean an end to social problems but also itself creates new ones.[†] The experience of countries in other parts of the world has included examples of social problems *created* by new wealth. Cocaine profits in the Andean nations provide the most extreme recent example.

Undeniably, postsurrender Japan is fundamentally more democratic, peaceful, and egalitarian than it was before 1945, and income-distribution is far more even, but it is not at all obvious, either theoretically or empirically, how this situation is related to economic growth. Studies of wealth inequality show that much of the redistribution took place in the first postwar years, particularly as a result of land reform: that is, redistribution occurred *before* economic growth began.[‡] In fact, consistent with Bennett and Levine's argument, not only have inequities in the system not disappeared, but many have grown worse during the last thirty years. Systemic

[*] Yoshihisa Ojimi, "Basic Philosophy and Objectives of Japanese Industrial Policy," in *The Industrial Policy of Japan*, ed. Organization for Economic Cooperation and Development (OECD) (Paris: OECD, 1972), 15.

[†] John W. Bennett and Solomon B. Levine, "Industrialization and Social Deprivation: Welfare, Environment, and the Postindustrial Society in Japan," in *Japanese Industrialization and Its Social Consequences*, ed. Hugh Patrick (Berkeley and Los Angeles: University of California Press, 1976), 439–92. See also Solomon B. Levine, "Social Consequences of Industrialization in Japan," in *Productivity: A Concept in Political Economy Reconsidered*, ed. Michael Sherman (Madison: Wisconsin Humanities Committee, 1984).

[‡] Toshiyuki Mizoguchi and Noriyuki Takeyama attempt to quantify the level of postwar poverty in *Equity and Poverty under Rapid Economic Growth: The Japanese Experience* (Tokyo: Kinokuniya, 1984), but say data are lacking. For an earlier effort, see Akira Ono and Tsunehiko Watanabe, "Changes in Income Inequality in the Japanese Economy," in Patrick, *Japanese Industrialization*, 363–90. See also Margaret A. McKean, "Equality," in *Democracy in Japan*, ed. Takeshi Ishida and Ellis S. Krauss (Pittsburgh: University of Pittsburgh Press, 1989), 201–24.

dilemmas include urban density and its consequences,* pollution of the environment,† and wealth inequality.‡ Japan is no closer than it was forty-five years ago to solving these problems. The inequality that has grown most startlingly in tandem with Japan's GNP is the effect of skyrocketing urban land prices. While the family income of workers' households increased about thirteen fold between 1960 and 1990, urban land prices increased about twenty-eight-fold.§ This development

---

* Problems of urban density include high land prices, cramped housing, miserable and long commutes, no place for children to play, and perennially congested roadways. This problem has become much more severe since the end of the war, particularly in the greater Tokyo area.

† This category includes severe cases of pollution of the air, water, groundwater, land (both subsidence and heavy metals pollution), nuclear radiation potential, decommissioning of nuclear plants, direct poisoning of people, and noise pollution. See the essays by Upham and Taira in this volume for explicit ways in which these concerns have been subordinated to economic growth.

‡ Taira's essay in this volume explores this issue in greater detail. Buckley demonstrates the growing participation of the female labor force in the postwar economy without equal compensation or opportunity. As in the United States, the middle-class ideal of supporting a family on one income is moving out of reach for more and more Japanese families.

§ Family income of urban worker households increased from an index of 11.7 in 1960 to 100 in 1980 and then jumped to 127.2 in 1985 and 149.2 in 1990. Meanwhile, the urban residential land price index has been calculated at 6.8 in 1960, with 100 pegged at March 1980. The disproportionate increase in land prices accelerated in the next decade, as the same index shot up to 137.7 in 1985 and continued its rapid climb to 189.5 in 1990. Land prices rose out of all proportion to other consumer prices in the same period. In 1987 alone, the consumer price index increased by 0.1 percent, but the cost of urban land (in the six largest cities) zoomed by 27 percent. For income and land figures, see Japanese Government Statistics Bureau Management and Coordination Agency, *Japan Statistical Yearbook* (Tokyo: Statistics Bureau Management and Coordination Agency, 1987), vol. 494:790; 1991, vol. 496:532; for comparison to consumer price index, see Japan Economic Institute Report No. 30A, 4 Aug. 1989, 5.

has made billionaires out of land holders and robbed middle-class Japanese who do not own property of the chance ever to do so. These issues are fundamental to any evaluation of economic success and call into question the ease with which we conflate economic growth and success.

Yet, rather than aiming for the complex and subjective goals of economic justice and economic success, many postwar Japanese (like postwar Americans and Europeans) accepted rapid GNP growth as a substitute. That such confusion was possible is in large part a tribute to the very real redistribution of wealth that did take place in postwar Japan and sets the postwar apart from economically undemocratic presurrender Japan. At the same time the removal of the economy (now presented as a technical problem of growth) from political debate was a profoundly political act—perhaps the most antidemocratic development of postwar Japanese history. As elsewhere in the technocratic world, decisions with major implications for Japanese society were recast as private, technical problems rather than occasions for public debate.

Nonetheless, this process of "political denaturing" was gradual and incomplete.¶ Various challenges have emerged throughout the postwar years, and the conflation of growth and success may not be sustainable. Tensions and contradictions over economic policy have continued to evolve in Japan at each stage of economic development. Some have been resolved, always through compromise, while others remain for the future. More and more, however, in recent years these tensions have been couched in terms of Japan's international relations rather than its domestic ones, obscuring the extent to which policy decisions stratify and divide Japanese from one another.

THE BIRTHRIGHT OF "POSTWAR JAPAN"

The postwar economy built on and broke with earlier Japanese history. Certainly 1945 presented a true

---

¶ Carol Gluck coined this term in a pretechnocratic context; *Japan's Modern Myths: Ideology in the Late Meiji Period* (Princeton: Princeton University Press, 1985).

rupture with the past for Japan both domestically and internationally. In the first few years after the war Japan suddenly became a fundamentally more egalitarian and democratic nation. Although this trend did not continue and gross inequities remained, as many of the essays in this volume demonstrate, the contrast to presurrender Japan was still stark. In the economic sphere this altered situation meant new attention to the desires of the general population for greater economic stability, higher wages, a better standard of living, and a larger role for nonelite groups in economic planning. This approach was a new postwar strategy, very different from the presurrender one. Moreover, early postwar Japanese debates on economic policy self-consciously addressed issues of justice, democracy, social responsibility, and political power. Without attention to these pressing matters—and resolution of some of the sharpest tensions in postwar society—rapid economic growth would have been impossible. As was unusually clear in the harsh environment of postsurrender Japan, economic decisions necessarily also shaped political and social choices.

Yet the postwar economy depended on powerful birthrights from both the prewar and wartime eras. Postwar Japan shared significant intellectual continuities with the prewar Japanese economy, as well as drawing on a strong presurrender economic base. Japanese in both presurrender and postwar Japan (and scholars today) debated the same central problems: how did their economic organization affect democracy, capitalism, war, and autonomy? For example, did the development of the economy foster or discourage economic and political democracy? Was a free market ideal for private enterprise, or should businesses cooperate rather than compete? What was the relationship between the Japanese economy and war? How much were Japan's economic and political choices constrained by international forces outside of its control? These questions suggest a continuity of debate, if not of strategies chosen, between pre- and postsurrender Japan. They also highlight the abiding problems of all advanced capitalist economies over the last century.[*]

This continuity of debate is visible in prewar writing about several specific areas of the economy. Throughout the reconstruction years the Japanese regularly drew on explanations of economic problems established before 1940, even when prewar practice was rejected. Experts on labor have attributed the development of postwar Japanese economic institutions to compromise born out of conflict rather than to a straight progression of positive innovations.[†] Thus; the strong emphasis on seniority in the Japanese wage system, for example, represents a historic compromise between managers'

Social Organization (Glencoe: Free Press, 1958), emphasizes traditional communal values. Johannes Hirschmeier and Tsunehiko Yui, *The Development of Japanese Business, 1600–1980*, 2d ed. (London: Allen and Unwin, 1981); Richard J. Samuels, *The Business of the Japanese State: Energy Markets in Comparative and Historical Perspective* (Ithaca: Cornell University Press, 1987); and Arthur E. Tiedemann, "Big Business and Politics in Prewar Japan," in *Dilemmas of Growth in Prewar Japan*, ed. James W. Morley (Princeton: Princeton University Press, 1971), 267–316, all stressed the pattern of business-government relations dating back to the Meiji era. W. W. Lockwood, *Economic Development of Japan* (Princeton: Princeton University Press, 1954); Kazushi Ohkawa and Henry Rosovsky, *Japanese Economic Growth: Trend Acceleration in the Twentieth Century* (Stanford: Stanford University Press, 1973); and G. C. Allen, *A Short Economic History of Modern Japan*, rev. ed. (London: Allen and Unwin, 1972), all focus on slow, rational modernization, while Kozo Yamamura, "Japan's Deus ex Machina: Western Technology in the 1920s," *Journal of Japanese Studies* 12, no. 1 (Winter 1986): 65–94, makes a case for the singular importance of technology transfer from abroad. Jon Halliday, *A Political History of Japanese Capitalism* (New York: Pantheon, 1975), and Jon Woronoff, *Inside Japan, Inc.* (Tokyo: Lotus Press, 1982), stress traditional forms of exploitation in the modern era.

† Representative sources in English include Mikio Sumiya, "The Development of Japanese Labour Relations," *Developing Economies* 4 (1966): 499–515; Kazuo Okochi, Bernard Karsh, and Solomon B. Levine, eds., *Workers and Employers in Japan* (Tokyo: University of Tokyo Press; and Princeton: Princeton University Press; 1974); Andrew Gordon, *The Evolution of Labor Relations in Japan: Heavy Industry, 1853–1955*, East Asia Monograph Series (Cambridge: Harvard University Press, 1985).

---

* Considerable Western literature attributes postwar growth to prewar factors. James Abegglen, *The Japanese Factory: Aspects of Its*

desire to reward skill and workers' wish for an objective, rational basis for wage payments.[*] The seniority system was the culmination of a long battle over the criteria for wage payments, reaching back several decades by the 1950s.

Another example highlights a major difference between the United States and Japan. The ongoing debate through the first postwar decade between business leaders and bureaucrats about the proper role of the state in the economy revolved around the central prewar dilemma—maintaining stability. Although Japanese business leaders rejected the heavy-handed state interference in their firms that they had experienced during the war, they also feared a return to the chaotically competitive conditions of the 1920s. Managerial autonomy in a stable environment, rather than a free market, was their goal precisely because of their dual prewar and wartime experiences. Their search for stability meant that the business community cast the state as an ally as much as an ideological adversary; this was perhaps the most important prewar economic legacy to postwar Japan. Their prewar experience led Japanese government and business leaders after the war to resist American laissez-faire principles (though not technocratic ones), while the failures of the wartime economy soured the Japanese on strictly centralized planning.[†] Presurrender experiences set the boundaries of debate over economic strategies since 1945. That is, postwar policies have operated within the intellectual framework established between 1920 and 1945—one of capitalism within certain policy limits. This diverse legacy, emphasizing long-term indicative planning, cooperation between private firms and government officials, and establishment of common goals, rather than any specific solution, was Japan's heritage from the first forty-five years of the twentieth century.

Some of the most celebrated aspects of the postwar economy developed during World War II itself, which left Japan not only destroyed but also transformed. Total war required that the national economy be restructured to serve military needs. By August 1945 the Japanese economy could no longer provide consumer goods or even feed the Japanese population. Instead, it had been transformed, as best the Japanese knew how, into a huge military supply unit. These changes were structural and could not easily be reversed. They had significant implications for postwar development, including economic centralization through bureaucratic controls, standardization of production processes, and increased reliance on industrial policy—all changes dictated by the need to mobilize for total war. Often these policies and controls were militarily inadequate, but they did serve to legitimate the process of economic planning. In another important shift, the war encouraged a bias toward those goods used by the military, that is, heavy industrial products rather than textiles. These wartime economic transformations were not in themselves negative; indeed, some aspects clearly hastened later economic growth. For example, the war encouraged new developments in such areas as subcontracting, in-firm production techniques, product standardization, seniority-based wages, and technical trainings all of which became key factors in Japan's postwar economic growth.[‡] These features are attributable not to Japanese culture, not to a miracle, not to the slow, rational modernization of the prewar economy, but to military mobilization and the reorganization of much of Asia for the purpose of further military conquest.

There are many interesting features of this wartime bequest. One is the extent to which Japan's postwar success was based on its presurrender exploitation of the rest of Asia (and of Koreans brought to Japan). Bruce Cumings argues in this volume and in greater detail elsewhere that Japan's economic relations with East and Southeast Asian countries today reproduce a pattern of Japanese capital control and reliance on other countries for cheap labor that was developed by

---

[*] Andrew Gordon, *Evolution of Labor Relations*, 380.

[†] See William Miles Fletcher III, *The Japanese Business Community and National Trade Policy, 1920–1942* (Chapel Hill: University of North Carolina Press, 1989).

[‡] For a longer discussion of the historiography of World War II and the postwar economy, see Laura E. Hein, "The Dark Valley Illuminated: Recent Trends in Studies of the Postwar Japanese Economy," *Bulletin of Concerned Asian Scholars* 16, no. 2 (1984): 56–58.

colonial bureaucrats in the presurrender years.[*] Another interesting and quite separate feature of the importance of military mobilization to postwar economic growth is that it mirrors the changes wrought by the war on the *American* economy. Although Japan's specific forms of subcontracting or the seniority wage system may be unmatched in other nations, the impact of total war mobilization on Japan closely resembles the effect on other industrialized, capitalist countries. Victor and vanquished were similarly transformed by the experience.[†]

Nonetheless, this analogy can be carried too far. Crucially, the Japanese experience also included losing the war. Defeat implied a discrediting of the Japanese military establishment and, more generally, a shift of social and political power within Japan. Surrender marked the failure of a national economic strategy that had relied on imperial expansion, oligopoly, and tight control at home. Domestically the Japanese elite could no longer enforce very low wages on the urban population nor very high rents and taxes on the rural one.[‡] All major industrialists and bureaucrats had based their economic plans on these assumptions. Thus, at micro- and macroeconomic levels, presurrender solutions to economic problems—indeed, much of the shape and direction of the presurrender economy—suddenly had become inappropriate to postwar conditions. These political power shifts triggered by defeat had enormous economic repercussions. The Japanese were forced to undertake a qualitative reordering of the political economy as much as a simple quantitative rebuilding.

The end of the war also meant that the Japanese economy now operated in a fundamentally different international context than did presurrender Japan. Probably the idea of a "Japanese economy" after World War II is misleading. Japan has not had a truly independent domestic economy at any point since 1945. Rather, the Japanese economy has been inextricably twined with the international one, and especially with the economies of the United States and, to a lesser extent, other Asian nations. It seems inappropriate to discuss the domestic aspects alone of such an export-oriented economy without considering Japan's position in the world as a fundamental part of the *definition* of Japan's economic growth.[§]

Without question, the most important international aspect of Japan's postwar economy was its connection to the United States. Although Japan's relationship with the United States is not now—and has never been—that of full ally, American patronage has been crucial to Japanese economic development. After the war this patronage more than compensated for disruptions and hostility to Japanese by other Asians, for the shrinking silk market, and for the loss of the imperial economy. It is hard to imagine what Japan would be like today in the absence of this patronage, particularly in the pivotal years of the early 1950s.

Moreover, the United States was not just the occupying power in Japan; it was also the hegemonic power of the postwar world. The international ethos of power changed after World War II, as did Japan's specific opportunities within the U.S.-dominated system. Although the Japanese consciously rejected some American approaches to organizing their economy, such as pitting

---

[*] This postwar relationship between Japan and its former colonies is discussed in Bruce Cumings, "The Origins and Development of the Northeast Asian Political Economy: Industrial Sectors, Product Cycles, and Political Consequences," *International Organization* 38, no. 1 (Winter 1984): 1–40.

[†] See Michael S. Sherry, *The Rise of American Air Power: The Creation of Armageddon* (New Haven: Yale University Press, 1987), and Charles Maier, "The Politics of Productivity: Foundations of American International Economic Policy after World War II," in *Between Power and Plenty*, ed. Peter Katzenstein (Madison: University of Wisconsin Press, 1978), 23–49.

[‡] See comparative presurrender and postwar data on household consumption presented by Horioka in this volume.

[§] Integration into the world economy was always part of national economic planning, as is clear from the annual Japanese government white papers on the economy, which consistently have incorporated analyses of the interaction of the Japanese and the world economies for forty years. And, as Dower and Cumings stress in this volume, the Japanese economy was tied not only to American economic policy but also to U.S. global military policy.

firms against government regulators, they were deeply influenced by other economic concepts and practices exported from the United States. These included a faith in capitalist reconstruction to solve not only economic problems but also political ones, the belief that science and technology held the answer to social inequities, and the transformation of economic language from one that recognized the relevance of the economy to political and social issues to one that accommodated only administrative and technical problems. This constellation of beliefs, often called technocratic, was exported not only to postwar Japan but also to postwar Europe, sometimes by the very same American individuals.* Technology was an important intellectual *and* practical element in Japan's integration into the new hegemonic world order.[†]

In fact, Japan prospered within the U.S. designed postwar world environment. This environment was predicated on the assumption that unfettered trade among noncommunist nations was the appropriate global economic structure. The United States and its brainchildren, the General Agreement on Tariffs and Trade (GATT) and the International Monetary Fund (IMF), maintained free trade and capital movement across national boundaries at a time when Japan was in no position to negotiate such privileges for itself. Moreover, the United States softened the impact of free trade policies for Japan with a number of specific policies, such as a generously high exchange rate for the yen between 1949 and 1971. These measures were designed to offset the fact that, although Japan had been a strong Asian power in the presurrender years (although weak vis-à-vis the West), it was much weaker in the immediate postwar era. Later, after the Japanese economy had grown at unprecedented rates, it became strong in relation not only to other Asian nations but also to the Western powers. This, too, was a new and unexpected development of the postwar era. United States global strategy to internationalize the capitalist economies provided a historic opportunity for Japan, although actual Japanese economic performance was completely unanticipated by the Americans, the Japanese, or anyone else. Nonetheless, Japanese economic growth ultimately rested on that particular international environment and was thus very much part of the global development of advanced capitalism in the twentieth century.[‡]

Thus, postwar reconstruction required a new economic vision to accommodate international as well as domestic changes. This was the real challenge facing the Japanese in 1945. Somehow they had to create a social, political, and economic strategy that was appropriate to the new context of the postwar world. As early as 1946 many Japanese understood that this vision necessarily had to include economic growth, a higher standard of living for the Japanese people, open international trade, and accommodation of U.S. policy in Asia. Many questions were still undecided, however, such as whether or not to nationalize major industries, what goods to export, where to sell them, how industry should be regulated, or who should make all of these decisions. The Japanese by no means had a clear blueprint for their economic future, nor did all of their efforts succeed. The postwar world presented new problems, and the Japanese disagreed among themselves over how to approach them or respond appropriately. Like economic

---

* At the more specific level, this technocratic approach included exports of methods of product standardization, public relations strategies, and employee management theories. Volker Berghahn, author of *The Americanisation of West German Industry* (Cambridge and New York: Cambridge University Press, 1986), who commented on an earlier draft of this paper, noted that the economic debates and the phases of development described here for Japan exactly mirror developments in postwar West Germany.

† See the essays in this volume by Allinson, Gluck, Gordon, and Koschmann and Ivy's comments on the way in which American television images of idealized middle-class life shaped the aspirations of Japanese who were just learning how to use consumer goods as their definition of success.

‡ To some extent, economic growth rested on good timing and the sense to recognize an opportunity. The Japanese were able to seize the fleeting historic moment when free trade, an expanding international economy, a large technology gap, extensive American political and financial support, and cheap oil meant that economic growth was closest to the nation's grasp.

policymakers everywhere, they were reduced to trial and error.[*]

CENTRAL ECONOMIC PLANKS: GROWTH AND TECHNOLOGY

Simply deciding whether or not to focus on the economy was the first major debate right after the war. In late 1946 the Japanese government under Yoshida Shigeru officially promised to maximize economic growth. The commitment to growth was a specific strategy chosen by the Yoshida cabinet, not an automatic development. Rather, this decision was made in order to reconcile or at least defuse deep political conflicts in postwar Japan. Like other postwar economic policies, it reveals contention rather than a natural consensus. From late 1946, with the adoption of the priority production policy, which concentrated all available resources in the coal and steel industries, the Japanese government strove not just for recovery or reconstruction but for growth and development in the direction of a sophisticated, high-wage economy. As such, it drew from a variety of constituencies, such as labor, business, academics, and bureaucrats, in part explaining how growth became the basis of a general postwar strategy. In other words, the acceptance of economic growth as a *primary goal* was itself a historical development during the postwar era.[†] This focus on economic growth was the first important feature of the economy to develop during the postwar era.

The Japanese had no clearly defined plan for economic development, but by 1949 the commitment to a high-valued-added economy with sophisticated export goods had also been added permanently to national economic policy. Their "rationalization" plan involved upgrading the quality of goods produced through infusions of technology in order to sell abroad. Again, this was a way of dealing with conflicting demands of different groups of Japanese, and economic policy development rested squarely on a historic compromise. This new policy, although frequently repressive in practice, contained promise for working-class Japanese, it inherently required the cooperation of industrial workers on a broad level and a literate, trained work force because the 1949 rationalization strategy depended on improving the *quality* of goods produced in order to win the essential export market. Elite Japanese took comfort from the widespread assumption that technology could enhance economic justice while avoiding redistribution of wealth. This dream of a technological fix for social problems was shared by the Americans in Japan and Americans at home.

Although developed as a proposal in 1949, rationalization was not easily accomplished. Conceptually, rationalization went through several stages and much debate. In its first incarnation it was designed to upgrade two basic industries: coal, and iron and steel. The coal half of this plan was a dismal failure, a fact rarely noted since attention has been riveted to the successful half, the iron and steel industry. Rationalization was later implemented in numerous other industries, but often in unanticipated ways. The blossoming of the oil refining industry, for example, surprised most Japanese planners. Its unexpected success created tension between the pro-coal and the pro-petroleum thinkers in Japan, a tension that took over a decade to resolve and has not fully disappeared more than thirty years later. Moreover, the Japanese were not at that time confident that the rationalization strategy was appropriate for their economy, nor was it fully developed. Fifteen years later they could present it as a unified theory, but it was still only one hopeful idea among many in 1950.[‡]

---

[*] This was an enormous challenge for all nations after the war. Yet in some ways defeat freed the Japanese to jettison their old strategies, while victor nations, such as Britain, were far less willing to accept the new global environment. This psychological attitude is probably the kernel of reality within the commonly expressed fantasy that losing World War II was economically better than winning it.

[†] See Laura E. Hein, *Fueling Growth: The Energy Revolution and Economic Policy in Postwar Japan*, East Asia Monograph Series (Cambridge: Harvard University Press, 1990).

[‡] See Hein, *Fueling Growth*. The fortunes of coal and iron and steel diverged so much that by 1960 they were rarely discussed together, in sharp contrast to almost all discussions of the economy until 1951. Interestingly, the two sectors are

The rationalization policy also required extensive American supplies of both capital and technology, involving complex interactions among American and Japanese government agencies and private groups, which all worked to upgrade the quality of Japanese goods. For example, in 1949 and 1950 occupation officials invited numerous American management training experts, industrial statisticians, and other specialists across the Pacific to advise the Japanese. The most famous of these, W. Edwards Deming, introduced the concept of quality control systems to Japan. He did so on his third trip to Japan, this time invited by the Japan Union of Scientists and Engineers, after approval from Supreme Command for Allied Powers (SCAP) officers. His ideas about quality control fit neatly with then-developing Japanese government rationalization policy and were officially encouraged. All parties agreed that Japan had to improve its ability to sell abroad if it was to survive economically and function as an effective economic and strategic ally in the Pacific. Deming's approach to quality control provided a concrete strategy on which U.S. and Japanese business leaders and officials from both governments could cooperate.[*]

Even in that archetypal success story, iron and steel, the best efforts of Japanese rationalization-policy planners and effective application of Deming's ideas were not sufficient. Recovery was possible in 1950 and 1951 only because of the unusual demand created by the Korean War. Without the specific efforts of the American government to funnel dollar sales to Japan, it is not at all clear that the feeble economy of that era could have achieved industrial rationalization. The vital problem of export markets was not even partially solved until the Korean War, and its outbreak on 21 June 1950 was certainly more important to Japanese economic history than was the political milestone of independence in April 1952.[†]

The Korean War was a key moment for Japan's reintegration into the international economy after the long decades of autarky and war. American military orders were purposely placed with Japanese firms to provide them with precious "overseas" customers. This tactic allowed the Japanese companies to import American technology for more sophisticated future exports, a development encouraged by U.S. foreign policy makers. It was only after those last pieces of the puzzle of economic recovery—access to technology and markets—were in place that the Japanese could implement their own economic rationalization policy. In 1951, the first full year of the Korean War, the Japanese economy recovered to its pre–China War level. This lucrative relationship continued beyond the formal cease-fire in Korea. Between 1951 and 1956 U.S. military purchases in Japan paid for more than a quarter of Japanese imports. This rate of spending tapered off in the late 1950s, but then the Vietnam War jacked up U.S. military procurements again in the mid-1960s.[‡]

---

once again linked in recent discussions, this time as declining industries. For example, see Yoko Kitazawa, "Setting Up Shop/ Shutting Up Shop," *Ampo: Japan-Asia Quarterly Review* 19, no. 1 (1987): 10–29. For works that credit rationalization policy for economic success, see Chalmers Johnson, *MITI and the Japanese Miracle: the Growth of Industrial Policy, 1925–1975* (Stanford: Stanford University Press, 1982); see also Hideichiro Nakamura, "Plotting a New Economic Course," *Japan Echo* 6 (special issue, "Economy in Transition"; 1979): 11–20.

[*] Mary Walton, *The Deming Management Method* (New York: Dodd, Mead, 1986), 10–15; W. Edwards Deming, *Out of the Crisis* (Cambridge: Center for Advanced Engineering Study, MIT, 1982), 2–6, 486–92.

[†] To an unusual degree the periodizations generally used in discussions of postwar Japan are based on economic events, such as trade liberalization in 1960 and the oil shock in 1973–74. Considering that most historic turning points in any country are defined by political events, this economic periodization is eloquent testimony to the primacy of economics in discussions of postwar Japan. One exception is 1955, which Junnosuke Masumi and many others have used as a pivotal moment on the basis of political events. See Junnosuke Masumi, *Postwar Politics in Japan, 1945–1955* (Berkeley: Institute of East Asian Studies, University of California, 1985).

[‡] Thomas R. H. Havens, *Fire Across the Sea: The Vietnam War and Japan, 1965–1975* (Princeton: Princeton University Press, 1987), 92–97.

Once again, the relationship of Japanese economic prosperity to war emerged as an issue. There was a moment just after World War II when this pattern had been criticized not just in Asia but also by the U.S. Pauley Commission on reparations, sent to Japan to redress the historic imbalance created by the Japanese military in the economic realm. The Pauley Commission's report wrestled with the problem of global economic justice and Japan's historic and future relationship with the rest of Asia, although it was soon superseded by American policy calling for Japanese economic recovery.* But Asian memories are longer on this point. Japan's former colonies have prospered since 1945 but have retained their subordinate relationship to Japan, perpetuating Asian tensions. The complexity of these relationships harks back to the presurrender era and immediate postwar settlement and keeps alive the issue of economic and social justice on an international scale.

Even after the occupation ended and the Japanese were freer to pursue their own economic goals, how to achieve them remained a lively subject of debate. For example, the Japanese debated through the 1950s whether they should emphasize natural resource development within Japan or export industries. The first position meant supporting the domestic coal and hydroelectricity industries whereas the second implied an expansion of petroleum and coal imports. Men like Arisawa Hiromi, Tsuru Shigeto, and the officials at the Economic Planning Agency within the Japanese government argued that import minimization projects, like the Tennessee Valley Authority in the United States, should have first priority. Worried about the expense and instability of overseas fuel supplies, they wanted less vulnerability to changes in foreign political and economic climates. Undoubtedly, Japan's prewar experience with autarky

influenced their thinking. These men believed that minimizing imports would protect them from overreliance on exports and that alternative development of hydroelectricity would help develop the nation's sadly inadequate infrastructure. They also hoped that new technology would yield previously undiscovered energy resources in Japan. This attention to the foundations of the future economy—with its implicit acceptance of planning—continued to be an important element of Japanese economic policy.

Nonetheless, the other side of the debate carried the day. Nakayama Ichirō, the primary spokesman, argued that the nation should focus first on expanding exports because that was the *quickest* path to self-sufficiency. Nakayama argued that Japanese economic conditions were very like those of nineteenth-century Britain and that the limitations of a large population and few natural resources were best resolved by embracing foreign trade rather than limiting it. Like the British economy of a century earlier, the Japanese economy would be sustained by processing imports and selling manufactured goods. Japan had no choice but to trade in the world economy and thus had to accept vulnerability to events over which it had no control, Nakayama argued. The debate was eventually resolved in favor of Nakayama when the Japanese were forced to accept the physical limits of the domestic resource base. Even so, the Japanese were very reluctant to give up the psychological comfort of energy and food self-sufficiency. The Arisawa Nakayama debate dragged on for nearly a decade, reflecting this discomfort. This and other debates on the fundamental nature of their economic policy reveal the many areas of continuing uncertainty over economic strategy well after the occupation years.†

During the 1950s the rate of GNP growth of the Japanese economy also began to increase. The period

---

* Edwin Pauley, "Pauley Interim Report to the President," 6 Dec. 1945, *Foreign Relations of the United States, 1945* 6:1004–9. For a detailed history of reparations policy, see Ōkurashō Zaisei Shishitsu (Ministry of Finance, Financial History Group), ed., *Sōsetsu: Baishō shūsen shori* (General introduction: Reparations and termination of war measures), vol. 1 in *Shōwa zaisei shi: Shūsen kara kōwa made* (Tokyo: Tōyō Keizai Shinpōsha, 1984).

† Nakayama Ichirō, "Nihon keizai no kao," *Hyōron*, Dec. 1949, 1–9. See also Economic Stabilization Board, "Stabilization as We See It," 1 Mar. 1949, 9; Arisawa Hiromi, "Nihon shihon shugi no unmei," *Hyōron*, Feb. 1950, 5–14. For comments on the influential nature of these articles, see the discussion in Tsuruta Toshimasa, *Sengo Nihon no sangyō seisaku* (Tokyo: Nihon Keizai Shinbunsha, 1982), 24–31.

of "high-speed growth" began gradually since Japan still required economic recovery. With the population swollen by 25 percent over prewar figures, the Japanese economy had to grow simply to provide the same per capita output. When 11 percent annual growth arrived in the 1960s, it surprised most Japanese.[*]

THE FINAL KEY TO HIGH-SPEED GROWTH: DOMESTIC CONSUMPTION

High-speed growth was achieved only after at least two important changes in official economic strategy in 1959–60. Like earlier policies, both changes developed out of conflict, in response to political challenges to the dominance of growth and technology in Japanese economic strategy. Ironically, although these challenges forced official strategy to include some redistributive functions, the new compromises encouraged even faster growth, cementing Japan's commitment to higher GNP levels.

The first policy change was the transformation of the 1949 rationalization policy into a new concept—industrial structure policy. The recent collapse of the coal and textile industries had shown that rationalization was not equally possible in all sectors. Each had become a declining industry; that is, neither could be made internationally competitive through injections of technology. The success of rationalization policy had depended partly on world trade and technology markets, over which the Japanese had little control. Although the Japanese knew this, they had assumed originally that foreign technology existed to upgrade all industries. Recognition of the problems of declining industries required a new policy. By 1959 the Japanese had also learned to study the effects of rationalization

itself, based on their experiences in such successful industries as electric power, oil refining, and machine tools. Rationalization of one industry could either help or hinder rationalization in another, and the Japanese were only beginning to understand how to manipulate these interindustry linkages in 1959. The problems of decline and linkage had to be addressed before the Japanese could transform their policy for economic reconstruction into one suitable for producing growth. Otherwise, some economic sectors would grow while others would falter.

The new "industrial structure" policy emerged out of MITI in late 1959. It used the metaphor of a biological life cycle to define and justify criteria for rationalization.[†] Industries at the beginning and end of their life cycle—like infant and aged humans—require more care than do mature sectors. From 1960 government assistance was increasingly targeted toward those two classes of industries. This was an important refinement of rationalization policy, which had previously emphasized basic industry. Although the two original declining industries were textiles and coal, the mature adult industries of one era are the pensioners of the next, as the oil refiners and petrochemical firms discovered in the 1970s. In fact, the policy implications of this analysis did not fully develop until these and other major industries began to suffer in the 1970s.[‡]

Social welfare provisions were added to the policy after labor unions teased out a new economic justification for reincorporating social welfare and redistribution of wealth into discussions of the economy. Technology's inability to resolve all social ailments was laid bare by

---

[*] For discussion in English, see Yutaka Kosai, *The Era of High-Speed Growth: Notes on the Postwar Japanese Economy* (Tokyo: University of Tokyo Press, 1986); Takafusa Nakamura, *The Postwar Japanese Economy: Its Development and Structure* (Tokyo: University of Tokyo Press, 1981); Tatsurō Uchino, *Japan's Postwar Economy: An Insider's View of Its History and Its Future* (Tokyo: Kodansha International, 1983). For GNP growth statistics, see Nakamura, *Postwar Japanese Economy*, 112.

[†] Tsūshō Sangyō Shō, Shōkō Seisaku Shi Kankokai, ed. (Ministry of International Trade and Industry. Commission on the History of Trade and Industry Policy), *Sangyō gōrika (sengo)*, vol. 10 of *Shōkō seisaku shi* (Tokyo: Shōkō Seisaku Shi Kankōkai, 1972); see Johnson, *MITI and the Japanese Miracle*, 252–54, for a description of the development of this policy.

[‡] See Merton J. Peck, Richard G. Levin, and Akira Goto, "Picking Losers: Public Policy Toward Declining Industries in Japan," *Journal of Japanese Studies* 13, no. 1 (Winter 1987): 79–123.

industrial structure analysis, and union members refused to shoulder the whole burden of their industries' reduced fortunes. The sharpest conflict occurred at the Miike coal mine, where the miners waged a six-month strike over job security and wages. All parties understood that this was not simply a debate between management and labor but intimately concerned government policy toward "sunset" industries. Labor's main accomplishment in that clash was to reintroduce debate on the relationship between economic justice and economic growth.* Recognizing that declining industries were part of the industrial life cycle eventually led to the development of a "soft landing" policy for workers in those areas. Those provisions both redeemed and tempered the technocratic approach.

In an equally important refinement, industrial structure, unlike rationalization, is a dynamic concept: appropriate policies for any given industry will change over time. This understanding of the dynamic quality of economies was a key policy contribution to Japan's subsequent high-speed growth. The first true energy policy was associated with this development, when the lengthy troubles of the coal mines led the Japanese to this conceptual breakthrough. Moreover, the effects of rationalization within one industry on development of another has become a standard aspect of study for industrial structure policy, providing an analytical framework for Japanese planners then and now. Industrial structure policy also assumed a permanent need for economic planning and government assistance to all industries at some stage of the life cycle. Like wartime and earlier postwar policies, it incorporated long-term planning into the Japanese economy. In theory as well as practice, economic planning repeatedly has been institutionalized in postwar Japan.

The second major economic initiative of 1960, the Ikeda administration's Income Doubling Plan, also championed redistribution of economic benefits within the context of a celebration of economic growth. The plan was designed explicitly to quiet political protest after mass demonstrations against the government's foreign policy. The Income Doubling Plan reaffirmed government responsibility for social welfare, vocational training, and education and increased spending considerably in these areas. It also sought to eliminate low-wage jobs and regional income disparities.

Yet the plan's greatest innovation was to redefine growth to include Japanese consumers as well as producers. Indeed, the government promised to double average household incomes within a decade, and, gratifyingly, the standard of living did jump dramatically in the next few years. Not only was the new wealth pleasant for consumers, but it also created a mass market that at last made high-speed growth possible.† This "consumption boom" was the final key to Japan's economic growth. In larger cultural terms, Ikeda and his allies transformed the image of consumer spending into a positive, officially sanctioned one. After decades (even centuries) of government exhortations to Japanese citizens to be thrifty and avoid ostentation, the invitation to spend meant an enormous shift in the ethics of economic behavior. In a suggestive correlation, mass consumer society, consumer consciousness, and consumer protest developed in Japan only after this point.‡ Most strikingly, although the official policies of 1960 were profoundly political responses to Ikeda's critics, 1960 marked the turning point in acceptance of technocratic thought and acceptance of growth as a goal in postwar Japan. High and continually expanding personal consumption satisfied most people.

Over the next decade the economy grew at an unprecedentedly high rate. Consumer goods proliferated and wages rose because of both the boom conditions

---

* On this episode, see also the essays by Garon and Mochizuki and Gordon in this volume.

---

† For the Income Doubling Plan, see Arisawa Hiromi and Inaba Hidezō, eds., *Keizai, Shiryō sengo 20-nen shi*, vol. 2 (Tokyo: Nihon Hyōronsha, 1966); Keizai Kikakuchō (Economic Planning Agency), *Gendai Nihon keizai no tenkai: Keizai kikakuchō 30-nen shi* (Tokyo: Ōkurashō Insatsukyoku, 1976); Nakamura, *Postwar Japanese Economy*, 83–89; Harry T. Oshima, "Reinterpreting Japan's Postwar Growth," *Economic Development and Cultural Change* 31, no. 1 (Oct. 1982): 1–43.

‡ See the essays by Ivy, White, Taira, and Upham in this volume, especially on antipollution and citizens' movements.

and a growing labor shortage. Meanwhile, the ties between the Japanese and the international economies became increasingly complex, as various new trade and capital relationships developed. That period ended in 1973–74 with the OPEC oil embargo, which clearly signaled a new relationship between Japan and the rapidly changing world economy. The high-growth period ended then, and to a considerable extent "postwar Japan" ended with it.

The 1946 strategy had worked politically through 1973 to elevate economics as a central political theme of Japanese society. It also mediated political tension by taking elements proposed by various different groups and weaving them together. In so doing, this strategy also created the shape of the postwar settlement in Japan. By the early 1970s, after a decade of high-speed growth, the focus on economic administration and technology itself obscured the highly political dimension of postwar economic decisions—even when those decisions were the product of intense political debate. This economic strategy worked reasonably well as long as high-speed growth persisted. By the early 1970s clearly articulated, self-conscious opposition groups had begun to disappear from the Japanese economic debate.* Many of their most acute economic grievances had been redressed as wages, household goods, and social services all improved through the 1960s. Nonetheless, although those opposition voices subsided, statistical inequalities lingered, suggesting that the possibility for profound contention also still remained. That possibility took on new immediacy when economic growth dramatically slowed in the 1970s.

---

* In this volume, Dower outlines some reasons why it grew harder to focus political debate after several major symbols rallying opposition groups lost their potency. Opposition groups include the worker/artisan culture described by Gordon, the anticapitalist intellectuals described by Koschmann, the critical historical visionaries described by Gluck, the independent producers of popular culture described by Ivy, and the peace activists who appear in Dower (all in this volume). See also Kelly and Taira on the developments of middle-class or middle-stream consciousness as distinct from achievement of middle-class status.

SLOW GROWTH: THE JAPANESE ECONOMY AND ITS PLACE IN THE WORLD AFTER 1973

A number of trends culminated in the early 1970s to bring an end to high-speed growth and, for a short time, stop economic growth altogether. One was that Japan had closed the technology gap that had powered high-speed growth for twenty years. For the first time, heavy manufacturing industries (such as aluminum and fertilizer production) were becoming *less* competitive internationally. Moreover, agriculture had shrunk so much that it could no longer provide a pool of low-productivity workers available for absorption into more high-productivity jobs. Another change was that American economic hegemony no longer rested on a firm foundation. The United States could no longer afford to prop up the international capitalist economy and act as the "free world's policeman." The climate that had nurtured high-speed growth within Japan disappeared with those changes.

The Japanese, who had not thought much about the end to high-speed growth, were not intellectually prepared, nor did they have policies ready for this development. They were stunned when the United States acted unilaterally to change its economic relationship with Japan. These U.S. actions, known as "shocks" in Japan, forced the Japanese to reevaluate their place in the world political economy. First, in July 1971 the U.S. government recognized the People's Republic of China without alerting Tokyo to that major policy shift. In the next "shock," on 15 August 1971, the U.S. devalued its currency against the yen by 17 percent, again without consulting its Pacific ally. The Japanese were completely unprepared for the corresponding yen revaluation because they had continued to underestimate the real strength of their economy. As late as 1967–68 many Japanese officials were arguing for currency *devaluation*, even though the yen was almost certainly already too low.† Then in late 1972, after a poor harvest, the Americans embargoed exports of soybeans, threatening

---

† Uchino reports that Ministry of Finance officials secretly considered a yen *revaluation* in late 1969, but this move was vetoed for political reasons; *Japan's Postwar Economy*, 155. See also 175, 274–75.

a traditional staple of the Japanese diet. Nor did the rest of the world look more hospitable. Just as the Japanese were adjusting to these changes, they confronted the biggest disruption of all—the OPEC oil embargo of 1973–74. Japanese leaders had not expected to be included in the embargo and, as with the "shocks," were thoroughly unprepared.

Thus, despite a decade or more of high-speed growth, most Japanese felt increasingly *insecure* about their place in the global economy. This sense of insecurity led to a new debate about Japan's place in the world, as the real consequences of Nakayama's economic strategy—a fundamental interdependence with the international economy—became vividly clear. A sense of vulnerability over vital imports of food and fuel swept the nation. Anxiety was equally strong over the postwar decision to follow the United States' lead, given that America's first priority clearly was America, not Japan. Even ostensibly faraway events, like the war between the Israelis and the Palestinians, had become central to Japan's economic health. Wealth without economic security suddenly seemed pointless.

Although nationalist rhetoric gained new legitimacy, renewed unease about Japan's place in the world economy and the terms of the U.S.-Japan partnership did not prompt Japanese leaders to radically change their foreign policy. They were reluctant to abandon the precedent established after the war by Prime Minister Yoshida Shigeru to accept American protection in return for prosperity, although Japanese trust in American benevolence decreased. Partly because the Japanese were so unprepared for changes in the international political economy, they had not (and still have not) found a viable alternative to life under the U.S. hegemon. Rather, these anxieties worked to obscure for most Japanese the fact that by 1973 Japan boasted one of the world's largest and most sophisticated economies. Few Japanese examined the effect of their economic actions on the rest of the world. Japan retained a curiously anachronistic insular quality. While alive to every pressure from overseas, most Japanese lacked a strong sense of reciprocal power.

Although Japanese foreign economic policy continued to be based on the fundamental assumptions of capitalist interdependence, open world markets, limited access to countries allied with the Soviet Union, and U.S. hegemony that were established in the early 1950s, anxieties over foreign economic pressures recast internal debates over political and economic problems into international ones. The pressures from overseas—to support one side or the other in the Mideast conflict, to open trade and capital markets, to maintain the embargo on certain goods to the Soviet Union and the Peoples' Republic of China*—served to defer domestic political debate just as economic growth had in the previous decades. Ironically, the growing fear of foreign domination occurred at a time when the Japanese economy was weathering realignments caused by the two oil embargoes better than most of the other major capitalist economies.

Fear of foreign economic power is not a new theme in Japan. On the contrary, it was a significant component in the prewar decisions to develop an empire and widen the war in 1941. Nonetheless, it had abated somewhat during the postwar era until the economic disruptions of the early 1970s gave anxieties about foreign domination of Japan renewed legitimacy and urgency. Those events brought home to the Japanese the inescapable relationship between economic diversification and increasingly complex ties to the global economy. At the same time, because those disruptions were interpreted widely as opportunities for foreigners to dominate Japan, they served to contain domestic political debate on economic strategy within a defensive, nationalistic framework.† Precisely because that transmutation of

---

* The embargo on strategic goods to the USSR was a major international issue as late as 1987, when revelations that Toshiba Corporation had sold sophisticated military machinery to the Soviet Union touched off an international scandal.

† These themes emerge in Yasuhiro Nakasone, "Toward a Nation of Dynamic Culture and Welfare," *Japan Echo* 10, no. 1 (Spring 1983): 12–18. In this volume, Kelly makes a similar point, as does Taira in his discussion of "Nipponists versus people." Note that Kelly and Ivy, who also argues that economic anxieties in the 1970s turned the Japanese culture introspective, both discuss the celebration of a new diversity within Japan in the 1980s, but both see it as fake, based on target markets and consumption patterns rather than any real distinction among the

international tension into pressure for domestic unity echoed the prewar nationalistic strategies of mobilizing the population, the tendency to subsume divisions within Japan and focus on threats from abroad is disturbing. Such use of global economic friction to fend off domestic criticism can threaten democracy and peace.

The political uses of this conflation of foreign economic pressure and the need for domestic unity were obvious; they served to entrench the status quo, including the authority of existing government and business leaders. Yet few Japanese focused on the conservative implications of this development, partly because their attention was drawn to the diffuse nature of the boundaries between Japan's domestic economy and the international one. Since Japan's prosperity depended on the survival of the existing international order, Japanese inside and outside the government saw domestic and international problems as one and the same. Any changes to the broad outlines of the postwar international economic order, because they would profoundly affect the domestic economy, were potentially threatening. Given the growing perception in other nations of Japan as a great economic success during the 1970s, this was a surprisingly pessimistic evaluation.

In the case of Japanese officials, perhaps this pessimism developed in part from the fact that they were losing control over the domestic economy. Not only did their high-growth-era policies become inappropriate for the 1970s economy, but the changes wrought by high-speed growth had themselves loosened the government's grip on economic activities of Japanese firms. For example, one of the main methods the Japanese government had used to influence Japanese businesses throughout the postwar era was strict control of foreign exchange reserves. This technique was extremely effective while reserves were scarce, but by the late 1970s Japanese export industries no longer needed to beg for foreign exchange allocations. The growing level of offshore production by Japanese firms also removed many activities from Japanese government scrutiny.[*] In these and other ways the inevitable global interdependence accompanying Japan's postwar economic strategy obscured real centers of Japanese power at home and abroad.

Not only were government officials far more conscious of their loss of control over the domestic economy than of their increase in influence over the international one, but they also were less aware that they shared this diminution of control over transnational corporations with Western governments. Because of this blind spot, nationalist political leaders inappropriately began to compare the current configuration, in which all transnational corporations are becoming more powerful and more independent of their home government, with the pre–World War II system in which Japan—the state—was weak in comparison to Western nations. The essentially domestic government-business conflict was redefined as an anti-Japanese attack. The prewar analogy was eerily reflected by the West's mirror image of Japan as a rogue economy (in which government and large corporations are entirely undifferentiated) bent on world conquest, just as the Japanese state was viewed as a rogue military force before 1945.[†] Japan's interdependence with the global economy accelerated in the mid-1980s with a massive yen revaluation and serious labor shortages. Deindustrialization, or the "hollowing" of the Japanese economy, took place at an

population. Indeed, these spurious differences serve to mask real divisions.

[*] T. J. Pempel, "The Unbundling of 'Japan, Inc.': The Changing Dynamics of Japanese Policy Formation," *Journal of*

Japanese Studies 13, no. 2 (Summer 1987): 288; Hugh Patrick and Henry Rosovsky, "The Japanese Economy in Transition," in *Economic Policy and Development: New Perspectives*, ed. Toshio Shishido and Ryuzo Sato (Dover, Mass., and London: Auburn House, 1985), 160.

[†] For example, see *Japan Echo* 4, no. 3 (1977), especially Naohiro Amaya, "Cyclical Twenty-Five-Year Periods in History and the Present Age," 16–28, and Toyoaki Ikuta, Nobuyuki Nakahara, Taichi Sakaiya, and Ken'ichi Koyama, "The Day Japan Dies for Want of Oil," 78–85. For a more recent U.S. example of the many political statements on this theme, see the cartoon by Mike Luckovich of the *Atlanta Constitution*, depicting two identical newspapers, one dated 7 December 1941 and the other 7 December 1989; the two headlines are "Japan Bombs Pearl Harbor" and "Japan Buys Pearl Harbor." (This cartoon appeared in the *Chicago Tribune*, 13 Nov. 1989.)

unanticipated rate because of yen appreciation.* That is, Japanese manufacturers began moving to low-wage, pollution-tolerant sites in Asia. Other Japanese firms accelerated plans to build manufacturing plants in North America and Europe to fend off potential protectionist legislation, many rushing to enter Europe before the economic reorganization there in 1992. Meanwhile, the U.S. government, burdened with a swelling federal deficit, demanded greater economic concessions from the Japanese state.

Japan's new involvements coincided with a reemerging debate over Japan's proper stance in the global political economy, confirming the sense of vulnerability for some Japanese and dispelling it for others. The debate in Japan over this economic configuration centered on whether to evaluate it as a sign of Japanese strength or of Japanese weakness.† Some Japanese responded by worrying that the high value of the yen relative to other world currencies was as destabilizing as was the earlier era of economic weakness. Other, more self-confident individuals comforted themselves with the thought that U.S. economic decline was due to American laziness and ethnic diversity rather than any structural economic factors—factors shared by all capitalist economies. Meanwhile, economic muscle

was increasingly attributed to the inherent superiority of Japanese culture and tradition. The focus shifted from Japanese perceptions of themselves as weak in the world to a self-definition of themselves as righteously strong but thwarted by malevolent outsiders. Japanese "subordinate independence" vis-à-vis the United States came under growing criticism. The runaway popularity in 1989 of *"No" to ieru Nihon*, which argued that Japan should say no to the United States, was graphic evidence that criticizing U.S. hegemony struck a responsive chord among millions of Japanese. Such criticism had emerged earlier from progressive critics of American cold-war and anticommunist policy, but it was now taken up by conservative elites, who were angered more by continued U.S. arrogance in the face of economic decline.‡ Nonetheless, Japanese leaders were still not ready to articulate a new bilateral relationship or a significantly new role in international affairs despite (or perhaps because of) the enormous shift in the international context caused by the collapse of the Soviet bloc and then the USSR itself between 1989 and 1992.

UNRESOLVED PROBLEMS

Despite this new level of confidence as Japan began the 1990s, several unsolved problems remained that had developed directly out of the economic strategy of the previous forty-five years: to achieve prosperity and political stability through economic growth, technology, and consumption. These problems included structural demands for ever-increasing cycles of investment, ecological destruction, and growing political estrangement between Japan and much of the rest of the world.

Japan was still locked into a dizzying cycle of new product development in the early 1990s. The Japanese high-growth system was based on the recognition that

---

* The yen was pegged at 360 to one U.S. dollar from 1949 to 1971. It then rose gradually to about 238 to the dollar in 1984 and 1985. Late in 1985 the yen's value began to shoot up, averaging only 128 to the dollar in 1988. In 1989 it dropped slightly, for an annual average of 138 yen to the dollar, but rose again in late 1990 to 1985 levels. The 1991 average was 135 yen per dollar. See Japan Economic Institute, *JEI Report* no. 2B (12 Jan. 1990), 2, and no. 2B (17 Jan. 1992), 11.

† Recent work by Western analysts also has concentrated specifically on this shift of the international economic environment, either gloomily suggesting that Japan will have difficulty responding to it or, in a more sanguine analysis, emphasizing Japan's capacity to adapt. For gloomy analyses, see the special issue *of Journal of Japanese Studies* 13, no. 2 (Summer 1987), especially Kozo Yamamura, "Shedding the Shackles of Success: Saving Less for Japan's Future," 429–56. In contrast, see Ronald Bore, *Flexible Rigidities* (Stanford: Stanford University Press, 1986), for a more hopeful analysis.

‡ The complaint is as much about America's loss of hegemony (without development of any new modesty) as about its perpetration; see *"No" to ieru Nihon*, by Morita Akio, chair of Sony Corporation, and Ishihara Shintarō, a prominent Diet member (Tokyo: Kobunsha, 1989). The best-seller went through ten printings in 1989 alone.

economic development is dynamic: new industries and processes must be introduced continuously to maintain growth within an international system. This was one of the great insights of the industrial structure policy of 1959. The strategy of constantly developing new products (including meaninglessly differentiated ones) was crucial to Japan's becoming an economic power and certainly contributed to the growing integration of the global economy. Yet that dynamic contained its own dangers. The rate at which industries matured and declined in Japan accelerated steadily—perhaps beyond the point where it should. This speed-up of the industrial life cycle has harmed communities, especially ones dependent on a single industry. Whole regions of Japan were depopulated as rapid shifts in industrial production rendered the plants and equipment there useless. Meanwhile, in the big cities negative effects included overbuilding, planned obsolescence, congestion, and the growing stress of urban life.[*] Too rapid economic change stood in the way of full employment as worker training became obsolete at an increasingly rapid rate. The aging of the population made it harder to shift workers to new skills quickly, creating an atmosphere of human disposability with painful implications for both economic efficiency and personal satisfaction.[†]

More generally, the implicit—and unsustainable—postwar assumption that rapid economic growth is normal and infinitely maintainable led to long-term neglect of the environment and of the quality of life. The continued emphasis on growth threatened the future standard of living in Japan and abroad. Even the newer, "knowledge-intensive" industries contributed to environmental degradation. The Japanese were very slow to appreciate the ecological effects of their industries on land, sea, and air. The government never threw its full weight behind pollution control or

compensation to those poisoned by industrial waste. As late as 1990 the central government refused to negotiate compensation for some sufferers of Minamata disease.[‡] Sadly, the natural beauty of Japan itself is nearly obliterated, while Japanese fishing, turtling, lumbering, and ivory-purchasing practices ravage the oceans, forests, and savannas of the world.[§]

The assumption that growth can last forever has also allowed the Japanese to indulge in a search for overseas scapegoats rather than accept the limits of the biosphere. For example, the common Japanese insistence that criticism of whaling is based on Western cultural taboos against eating whale rather than concern about decimation of the global whale population neatly illustrates the deflection of both domestic and international criticism of the official policy of maximizing economic growth. Prophecies of extinction—and thus the unavailability of whale meat to future generations of Japanese—have been transformed into racial criticism of Japanese custom. This mutation silences ecologically minded Japanese, particularly since foreign criticism often *does* include an element of disgust, reinforcing Japanese perceptions of themselves as buffeted by the outside world.

High-speed growth was possible because of the confluence of a specific set of international and domestic opportunities. But by the early 1990s the Japanese economy had grown so much that its sheer size alone profoundly affected the world economy—and made

---

[*] Note Ivy's argument (in this volume) that the increased speed of consumption of cultural images serves to blur the line between reality and images, reducing the space available to recreate nonhegemonic images.

[†] Yutaka Kosai, "The Reasons That Unemployment Must Rise," *Japan Quarterly* 34, no. 3 (July–Sept. 1987): 234–40.

[‡] This decision occurred within the context of a legal suit for compensation by some people who wanted legal recognition as Minamata disease victims. Four separate courts recommended that the defendants in the long-running case accept mediation because the plaintiffs were beginning to die of old age. Two of the defendants, the prefectural government and the polluting corporation, agreed, but the central government preferred to pursue its case in court, adding several years before the matter could be resolved. Whereas the government had earlier tried to avoid the legal system, it was now to its advantage to embrace it. *Japan Times*, 19 Oct. and 30 Oct. 1990.

[§] "The World's Eco-Outlaw, Critics Take Aim at Japan," *Newsweek*, 1 May 1989; "Environment: Putting the Heat on Japan," *Time*, 10 July 1989.

further high-speed growth much more difficult to attain. Attention to this fact, however, would demand a major debate about growth policy, something the Japanese have been unwilling to do. Rather, world events are still perceived as things that happen *to* Japan, all of which potentially threaten domestic prosperity. By ignoring Japan's growing role in shaping the global political economy, Japanese leaders deflected domestic dissent but also left themselves intellectually unprepared for new developments. Their conceptual myopia revealed itself in both general attitudes and responses to specific events. Japanese assumptions that their economic power derived from racial purity or cultural superiority suggests an absence of intellectual tools to explain inevitable future problems (such as growing competition from the Republic of Korea). In a more concrete example, when Iraq invaded Kuwait in 1990, the Japanese government seemed surprised that its citizens were treated as political pawns along with Western nationals. Despite the long alliance with the United States and Japan's eager participation in the international petroleum market, few Japanese understood that their economic power largely determined the image Japan presented to the Arab world. This is disturbing: as long as the Japanese ignore the consequences of their own economic growth, their ability to meet future challenges will diminish.

DEMOCRACY AND HIGH GROWTH

Edited by William Theodore De Bary, Carol Gluck, and Donald Keene

ENVIRONMENTAL ACTIVISM IN POSTWAR JAPAN: MINAMATA DISEASE

In the 1950s, the devastating symptoms of what later was identified as mercury poisoning began to destroy the health, lives, and livelihoods of fishermen, their families, and the residents of Minamata City in Kyushu. The mercury was discharged into the bay by the Chisso Corporation as a waste by-product in the production of chemical fertilizer. Local residents and then a network of supporters nationwide organized a movement to provide compensation and redress and to prevent future pollution. A settlement reached in the 1950s offered meager payments to a small number of recognized victims and half-measures of prevention. The company denied responsibility and covered up evidence of the link between its production process and mercury poisoning. Then, from the late 1960s into the 1970s, a far more effective protest movement developed in a changed context. Economic growth had made compensation easier to afford, and it also made it easier for activists to communicate to a broader audience. The settlement was a landmark in the history of political activism by pollution victims and ordinary citizens, a case of effective mobilization outside the frame work of both parliamentary politics and the mainstream political parties. The following statement conveys something of the emotional appeal to a broader constituency and the sense of betrayal and anger felt by citizens toward the corporation and the state. (The title of the book of Minamata-related documents that contains this statement is a grim pun. The word *shimin* in the title normally means "citizens" but here is written with the characters that mean "dead people." "We citizens" thus becomes "We dead people.")

WE CITIZENS: SIT-IN STRIKE DECLARATION (WAGA SHIMIN)

As we who suffer from Minamata disease and our families continue our sit-in strike in front of the company president's office at Chisso headquarters [in Tokyo], how can we possibly thank the many people throughout the nation who have provided us with their warm support?

Although we began our negotiations with Chisso this past December 6, we have met nothing but a scheme to avoid us, in the form of a note mentioning the company president's (feigned?) sickness. From Minamata to Tokyo, even if we families and victims did not expect to reach a final solution thereby, we did hope that our path would lead us to some tangible hint of a solution. These hopes were brutally shattered. What became clear, what was proved to us in Tokyo, was the immorality, the inhumanity, uncivility, the utter depravity of Chisso's leadership. These robotlike men raised a storm and tried to intimidate those of us who suffer from Minamata disease, our families, and all those who fervently love humankind. The cacophony of their pleas to "Let us do our job," uttered in unison by these robotlike men, has ignited the wrath of the many who suffer or who have died from Minamata disease. Our five or six encounters with Chisso's executive board have only strengthened our resolve and made us even more adamant in our determination. A string that is stretched to the limit is about to break. Even though we are in such an overextended state, we strive to retain our flexible and rich humanity and the abundant fighting spirit that lies hidden deep within us.

Our conversation with Mr. Sato continued far into the night as we talked about soothing our pain, gaining foresight, and repaying all the people throughout the nation for their cherished support. ... As we enter the fifteenth day [of our sit-in], we continue to shout our "gratitude and appreciation for the privilege of life, health, and livelihood." Even if our voices may sound faint, from the site of our sit-in in front of the company president's office, we rejoice day by day in our fortitude. In Tokyo, the center of a Japan fast becoming an archipelago of pollution, an archipelago of wrath, we are able to meet our daily needs in the "Chisso Central Headquarters" building due to your kind support. ...

A new year is about to arrive. We hereby solemnly declare that we will continue our sit-in strike into the new year, just as we continue it this day today with the support of people throughout the whole nation. We rely on the mighty tree of material and spiritual help of the people from the "Committee to Publicize the Minamata Disease."

(December 24, 1971. Issued by Kawamoto Teruo and other sufferers from Minamata disease taking part in the sit-in demonstrations)

[Ishimure, ed., *Waga shimin,* pp. 333–34; AG]

BULLDOZING THE ARCHIPELAGO: THE POLITICS OF ECONOMIC GROWTH

A little more than a decade after the income-doubling plan was announced, the newly installed prime minister, Tanaka Kakuei, issued his plan to "remodel" the Japanese islands. His *Building a New Japan* quickly became a best-selling book. Tanaka was adroitly responding to the growing popular unease at the price of affluence, in the form of environmental destruction in the industrial centers of Japan and the decline of rural areas. With this project to invest huge sums in roads and high-speed railways to reverse the flow from country to city that he lamented, Tanaka was also aiming to serve the construction industry, which had so richly supported his political machine. Scandal tarnished Tanaka's own career a few years after this declaration, but over the following decades the government indeed poured billions of dollars into public-works projects throughout the archipelago. These investments did not in fact stop the exodus of people into urban and industrial centers, but they did lead rural communities to undertake numerous projects to bring tourists "home" to the countryside.

EPILOGUE OF *BUILDING A NEW JAPAN*

Those born in the Meiji (1868–1912) and the Taisho (1912–1926) eras have a deep sense of love and pride in their native locales. While life in these rural villages may not have been rich, it was home. Home was the place where your stern father and gentle mother lived, where you could always find your childhood friends, and whose green fields, rolling hills, and fresh streams remained with you forever. Seeking their fortunes, village youths left their ancestral homes for faraway cities where they studied, worked, married, and followed the course of their lives. Saisei Muroo, a poet of those days, sang in praise of his homeplace, "It is where my mind travels from afar." Whatever their fate, whether in success or failure, they always remembered the people and scenes of their unchanging homeplace.

I believe that the endless fountain of energy which has built today's Japan derives from the cherished and respected rural homes from which all of us have originally come.

In this great enterprise of remodeling the Japanese archipelago, I am motivated by a strong desire to rebuild the home of the Japanese people, which has been lost and destroyed and is declining today but which, once restored, will again give to our society a sense of tranquillity and spiritual enrichment.

It is true that the urban concentration of both people and production has been the driving force in building today's prosperity. The process of this massive flow has given rise to many whose only home is a two-room apartment in a big city, sapped the villages of their youth, and left behind only the aged and housewives to sweat and toil in back-breaking labor. How can such a society generate the energy necessary to build a new Japan in the next hundred years?

It is such considerations as these that have impelled me to work on the policy of "dispersion" to reverse the tide of people, money, and goods and to create a flow from urban concentrations back to outlying areas, using industrial relocation and the nationwide communication and transportation networks as the main tools.

This plan for building a new Japan is a set of policy programs to solve simultaneously both overcrowding and underpopulation through the relocation of people and industry into less populated areas. It is, more importantly, an action program to implement these prescribed solutions.

I wish to activate the dynamo of our nation's powers to revitalize the declining rural areas of Japan. By moving pollution-free industries from large cities to outlying areas, local cities can be made strategic cores of development with improved income opportunities. Educational, medical, cultural, and leisure facilities will be adequately provided to enrich the local life environment. Those leaving the farm will find new jobs in local factories and stores while still being able to cultivate enough land to produce some rice and vegetables for their own consumption. Land they do not need can be leased for salaried cultivation. No longer will they have to leave their villages to seek seasonal employment in the large cities.

Japanese farms of fifty to seventy-five acres will be mechanically cultivated by a small number of highly efficient farmers raising stock in spacious pastures, growing fruit and rice in well-tended fields and paddies. Life in the large cities will also be improved. By relocating those industries and universities no longer needed in big cities, urban areas will be freed of pollution and high costs and made comfortable places to live in. City dwellers will work five days a week at worthwhile jobs. While they will live in apartments near their work in their twenties and thirties when they are in the prime of life, in their forties they will have homes in suburbia where they can take care of their aged parents. On weekends, they may enjoy family outings by car to nearby mountains, rivers, or beaches, or they may choose to engage in do-it-yourself carpentry or agriculture in their spare time.

Only when life in both metropolitan and rural Japan is reshaped into one humane, livable environment will the people take pride in their own communities and develop a strong sense of solidarity and mutual cooperation. So long as the people can enjoy the same conveniences and opportunities for self-development wherever they may live, their love for their homeplaces will be firmly restored and will develop into an abiding love of their homeland Japan.

The road before us is steep and rocky. Yet both the necessary funds and ingenuity for this great enterprise can be found if we remain a peace-loving nation and if, on the strength of our high growth potential, we manage our economy to make growth and welfare compatible.

If we join together to consolidate the energy, wisdom, and technology that enabled us to construct today's Japan from the ashes of World War II, I am confident that it is possible to bring about a new era, a renaissance in which man and sunshine and verdant surroundings will replace big cities and industries as the rightful master of society. Japan will indeed be in the vanguard of civilization when the more than one hundred million intelligent and hardworking Japanese people put all of their strength together to solve the problems of inflation, pollution, overcrowding, depopulation, agricultural stagnation, and generation gaps common to all developed countries and do this without following the path to militarism. As a free nation which knows no social prejudice, which gives its citizens every opportunity for success if they are creative and work hard, Japan will be a trusted and respected member of the international community and will enjoy fraternal relations with all nations regardless of ideological differences.

For the past twenty-five years, I have done my best as a statesman to make Japan a well-balanced, comfortable place to live in. And I shall dedicate the remainder of my life to the consummation of this task. A society where every home is filled with laughter, where senior citizens live peaceful, restful lives, where the eyes of youth shine bright with the light of hope—such is my dream for remodeling the Japanese archipelago.

[Tanaka, *Building a New Japan,* pp. 217–20]